Kings of the County League

One Summer, One Team, One Dynasty

Craig Ohlau

Black Rose Writing | Texas

Some names and identifying details may have been changed to protect the privacy of individuals.

ISBN: 978-1-68433-581-7
PUBLISHED BY BLACK ROSE WRITING
www.blackrosewriting.com

Printed in the United States of America
Suggested Retail Price (SRP) $20.95

Kings of the County League is printed in Palatino Linotype

*As a planet-friendly publisher, Black Rose Writing does its best to eliminate unnecessary waste to reduce paper usage and energy costs, while never compromising the reading experience. As a result, the final word count vs. page count may not meet common expectations.

This book is dedicated to Vern, Lucy,
and all the Buds who live within its pages.

"Playing for Waterloo was like playing for the New York Yankees. The Mon-Clair league was hardly a replica of the majors, but the Buds definitely possessed that kind of domination."
— Randy Wells, Waterloo Buds Catcher 2001-2003, Chicago Cubs Pitcher 2008-2012

"Ohlau hits it out of the park in this touching memoir of a man, a team, and a legendary baseball club."
— Mike Sabatino, 3-time Illinois State Baseball Champion Coach, Lindenwood University Pitcher 2012-2016, St. Louis Spikes Pitcher 2014-2015

"Vern Moehrs was an icon in the league. He was the Billy Martin, fiery and competitive. Your team was measured for how it stacked up against the Buds. You learned to hate them but loved the way they played. I always loved the challenge of pitching against them."
— Randy Martz, Lewis and Clark Community College Head Baseball Coach, Chicago Cubs/White Sox Pitcher 1980-1983, East Alton Silver Bullets Pitcher 1988-1993

"It was a tremendous honor playing for Vernell Moehrs. He was like a second dad to me in my early days. He taught me the most important thing a coach can teach a young man. He taught me how to win."
— Jimmy Wahlig, Semi-Pro Baseball's All-Time Home Run King, Waterloo Buds Slugger 1977-2003

"My time in the Mon-Clair League both playing for and against Vern was easily the most fun of my days. Vern was passionate about the game like very few and I enjoyed that about him. When we beat Waterloo, it was always extra nice, and when I played for him and lost, let me just say we didn't take it very well."
— **Darin Hendrickson, St. Louis University Head Baseball Coach, Waterloo Buds Pitcher 1998-2001**

"Vern Moehrs has had a longevity that will never be seen again in baseball. In his 70+ years, he has touched countless lives on and off the field."
— **Neil Fiala, St. Louis Cardinals/Cincinnati Reds 1981, Waterloo Buds Infielder 1993-1999, NJCAA Coaching Hall of Famer**

"In tiny pockets of middle America, the game of baseball still evokes a layered passion, where individual stories and the meaning of "team" unite behind a shared summer dream. Craig Ohlau's *Kings of the County League* took me to that place, page by page, in an achingly powerful account of friends, a legendary manager, and 'the best damn game in the world.'"
— **Brian Kaufman, author of** *The Fat Lady's Low, Sad Song—Kirkus Reviews'* **Best Books of 2018**

"*Kings of the County League* is a classic brew of love, leadership, and one man's lifelong journey creating amateur baseball's greatest dynasty."
— **Bret Burris, Team Leader ISP Swat, Alton A's and Granite City Steelers Outfielder 2001-2006**

Kings of the County League

THE MON–CLAIR BASEBALL LEAGUE
FIELD LOCATIONS

INDEPENDENTS
CAPE GIRARDEAU CAPAHAS
ST. LOUIS PRINTERS

MONROE DIVISION
COLUMBIA SAINTS
MARISSA YOUNG GUNS
MILLSTADT VFW
VALMEYER LAKERS
WATERLOO BUDS

ST. CLAIR DIVISION
ALTON A'S
EAST ST. LOUIS COLTS
GRANITE CITY STEELERS
FAIRVIEW HEIGHTS REDBIRDS
ST. LOUIS SPIKES

PREFACE

I had fallen in love with the game at eight years old watching Ken Griffey, Jr. I wanted nothing more than to play centerfield for the Seattle Mariners, the St. Louis Cardinals, the Chicago Cubs, or any other Major League baseball team for that matter. Me wanting to be a baseball player was different than my mom wanting her middle son to become someone prominent, a doctor, or a lawyer. My gosh, she would have even settled for a teacher. Playing ball for a living—now I could actually work every day at that, and I grew up truly believing in the idea. My father never played the game after Little League, and my mother knew only a little about it, though she kept the score book at most of my brothers' and my games. Dad always said she was good at Wiffle ball.

When I was ten, my brothers and I started a sandlot league, with only the three of us participating. Well, two of us really, for Kurt, our baby brother, kept score. The joke was we sometimes let Kurt play third base as the base itself. And we loved to tag up on fly balls.

In our grass-depleted backyard, we played a 162-game, five-inning-per-game schedule, keeping the stats of all the players on our team by categorizing them in a neatly bound binder. We attended church every week, mainly because Mom promised a pack of Topps for our participation. We sold and traded the cards we earned from weekly catechism religiously out of our "card shop," a beat-up office upstairs in our two-story house hung with curtain rods to hold the cards we were "selling." We played the game we loved all summer freely in the sandlots, farm lots, and parking lots throughout our town. I lived for baseball. Everything I did, every food I ate, every dream I had, every girl I dated was based on how it might affect my playing. I was a shy kid, and I never liked drawing attention to myself, unless of course if it was on a baseball field. There I felt comfortable, at home, and able to show off. I felt the confidence that comes from applause, having success, being singled out. I played in college—a rare occurrence for athletes from my small hometown—and it was there that I first heard of the Summer League on which this story is based.

I was an outfielder and leadoff man at Southwestern Illinois College during the first year of the new millennium. Our team, the Blue Storm, was good—good enough to be ranked top ten in the country among D-I Junior Colleges and good enough to be called Midwest Regional Champions and play for a chance to go to the World Series in Grand Junction, Colorado. In our free time and on the long baseball bus rides, "summer ball" options were discussed regularly by the guys that made up the 24-man roster—as if we hadn't played enough ball in our 65-game college schedule. We never lauded the local county league back home in our talks the way we did the prestigious national summer leagues like the Cape Cod or the Carolina League. Or even some of the other regional leagues like the Northwoods League, the Jayhawk League, or the Central Illinois League. And rightfully so. The local county league was only a glorified "Beer League," "The Best Beer League in the World!" After much debate and questioning, one theme rang loud and clear, and we had reached our conclusion. "If you wanted to stay local and enjoy your summer without getting burned out . . . .. shiiit....Just play the Clair."

PROLOGUE

"Ohlau, you're up." A moment arrives in every ballplayer's story when the stakes suddenly change. For me, that moment came in early May on a cold, windy afternoon in a batting cage on the campus of Wisconsin-Parkside, a Division-II University in Somers, Wisconsin. The hitting session was focused simply on getting some pre-game swings. Scouts from the Baltimore Orioles and Minnesota Twins hovered behind the back screen, clipboards in hand. Every swing was analyzed. Every action noted and dissected. Bo Collins, longtime coach at Southern Illinois University in Edwardsville, machine-like, threw a pitch, and another, and another, and another, and for a combined total of five minutes, I swung.

To my way of regarding time, this all happened a long time ago — going for broke in the cage, attempting to impress the onlookers. College was winding down. It was my senior year. With two more weekends to play, it was now or never. The fate of my career, my dream, and the dreams of young hopefuls from all over the world would be decided next month during the two-day Major League Baseball Draft. That day in the cage seemed different. It *was* different. The scouts always kept their distance, observing me from afar. This time, however, was up close and personal.

As a hitter, I naturalized smooth hitting mechanics from the left side, converting each pitch to solid line drive after solid line drive off Coach's arm, which was chucking exquisite meatballs. I had led the area in hitting as a high schooler at Chester High and led my college team in nearly every offensive stat. I was leaving SIUE with a degree in education, but it was this tryout, this round in the cage, this next pitch that could be my last real shot at playing the game I loved for what seemed at the time a larger purpose. The pressures that a college senior puts on himself were mounting. My future was converging on me and fast. I didn't want to get a job, a real one, not yet anyway. I desired to hold on as long as I could to the game I loved. Just give me a chance at the pros, and I'll succeed, I always thought. Not making it, not getting drafted or signed, was never an option.

• • • • •

"Throw it to Daddy." The instinct to throw comes naturally to a boy. A toddler sees a rock, and he throws it. He picks up a ball. His dad claps and coaxes him, "Throw it to Daddy." It's the first confidence he feels by means of separation from his dad. He sees a river, and he thinks he can throw a stone across it. There's the story of the boy George Washington throwing a silver dollar across the Potomac. It doesn't matter whether it's legend or not. You know he thought he could do it.

At two years, three months, Corey Blackwell picked up a ball, a Nerf one, a turbo, a whistler, and chucked it across the room, a perfect howling spiral. His dad could only smile as the ball shattered the lamp on the far side of the room. One of his grandpas called him "The Prince," "The Chosen One," "The Boy with the Golden Arm," and from that moment on, everyone in the family knew the kid had a gift, throwing.

At 10, he dreamed of pitching in the big leagues. One loss in Little League caused him to cry hysterically. He vowed never to let it happen again. To lose. To cry. It was evident the love the little Prince had for the game. His father put a pitcher's rubber in the backyard. Stan Blackwell never had the arm, the ability, the love, but he had his son, and he knew the game. He had played in high school. He saw his son's talents. Fathers and sons— the theme is as old as the dirt the game is played on. The Prince played catch with his dad almost every night before dinner—sometimes even after—all the time with an enthusiasm only a certain love brings. The two made up a game called "What Pitch?"

"What pitch do you throw 0-2 when you've already thrown two fastballs?" "How about 2-2 when the hitter is on the fastball?" "2-2 to the best hitter on the team. What pitch do you throw, Son?"

They played the game constantly, even when actual throwing was impossible. In the car on vacation, before bed, in church, they played. The Prince learned to command his pitches and think the game. In Little League, where ten-year-olds were still working on the coordination to get the ball anywhere near the strike zone, the Prince threw strikes. He had a smooth, easy motion to his arm and a feel for situations and counts that eluded even the older players. He wasn't the flashy look-at-me type. People didn't look and say, "This one's surely going to play in the Bigs," or "Damn, that boy right there is a stud!" He wasn't that kind of Prince. He ate up the sports page of the Freeburg Tribune, memorizing the names and statistics of the local high school stars. His bedroom wall was a who's who of posters from Major League stars like Nolan Ryan, Dwight Gooden, and Roger Clemens. Between ten and eighteen, he grew, albeit not much. He stood at 5 feet 9 inches tall and weighed 150 pounds soaking wet, far from the imposing figures living on his bedroom wall. What he lacked in size he made up for in his loose arm and uncanny accuracy. Catch with his dad in the backyard ceased as his dad could no longer catch the heavy balls he was throwing. In his senior year, he led his team, tiny, unassuming Freeburg High, all the way to the state tournament. "A free college education," Stan told his Prince. "That is the best thing; you will go to college, Son."

"I don't want to go to college, Pop. I want to be a ballplayer."

After four years in the college game, which saw the Prince play at junior college powerhouse Southwestern Illinois, Division-I Austin Peay in Clarksville, Tennessee, and then back to Division-II Southern Illinois in Edwardsville, his moment had arrived. Unable to entice an MLB team to take a chance on him, he got his shot when he signed with the River City Rascals of the

Frontier League—an Independent Pro League consisting of teams ranging from Pennsylvania and Virginia in the East, Michigan to the North, Kentucky in the South, and Illinois and Missouri to the West. He needed to prove himself not only to his team but to himself. Two innings pitched, four hits, two walks, a wild pitch, and five runs was his line.

· · · · ·

"What do you want to do today?" Jeff Kaiser grew up in Hecker, Illinois, population 500. What did Kaiser do in Hecker? Play baseball, of course. "All we had was the old softball field. My brother Randy and I would get some buddies, and we'd go up there. We'd scrounge up all the balls we had. The cornfield in the outfield grass was the fence. We called it cornball. Randy and I threw batting practice to each other almost every day. I bet we lost fifty balls out there in that field over the course of our lives."

There was no batting cage in Hecker. Those thousand rounds of batting practice pitches made Jeff into an accomplished switch hitter. The son of a heavy machine operator and a church chef, Kaiser stood out at Waterloo High School, helping lead his team to the state tournament in 1984. His high school coach, Lon Fulte, knew he was special. "He got his hands from his father, the construction worker," he would say. Those hands would take him places.

Recruited to what was then Southwest Missouri State University in Springfield by legendary coach Keith Gutton, Jeff shined as a switch-hitting middle infielder.

He played lockdown defense up the middle and led the team in hitting with a robust .420 average. Pro scouts were on notice. His dreams were close.

His lifelong goal of playing baseball professionally came true. The San Francisco Giants drafted Jeff in the 6th round of the 1988 Major League Baseball Amateur Draft. He spent his first season split between two clubs, the San Jose Giants, a Class A affiliate, and the Pocatello Giants, a rookie ball club in the same organization. "Pro ball was different," he would say. "Everyone was always out to get their own, in it for themselves." Jeff struggled.

His moment came in the fall of '89. Playing in his first full season and 96th game for the A-Level Salinas Spurs of the California League's North Division, Jeff had had enough of the pro game. Or maybe the pro game had had enough of him. Hitting .150 in 255 at-bats, he was smack dab in the middle of a nightmarish slump and nearing the end of a long season. It was his second full year in the low minors. He was tired—he missed home. Holding a career batting average of .178 in his two professional seasons, he left himself no choice. He left the Spurs no choice.

CHAPTER 1
LEGEND

Players like the Prince and Kaiser often come together on one sheet of 20-year-old recycled letterhead Vernell Moehrs keeps in his bruised brown attaché briefcase. Vernell Moehrs, to this very day, manages the Waterloo Buds of the Mon-Clair league—often called the Clair. The Mon-Clair Baseball League is a county baseball league consisting of teams that range from the entire metropolitan St. Louis area on both sides of the Mississippi River and spanning to Cape Girardeau in the south. It is one of the few unlimited baseball leagues still around. This means it allows competitors of all ages a chance at participation. It is a league sweet enough to lure ex-big leaguers, grown men married with kids still living for the occasional square-up, college upstarts dreaming of the pros, and the blossoming high school hopefuls looking to hang with the "big boys" every summer to the scorched, dusty sandlots in the middle of America's heartland. It is billed as "The Best Men's Amateur League in the Midwest" by its promoters and simply as a great county "Beer" League by others.

Vernell pencils in his player's names and positions in handwriting resembling that of an advanced third grader with many experiencing a misspelling or two. The players mostly come from the surrounding and encompassing counties—from high schools, junior colleges, universities, the pro game, or full-time jobs. Some of the names on Vernell's tattered lined paper have existed there for years. Some have only recently been added to the list. Almost all of them, he either sees play personally, are recommended somewhere along the line by the different college or professional coaches in the area or are referred by local sports legends connected with the old coach. Vernell loves these facets of his hobby—watching the game, talking to coaches, recruiting, and working in the light.

Vernell Moehrs is a retired coal mine superintendent. He worked in a quarry, underground, for 30+ years. When asked by a reporter if he enjoyed his career as a miner, he quickly responds, "If I had to do it over again, I'd want to do that," spitting long cut tobacco juice into a red solo cup charitably given to him by his wife, Lucille. "I loved it...And all miners chew because it's not legal to smoke. They do slip a smoke in, but you're around explosives." "I've chewed since I was 14 years old," Vernell would later add. "I was born and raised on my Grandpa's farm. I'd skip rocks in the creek with my sister Audrie. We'd play stickball for hours. Homerun if the acorn made it on top of the barn. First home run I ever hit. Gramps had two sons; they weren't interested in horses and things like that. Grandpa was going down the road, and he had tobacco and cut a piece off. He couldn't say Vernell — he called me Viby. 'Viby, try this.' It was *goood*."

Vernell — Vern for short — is a husband to Lucille — Lucy for short — and a father to two, Gina and Clay, and a grandfather to three, Stephanie, Kennedy, and Grayson.

He is originally from Renault. "It's not much; it's between here [Waterloo, IL] and Prairie du Rocher, if you've ever heard of Prairie du Rocher," Lucy describes. Only 150 people reside in the little farming community. Vern said that when he was a teenager, "every town back there had a team. We went out and cut some posts, cut some chicken wire for a backstop and the bases were sacks. Dirt sacks. There was no money at that time. Nobody had a suit. You were lucky to have a pair of spikes. But guys played all the time." The manager of the town's grocery store also managed the local team, the Renault Ramblers. "During the week, he'd go to St. Louis haulin' cattle, haulin' pigs, groceries, all that stuff," Vern said. "So, on Saturday, all of us got together, and we scrubbed the bed of the farm truck and put benches in there. And on Sunday, he'd haul us to games."

As for Lucy and Vern, their love story budded at an old bar called the Old Shamrock off State Highway 13, a main artery zigzagging across southern Illinois from Belleville in the west to Harrisburg in the east.

"The dances were big then," says Lucy, who met Vern in 1956. "You'd have the big band sound. Back then, guys asked the girls to dance. He asked me to dance. Swing, jitterbug. Oh yeah. We were good dancers, *reaaallly* good dancers. Every weekend. He played ball, but in the evenings, dances, too. They were like five-, six-piece orchestras. Back then, there was Tommy Ryan."

"Al Ross!" Vern said.

"Collinsville Park Ballroom had Walt Schlemer," Lucy said. "Whitey [Herzog] was coming out there at Shamrock, too!"

Lucy and Vern were married in 1958. Thanksgiving Day. She was Catholic; he wasn't. Her hometown church wouldn't marry them. By that time, Vern was playing ball for Waterloo.

After daughter Gina was born in 1961, Lucy and Vern were unable to have more children. Eight years later, they found themselves sitting in the couple's living room both eerily silent—Gina sound asleep in the adjoining room. "I looked at Lucy," Vern recalls years later. "She looked back at me with tears in her eyes. We sat for a long moment just staring at each other." "What are you thinking?" she asked. "I've always believed in miracles. I told her we need to adopt a boy." They adopted Clay, an 11-day-old baby boy six months later. "When Gina was born and when we brought home Clay—those were the two best days of my life," the old man recalls, his voice cracking with emotion. "In the early days, Gina slept more in my back seat going and coming from games than she did in her bed." Family is undoubtedly the love of Vern's life, but anyone who has ever been introduced to the man knows what finishes a very close second.

Vern had been playing organized ball since his graduation from Waterloo High at age 17 in 1952 with the independent Waterloo Warriors of the old Monroe County League when only a few teams in the county competed. He played for nine years with the Warriors before taking over the team in 1961 as player-manager. He was replacing local baseball enthusiast Bill Mohr—the league and team founder. Bill Mohr stayed busy. He led a merger of the old Monroe and St. Clair Leagues to form the original Mon-Clair in 1961. Five years later, in 1966, the recently developed Mon-Clair merged with the Greater County League to form what is now the current Mon-Clair League. Trailblazer Mohr, who was running both leagues, served as the Mon-Clair League's first league president. "Baseball is here! And it is here to stay!" the local papers boasted.

Vern knew, if things were to be done right in his takeover of the Warriors, he needed a team sponsor. One phone call was all it took for the wordsmithing miner to establish a framework for partnership with the Ray "Slim" Koerber family, owners of a local Anheuser Busch distributor. The offer the Koerbers made was a simple one for the young Moehrs: "If we pay the annual budget, you rename the team, and we [the Koerbers] will be your proud sponsor. It didn't take long for Vern to agree. The Warriors were now called the Buds, after the beer, "The Undisputed King!" Everyone was happy.

Vern and his Buds won the first-ever Mon-Clair game on May 8, 1966. He has managed the club ever since. While you are reading his story, there is a good chance the old man is sitting in the comfort of his home, pondering roster moves for the upcoming summer, or maybe it's baseball season. His team, the league, and his place in it is the total package for him. It is as personal to him as a family vacation or a quiet night out with Lucy. His love for baseball is fabled in the Clair. He has managed in the league longer than the other nine current field managers combined. Vern's passion is unmatched in County League standards—in baseball standards. He spends countless hours recruiting his players. He works more than a season in advance. Getting leads on local high school seniors destined to star at the next level, forging relationships with local or statewide colleges or universities, seeding potential cuts from local Independent "Pro" Clubs, or even cherry-picking guys within the league. His scuffed and leather-splintered black book inside the attaché is a cultivation of his contacts in the game that seems to reach every corner of the Midwestern baseball world. Former St. Louis Cardinal players and managers Lonnie Maclin, Rich Hacker, Neil Fiala, and Whitey Herzog are just a few of the names scratched into his journal.

The roster of potential Buds in Vern's attaché resides next to a folder containing a stack of one-page player contracts—the contract every player has to sign before joining the club, releasing the league of certain liabilities and locking that player into an agreement with the club. The contract is strictly enforced. It sits by last season's score book and team program, an old beat-up three-ring notebook filled with the ridiculous worn-out, tattered pages of cross-outs, circles, and substitutions, and the black book of player contacts. It is this love affair with the simple workings of managing his club that best captures Vern's true spirit as a man. It is his love affair with his Buds. He sees the unbridled romance in the amateur game—the competition, the fun, guys hustling to the ballfield after a day of work, changing into their uniforms in their cars, the lights, the sounds, the smells, the beer afterward. While in a small way detesting the greed and ego that often seem to define most professional sports. This is Vernell Moehrs stripped naked. This is his life—sixty-plus years in baseball's bushes.

KOERBER DISTRIBUTING CO., Waterloo

Elected To Mon-Clair League Hall of Fame —
25 year Bud sponsor, Ray Koerber and Bud First
Baseman-Pitcher, Richard "Dick" Dillinger.

1986 Bud Program honoring inaugural and longtime sponsor
Ray Koerber

Waterloo Buds

1992 SEASON

Official Souvenir
SCORE CARD

Mon-Clair League
Gibault Athletic Field
Waterloo, Illinois

KOERBER DISTRIBUTING CO.. Waterloo

This 1992 Program is Dedicated to
Bill Mohr former Waterloo Manager

1992 Bud Souvenir Scorecard dedicated to trailblazer Bill Mohr

CHAPTER 2
"THE CALL"

The 2005 Major League Baseball First-Year Player Draft was coming to an end. Executives from Major League Baseball sat around conference room tables surrounded by papers, charts, computer screens, and phone lines connected to the draft rooms of all 30 big-league ball clubs. The amateur players whose names were being called were not yet household names. None of them would be seen walking across a stage, shaking hands with the commissioner like the NFL's or NBA's draft-day spectacles. During the baseball draft, teams announced their picks over a conference call, which was streamed live over Major League Baseball's website, MLB.com. The final five picks flashed on the bottom of my girlfriend's laptop screen.

1497 Justin Otto NO SCHOOL RHP R/R 6'2" 185
1986-09-14

1498 Mitchell Houck Cypress Bay HS LHP L/L
6'1" 200 1987-05-26

1499 Derick Himpsl Johnstown HS LHP L/L 6'4"
240 1986-06-04

1500 Colin Arnold Kings Academy LF L/L 6'2"
175 1987-08-16

1501 Blake Heym Grayson County Col C L/R 6'2"
195 1985-01-04

Son of a *b* —! I didn't make it, I thought. I wasn't surprised, and I began the second-guessing process of my school choice, my practice habits over the years, the girl(s) I was dating, and everything else under the sun. And just when I thought all hope was lost, the phone rang. I got the call. Could it be? Could it really be? Could I really be so lucky? This is it. My childhood dreams of signing with a Major League team were coming true. An old scratchy voice toiled through the line, not waiting for me to say Hello. "Ohlu, sorry to hear what happened...I was watchin'. You had a helluva tryout. Had no idea you could still run like that...and those home runs...now that was some real poppie, poppie!"

The voice wasn't that of general managers Jim Beattie or Mike Flanagan of the Orioles or Terry Ryan of the Twins. It wasn't Walt Jocketty of the St. Louis Cardinals, John Stockstill of the Chicago Cubs, or Brian Cashman of the New York Yankees. I knew subconsciously that this call would come. How could I have been so naïve? I immediately deciphered the familiar tone on the wire. I had heard the voice many times before during the previous four summers. Vern freaking Moehrs. I figured he was watching—he was always watching. It's not hard to miss the brown leather boots, flannel shirt, and overalls in a near-empty baseball stadium.

"So, Ohlu, what do ya plan on doin' now?" The voice inquired. He always pronounced my name wrong. Vern knew the answer. He knew damn well who he was talking to. Déjà-vu! I somehow knew this question was coming days before the tryout. And in predestined anticipation, I was somewhat happy that it did. The answer pegged before the question.

• • • • •

The Prince got his call much earlier. In the middle of a cornfield, to be exact, surveying property for a new housing development. He flipped open his Motorola. Vern didn't need to spit any pleasantries to sell the twenty-seven-year-old hurler on coming back for another summer. The Prince was already one of Vern's most loyal and dominant arms and more than happy to continue on his coquettish path to County League stardom.

Seven years prior, however, the Prince was unfamiliar with Vern. At that time, the Prince was pitching for the Sauget Wizards, a rival team in the league. Vern's Buds, amid a historic season, needed one more series win to cement itself as the best in the club's long and storied history. The best in possibly our nation's history. 45-0 and in game 1 of the best-of-three series facing the Wizards for the championship of the Clair, Vern's Buds were chasing perfection. With fire in his ass and NSAIDS in his veins, the Prince fired a complete game 5-hitter, beating a shocked Waterloo Club 6-2. Lucky for Vern and the Buds, it was a best-of-three. The Buds survived with a come-back win to take the series, and the championship, oddly enough, by beating the Prince (on one day's rest). The Buds ended the year 47-1, Vern's greatest season ever. He made one promise to himself after that unprecedented defeat, to never again lose to the Prince.

• • • • •

Jeff Kaiser didn't need a call from the old skipper. He knew he had one more year of ball left in him. 2005 was going to be his sixteenth season and his last in regard to his baseball career. The longtime shortstop knew his 38-year-old frame was aging and his skills were diminishing. The ever-mindful Vern knew it as well. He needed to make sure of one thing before he felt comfortable with Kaiser at shortstop. He required a complementary Jake Friederich to play second.

Friederich, called "Franchise" by his teammates, was a Saint Louis University graduate and former junior college All-American at second base. His sure hands and quick exchange would be the perfect double-play complement to the veteran Kaiser at shortstop—one problem—he needed Franchise back. The previous summer, Vern lost out on his second baseman, a rare occurrence for the acclaimed county league recruiter. Following Franchise's junior year at Saint Louis University, he hightailed it out of town with dreams of being noticed in a New York summer league. Regretting ever leaving Vern's side, Franchise answered the call and danced with Vern every summer thereafter.

• • • • •

Vern's recruits for the 2005 Waterloo Buds understood what a summer in the Clair meant, even if only intuitively. What we all didn't know exactly was how much fun we were going to have.

CHAPTER 3
BUDS

"My players never had to pay a dime to play for me. If I couldn't come up with the money, we wouldn't have been able to do it right. Father Edwin Hustedde, 'The Pitching Priest,' built the field...let us play for free. He played with us for years. He married Lucy and me. Later in life, when I converted, he baptized me, our children too—great left-handed pitcher! Without that great man and our many sponsors over the years (Koerber from '61-'05, Illinois Distributing in '06-'07, and Chick Fritz from '08-'20), we would have never had the success we've had. We were able to stay in the green, get the players we wanted, and win championships."

−Vern Moehrs

The attached, one-car garage at the Moehrs' house was our uniform supply closet. First up, a rack of perfectly organized uniform tops. Our only uniform was red with *Buds* sewn across the chest, a significant contrast from the long-held whiteys of the past. Grays were rare for county league teams as teams always operated on a limited annual budget. On a different rack next to the tops hung twenty gray pairs of stretchy lined uniform pants—a box of stiff, black-colored wool adjustable baseball hats, categorized by size, lined a wall—close to a package of dark expandable belts, a bucket of baseballs and an extra large duffel bag of headwear.

The basement had a different purpose. From wall to wall in the cinder block lower level, trophy after trophy after trophy decorated the mantles and many shelves that draped the room. Wood-framed photographs of the Buds lined the walls. Bud nostalgia and memorabilia drowned out almost everything else in the Moehrs' basement and evidenced Vern's obsession with his team. Most coaches in the league had their favorite hangout spots, but none were as inviting as the basement at the Moehrs' house.

On top of Vern and his three assistants, Harry Thompson, Mark Vogel, and bench coach Lon Flute, Lucy, the team president and always ahead of her time, seemed to carry more influence with the club than any of the three men combined. "She has put up with it all this time. Sometimes I think she is more interested in it than I am," Vern describes his dedicated spouse. Lucy wants the players to feel comfortable and relaxed. She makes them feel like family. She makes her rounds at the games talking to players and families with whom she is sharing her life. She doesn't hide from them the basis on which each player was selected to the prestigious club. "Now you all make sure you win two today. We want two wins. Remember that now. Two. Win 'em for Vernie."

In addition to the Buds' inner circle, local businesses pay homage to the team year in and year out. Whether it's the beer distributors, the bars, the local auto bodies, banks, insurance agents, car dealers, mom and pops, the quarry, the pizza joints, former players, or even the sheriff, no one wants to be left out. The town supports its Buds.

. . . . .

On the evening of March 23, 2005, Vern sat in the dimly lit, back room at the Knights of Columbus Hall in Millstadt, IL—another small German settlement ten miles northeast of Waterloo. He was fulfilling one of the unpleasantries of managing in the league—attending the preseason league meeting. He sat with Rich Fisher, "General Manager of Personnel" (a title bestowed mainly on paper), fellow hot stover, longtime friend and better known around Illinois baseball circles only as "Fish." "Want a beer?" Fish asked his old friend.

"One...I want ONE," emphasized Vern.

Never known as a drinker, Vern's habit was to drink a limit of one beer at any gathering, whether it be a wedding, birthday, or a championship celebration. Also customary was Vern's inability to reach for the tab at the end of the evening. "His arm shrinks six inches when it's time to pay," Fish joked while taking care of the bill.

At the yearly preseason kick-off, each of the league's ten managers previewed the forthcoming season. Each congratulated Waterloo resident and businessman Dave Powell on his most recent appointment to league president. The indifferent Powell thanked them, "Someone has to do it."

Fish, the persistent outgoing shit talker, was the first to make some comments to Powell. "You sure as hell better not let Valmeyer get away with the shit they pulled last year. Canceling those games with us because of the rain. Everyone and their brother knows Pieper could have gotten that field ready!" This rib was typical of Fish, stirring the pot for the sake of stirrin'. Most of the managers excused such comments—they knew the culprit. Others sat in shaken disbelief. Fish had made his point. The managers also excused in advance the probability of starting the season shorthanded due to the absence of certain college recruits still at school or in season. Denny Pieper, longtime manager of the Valmeyer Lakers, echoed the concern. Moehrs, annoyed by the annual excuse-making, whispered to Fish, "It is the same for every team in the league every summer." Before Fish could publicly respond, an affronted Vern stood and said, "So, are you all going to suck? Just forfeit then! Hell, why don't we just push the season back two weeks!" It was this unbridled passion and willingness to speak his mind that few understood; the kind of passion that most who knew him would describe as being, well...a major crab ass, as being, well...a leader, as being, well...RESPECTED. After the brief interruption, the meeting went on unchecked. Everything was set. The managers were ready. The season only weeks away.

CHAPTER 4
BANANAS

1932 Waterloo Baseball Club

The first organized baseball club in Monroe County was the 1894 Waterloo Elks baseball club consisting of team members J. Wallhaus, H. Oldendorph, L. Zimmer, A. Hermann, R. Sinclair, A. Reiffel, Vic Mitchell, Don Voris, Ed Jobusch, and L. Arns. Up until the year 1910, county teams played St. Louis teams and neighboring towns. In 1910 the M and O League formed, which included teams from Columbia, Waterloo, Red Bud, and Millstadt. In 1911, Waterloo entered the ILL-MO League, also known as the Trolly League, with teams from St. Louis and the entire Metro-Area. The popularity of this brand of ball grew to its peak between the two World Wars in the 1930s—as factories and mills across the country sponsored teams to advertise and promote their businesses. In addition to the advertising, the teams provided free entertainment, a civic interest, and a local pride to its fans. For several reasons, the heyday of semi-pro (often called amateur or sandlot) baseball passed long ago. There are aspects of this brand of baseball that remain irresistibly alluring. It's not so much the baseball as it is the towns and communities in which it is played. It's the devotion and spirit of the people who make it possible, who follow it, who play it, who live it, and who love it.

For Vern Moehrs the summer of 2005 officially began Sunday at noon on the 7th of May as he slowly strolled onto Saints Peter and Paul Field in Waterloo, Illinois. The field was purposefully cut from the woods—likely the work of a German immigrant in the late nineteenth century with one lumber saw clearing timber to make a field for corn. The park was donated freely by a local family to the Belleville Diocese in the early 50s. With Vern, and the famous Bud pitcher Father Ed. Hustedde — "The Pitching Priest" — leading the charge along with many townsfolk, the field began to take shape. They plucked the ground of every tree and stump, picked every fieldstone and pebble, and grated it as smooth as a tabletop by dragging it with a section of chain-link fence.

They would add, in the years to come, soccer fields — that will forever feel European, a playground, and a basketball court. But it's the baseball field and the perfect geometries of it that are the center of Vern's universe. Ss. Peter and Paul Field is what you get when sandlots are turned into visions. The home plate is located only a minute's walk from Vern's front door. Baseball has been Vern's religion for a half-century and the field, his chapel.

On this day, he wore his customary brown leather boots, blue jean overalls over a worn, red flannel shirt, and a crisp, brand new "W" hat on his head. A thick mouthful of finely cut *Skoal* lined and overflowed his bottom lip. He looked right at home as he made his way to the open area outside the home dugout, his face ruddy from the many years spent in the mines and at the countless sun-soaked baseball games, the thick lenses of his glasses aiding the vision that had long left him.

At 70 years of age, Vern had managed in Waterloo before his players were even born. He gathered the year's first arriving members of this year's team around him and welcomed them to the first of only two workouts scheduled prior to the summer opener in two weeks. "We're not gonna win any games by standing around bullshittin'! All you rookies get the balls and the screen; the platform is in the shed! We are taking batting practice!"

The 70-year-old couldn't run a full-scale workout with just six position players and four POs (Pitcher-Onlys), and he didn't even try. Player-led catch and batting practice on the field was the plan. Vern believed only a few light gatherings before the opener were needed to work out any kinks and tighten any loosened bonds between the players after the year away, more specifically for the guys who didn't have the luxury of a jam-packed college game schedule.

Like some of the other managers in the league, Vern had played in the Clair himself—over many summers in the sixties and seventies. He understood the need for a fun and relaxed "summer" atmosphere, a team-chemistry, a team purpose. He let his Buds flow in smoothly on different timetables. Some would show up for the pre-season workouts, some for batting practice before games, and some ten minutes before the first pitch—punctuality reserved only for real bananas. Vern knew his players. It was their team now. He brought them together, but only they could win the games.

He sat in a lawn chair just above the fourth stair, exiting the left-field side of the third-base dugout. He observed. He squinted through the thick sunshade lenses of his new prescription. He let the early arrivals know that the objective of pre-season workouts was to "Knock off the rust and get acquainted. Get ya some swings in." He scouted most of his recruits during the long college season and was fully aware of which ones would benefit the most from the reps.

The players readied the BP routine. Vern attracted players with a certain kind of swagger and, in more than one way, justified it. The guys invited to the team were bananas, at least by County League standards, and had been handpicked for the most select men's amateur team in a five-state region. There were no lemons in this group. Some of the early arrivals were as anxious as they were confident. Vern cross-checked the names off his sheet of 20-year old recycled letterhead. The names matched the bodies. They came from programs such as Truman State, Missouri St. Louis, Southwestern Illinois, Quincy, Mckendree, Missouri State, and Southern Illinois.

Jim Queern (Mckendree) and Pat Hardin (Truman State) had the most to prove. They were the newbies who had never played for Vern. With that being said, they were hardly rookies. Like most of the other players around him, Queern knew the faces and names of the players on this year's roster. These faces had been high school or college teammates, rivals from an opposing team, or lifelong friends. Queern and Franchise grew up as next-door neighbors. That familiarity charged the anticipation, to see how good they could be together.

Hardin seemed more uneasy. He had no conception of the players who practiced with him on this day. He stood next to utility man Charles "Chas" Wigger, who was also new to the Vern scene, in the outfield shag group. Chas was funny, easy to be around, and socially adept, the perfect sidekick to Hardin's calm. Chas, with a head full of ideas and zany, sarcastic humor, possessed the effortless ability to slip into or out of conversations and into new surroundings. Chas acted in no way like this was his first rodeo with the guys. He wasn't taken aback by the aura, the athletes, or the county league folklore that surrounded him.

Hardin and Wigger looked around at the cast of characters on the field that day. Corey "Prince" Blackwell (Southern Illinois), Brandon Waeltz (Quincy), Brandon Musso (McKendree) and Peter Buck (Gateway Grizzlies) were among the players prepping pens on the left-field line. Jake Hurst (Southwestern Illinois/Daytona State) was shagging in right field; Jeff Kaiser (Missouri State), the oldest rostered player on the team took care of the bucket; and Queern hit. The character of the players suited the town of Waterloo.

Waterloo's rich history dates back to the 18th century, with the French being the first Europeans to settle in the area. The French loved it because of its elevation and proximity to the Mississippi. It was also close to Fort de Chartres, a French stronghold which boasts the stone magazine, considered the oldest building in the state of Illinois. Word began to spread of Waterloo's fertility as the town experienced a population increase after 1840. The original German settlers arriving in the 1830s came directly from Germany in search of their own land, and to escape the widespread political unrest in the Motherland. Many of Waterloo's buildings and citizens, its local character, and even its team of baseball emigrants reflected the heritage left behind by those heroic settlers.

Vern left batting practice up to assistant coach, former Bud second baseman, and current Waterloo high school coach Mark Vogel. Vern sauntered toward his pitchers down the line to the bullpen — a small hill of grass in an open area with a hole kicked in the dirt beneath a buried pitching rubber. Pillowy clouds meandered across the radiant blue southern Illinois sky. Ping...Ping...Ping. The rhythms of baseball and summer drowned out the low croon of not-so-distant car motors and the wind in the trees. After catch and a little driveling, each pitcher threw off the mound, slowly at first, but as their muscles loosened and their imaginations came to life, they picked up steam. Vern stood off near the foul line, just in earshot. Brandon Waeltz, who old-timers may have once called a plow jockey, was a tall, broad-shouldered, heavy-handed farm boy from the nearby town of Marissa—a small farming community 25 miles to the east. He fired a couple of hard buzzers that cracked the catcher's mitt. "I'll be damn, his whistler looks good," said Vern as he stood, *Skoal* dripping from his chin.

Next up in the bullpen was 25-year-old Peter Buck. Vern continued spitting chaw and admiring his next summer catch. "I did good...I did reeaaal good with this one," he muttered to himself, showing his inner chesty watching Buck's three-quarter-arm fastball hum past. Buck, small for a pitcher, looked shorter than the six-foot-one advertised in the media guide of his old team. Coming off a more than stellar career in the Independent pro circuit where he won a career twenty-six games while striking out 316 batters in the process, Buck was primed for county league stardom. He was a pitching Picasso with a fast, funky delivery and a polished deception only the craftiest of veterans exhibit. His fastball touched 90 mph. Vern watched Buck throw three sharp tumbling yakkers in a row. "I'll be damned. He is gonna be a good one," the old crow muttered again to no one.

Six-foot-three inch, 270-pound Brandon Musso, called "Moose" by the rest of his Buds, drifted into the shag group while waiting his turn on the mound. Moose was the son of Tony, a former Bud pitcher and league Hall of Famer. Tony lived for Bud baseball almost as much as his favorite son. Moose stood on the warning track next to the 325 ft. sign airing out a long toss toward the opposite foul line in the direction of bookend Jake Hurst in right. One of his throws sailed an unbelievable 20 feet over Hurst's head. "Hey Moose, it's a shame you couldn't throw like that at McKendree. You wouldn't have to listen to Vern ride your ass in the pros," Waeltz harassed from his position in the pen. The same throw nearly drilled assistant coach Harry Thompson square in his head as he walked beyond the fence, hunting a foul ball.

"Harry wouldn't have missed a stride if it did hit him," the Prince mumbled facetiously while digging his cheek clear of *Red Man* long cut. "That dude's crazy!"

At the end of the workout, Vern brought his players together in front of the home dugout. Kaiser, with his Will Ferrell look-alike curly blonde hair and child-like, playful demeanor, couldn't stop talking. "Hey, Pete, tell us the story about Neil and the road trip to Kalamazoo." Kaiser, always inquisitive, wanted Buck to share with him some of the stories he had acquired while playing independent ball alongside Kaiser's old buddy— Gateway Grizzly manager and former Bud, Neil "The Real Deal" Fiala. Kaiser loved hearing dirt on his colorful friend. Before Buck could elaborate on his memory of when Fiala knocked on his hotel door wearing nothing but a male G-string, a familiar voice interjected. "Shut up Kaiser! If you want to be a barber during team meetings, go play for Valmeyer!" It was Vern. We laughed as we stood perplexed by how he decided on the term barber? I thought barbers cut hair.

We knew Vern's style, the old school authoritative kind that if you do well and win, everything is hunky dory.

But if not, well...you better be ready to pack your bag.

"We have one more workout scheduled for next Sunday. Now pick up the gear and take it to my truck. The red one."

• • • • •

More Buds poured into Waterloo for the team's second workout; Vern got his first look at the Thompson brothers. Aaron — "A.T." — was a confident, self-reliant, lefty-hitting two-sport athlete (Soccer/Baseball) from the University of Butler. "The best lefty swinger on the team," he always bragged. His younger brother Jordan — "Jordy" — was a two-sport star (Hockey/Baseball) at St. Louis' private Chaminade High. The brothers were the only townies on the team. They were born and raised in Waterloo. Aaron, almost six inches taller than his brother, had the look of his father, assistant coach Harry. With a square jaw, broad shoulders, and a face filled with stubble, he resembled a bantamweight fighter in the UFC's octagon. Younger and shorter brother Jordy looked more like his mother and acted like, well...like Aaron's younger brother.

As Jordy took his swings on the field, Eric Caby, a catcher from Quincy University, pulled his red Mustang into the parking lot. Five-feet-nine-inches tall with muscles on top of muscles popping through the invisible sleeves on his homemade cutoff coupled with severe Nordic features gave Caby the hard-nosed good looks of an authentic river rat from Chester, Illinois—a blue-collar Mississippi river town 25 miles to the south. There was nothing fake about the way Caby carried himself. What you saw is what you got. Caby greeted and answered Vern's questions punctually and with the utmost respect. "Hello, Vern." "Yes, Vern." "No, Vern." "OK, Vern." Before he took his turn in the batter's box, he put the donut on his bat, clipped on a shin guard to shield against unwanted foul balls—his shin didn't want to feel the concussion of a shot exiting his bat—and took two hard practice swings. He was ready for his hacks.

Vern sat on the bench behind the backstop next to Fish—he noticed certain nuances right away. Outfielder Jake Hurst ran to track down a fly ball. That rarely ever happened, at least in practices anyway. Kaiser ranged to his right on a ground ball in the hole backhanding it with smooth perfection. Vern hadn't seen him do that since '95. And Jordy was uncharacteristically quiet, shagging by himself in the outfield—this behavior was the rarest of all.

Ping...Ping...Ping. Caby was centering balls at a ninety-percent success rate while Franchise patiently waited his turn in the on-deck circle. After Caby's onslaught, Franchise raked and continued the hitting display. He peppered the field with line drive after line drive, and when it was all over, Vern gave his second speech of the short summer. It was one of the longer speeches of his career.

"I know all you studs are popular at school and have lots and lots going on this summer," he said with his trademark chubby sarcasm. "But if we want to win the Division, the Midsummer Classic, and the League championship—The Triple Crown—we need a real commitment from every guy here. I've had guys throw up in that trash can over there and play. Guys have played with broken bones, even a broken leg for heaven's sake, muscle tears, bumps, bruises, even piss drunk. Hell, Johnny Wahlig, one of the best damn hitters I ever had, postponed his honeymoon to play. All you rookies should talk to Hurst; he's never missed a game! Those are the types of guys we need on this team! Don't be a Wally Pipp!"

At the beginning of New York Yankee great Lou Gehrig's world-famous streak of 2,130 consecutive games in 1925, according to a popular legend, Pipp showed up at Yankee Stadium with a severe headache and asked the team's trainer for two aspirin. Miller Huggins, the Yankees' manager, noticed this and said "Wally, take the day off. We'll try that

kid Gehrig at first today and get you back in there tomorrow."
Gehrig played well and became the Yankees' new starting first
baseman. "I took the two most expensive aspirin in history,"
Pipp was later quoted to have said.

Vern's version was slightly shorter. He made his point.

"Now pat everyone on the ass and put your hands in and do a cheer," Vern acerbically commanded. "You know all that rah-rah college stuff you guys like to do." And with that, workout #2 was in the books. Only two more weeks till opening day.

Chapter 5
Opening Day

Lucy once described her idea of opening day.

"It's when we score five runs in the first, three more in the second, and then pull away and win in five. And of course, win 'em both!"

Wednesday, May 18, 2005

Vandals had spray-painted the dugouts. No one knew what the upside-down letters and symbols stood for, or why they chose these dugouts to deface. "It was probably those redneck hayseeds from Valmeyer," remarked Mark Mueller, a local pitching standout who was just joining the team. Mueller was unique in more ways than one. His old-school pitching style modeled after his longtime idol, his grandpa Les, resembled a hybridized technique of classic Walter Johnson and the "Far East" style of modern-day Japanese pitcher Hideo Nomo. With hesitations and inconsistent variating deliveries, his pitching style matched perfectly with his quirky personality.

"Come to think of it, the Lakers don't have the *cojones* to do this, probably just that group of burnouts that hang out up there on that corner," Mueller remarked, pointing towards the park's playground.

Mueller walked tall and lean, with wavy haired good looks resembling more a Hollywood star than a county league ballplayer. His genes displayed his big-league pedigree gifted for on-the-field greatness.

Grandpa Les Mueller, a national baseball legend, who in his prime pitched for the Detroit Tigers in 1941 and 1945, was born in Belleville, Illinois, like his son and his grandson after that. Les enlisted in the Army after the United States entered World War II, and it wasn't until a physical revealed he had a hernia that he was able to receive a medical discharge and return home. Les rejoined his Tigers for the 1945 season, putting in one of the most exceptional pitching performances in major league history. On July 21, 1945, he pitched the first 19-2/3 innings for the Tigers and left having given up only one unearned run. No pitcher has thrown as many innings in a major league game since. The game lasted 4 hours, and 48 minutes before the umpire called it a tie due to darkness at 7:48 p.m. When Tigers manager Steve O'Neill removed him, Les asked, "Gee, Steve, the game isn't over, is it?" After his baseball career ended, he returned to Belleville, where he worked in the family's furniture store, like his grandson Mark a half-century later, until he retired in 1974. Les's son Roger paid homage to his father in this 1983 poem.

THE PITCHER

Although my father had played ten years of professional baseball, I was too young to see him. Instead, I remember the summers I spent with him after he retired when I was the batboy for the local County League team on which he pitched.

As a batboy, I had more to do than take care of the bats. During the pre-game batting practice, I'd shag balls in the outfield or chase foul balls. If I were lucky, an odd number of players would be playing catch, trying to get loose. Eagerly, I would play catch with the extra man. Also, before the game, I'd fill the water bucket. The source of water, invariably, was a long way off. On the return trip to the bench, carrying the heavy galvanized bucket filled with water as well as an old-fashioned dipper, I would switch the burden from one hand to the other as the handle made deep creases in my palms. My legs would be bruised, and the pant legs of my jeans would be wet from the bumping of the bucket against my legs.

By mid-afternoon, the game would start; the wind would lift the dust from the infield and swirl it slowly toward right field. From the grandstands filled with spectators would come the shrill voices of women, the harsh, angry-sounding voices of men, and an occasional loud, slurred, and often absurd utterance of a drunk calling to a fielder who had erred. "Pay no mind, Ronnie, Pay no mind." If the home team rallied, the fans in their cars parked along the edges of the field would sound their horns in a cacophony of approval. But the clamor would die away after a strikeout or maybe a double play.

When the opposition was batting, there were no bats for me to gather, so I could sit on the bench and watch my father pitch. He was big, broad-shouldered, and just a little heavy in the middle. His arms were long, and his strong wrists and hands extended from the sleeves of a heavy sweatshirt. Everything about him seemed veteran, seasoned, and conditioned by long use: his faded cap whitened with salt residue, his spikes with the metal toe plate (the badge of the pitcher) on the right shoe, and his old-fashioned flat glove with its unlaced fingers and small web.

On the mound, he had an air of competence and grace, and the height of the mound made him seem even bigger than usual. After getting his sign, he'd rock forward and then back, his left knee and foot would come up as he'd roll his hips from left to right, and then as he pivoted and pushed off with his right foot, his right arm would extend and his right hand clutching the ball would drop behind him, but his eyes would remain on the target. Then as I would watch with awe (seeing something beautiful, graceful, and powerful and somehow poignant because that something was my father), he would uncoil his left leg and step toward the plate. His right arm would come whipping forward (accompanied in the late innings by an audible grunt indicating a supreme effort drawn from a tiring body by an indefatigable spirit), and then the ball would appear, not as a white sphere but as a linear, translucent blur that hissed toward the catcher for a fraction of a second before disappearing into the leathery pocket of the catcher's mitt with a startling pop. Again, and again. Hisssss...... . pop!

Soon, as the side was retired, our players would come to the bench. They were men with tanned faces and powerful hands and forearms. Some would chew tobacco and spit, producing in the dust a thin line and a circle of wetness which *they would unconsciously wipe away with their spikes. As I moved to the bat rack at the end of the bench, I would hear someone say to my father, "Way to go, Les." And to one another, "Come on: let's rattle those bats." Remembering each player's favorite bat, I'd give the right bats to the first batter and the on-deck batter. Then, I would stand and wait for the instant when I would have to run to the plate and quickly get the discarded bat, all the while keeping myself out of the way of the nonchalant swings of the on-deck hitter and watching the batter on each pitch to avoid getting drilled by one of those treacherous foul balls that come from late swings or half swings.*

Eventually, after three outs, the ebb and flow of the teams would recur. The afternoon would slip away. I remember it all: the long shadows of the grandstand stretching out to home plate, the sun rays slanting through the lazy clouds of dust, the smell of sweat and leather, the hoarse and shrill voices of the fans, and the whistles and the half-intelligible voices of the infielders "talking it up." But most vividly, I remember my father (quiet, splendid, heroic) hurling that sizzling white blur into the catcher's mitt. Hiss! Pop! Strieek three: Yer out!

— Roger Mueller, 1983

As for me, I had barely crossed into Columbia, IL, the evening of May 18, 2005, when I learned how unpredictable my $500 Salvation Army investment was. I had driven the 1986 Ford Tempo— dubbed "The Chick Magnet" by my college roommate —forty minutes down highway 255 to Illinois Route 3 into the town of Columbia. Columbia was seven miles from Waterloo—

my destination. I was already running late when disaster struck.

A busted water pump brought the clunker to a sudden halt. It wasn't enough that the car's ten-dollar rims had been stolen at the college laundromat a week prior, transforming the classic car's look to a mere junkyard piece — now its function was the way of its appearance. I had already missed the two opening pre-season workouts. It was seeming like I was going to be tardy for the summer opener against the club just added to the league this year — the St. Louis Spikes — a team filled with county league stars from the big city — Jay Davis, Steve Maher, John Altis, Mitch Thomas, and Mike Tallis.

I coasted the dead sedan toward the shoulder next to a line of twenty impatient cars finishing their commute from St. Louis after a full day's work. I pushed open the door, regrettably stepped out, and forced the lemon up the hill across the bi-way and into the free parking lot of a nearby gas station.

"How the hell am I gonna pay for this one?" I wondered.

I'd been fortunate enough with scholarships not to accumulate any debts at school and was counting on my summer job as an environmental trash man to dig me out of the hole of being the dead-broke college kid that I was. My parents had put me on my own after high school as a way of easing me into the natural world. Somehow, it worked, as I managed to become the responsible and frugal son, it seemed my dad had always wanted me to be. However, less than a week into summer, I was already hundreds in the hole. Thankfully, I had just enough time to call Harry.

I can still make the game, I thought to myself. Harry will surely come if he answers—if my Kyocera has a signal and a charge. Two bars and 6%. I was in business.

Harry, reliable to a fault, picked up after one ring. It took him 5 minutes to travel the 7 miles to the station. The rumbling of Harry's Camaro pulling into the Phillips 66 let me know that it was time to go for a ride. "Cam can!" we hollered as we peeled out. He bested his time on the return trip. Four minutes seemed like an eternity. "Cam can!"

The parking lot at Ss. Peter and Paul Park, tucked in among the old homes and the decades-old maples, extended back from a chain-link fence lining the right side of the diamond. Harry sped Cam into one of the last remaining spots.

I saw the rest of the guys grouped up near the dugout, itching to take the field as the umpires trudged in from beyond the right-field fence, ready to "play ball." I quickly grabbed my gear out of the trunk, thanked Harry, and hustled to the guys. I dropped my bag on the bench. The Prince was the first to greet me. He looked me straight in the eyes with what had to be a Mississippi-sized grin. Or was it a glare? I couldn't tell.

"Ohlau, you mother f—er! Ask out my girlfriend, you son of a b—?!! And have the nerve to come back here!?" the Prince fumed. Jokingly, I presumed.

"Come on, man," I desperately pleaded, smiling from ear to ear. "That was months ago...and...I had no idea you could get a girl like that. She is beautiful!" referring to the Prince's newfound younger love interest.

We both laughed out loud at the ironic and seemingly unforgettable circumstance of me mistakenly asking out his girlfriend eight months prior in the campus gym. We slapped hands in welcome.

Cool, sunny, and calm ruled the evening. It was Opening Day. The initial unease of the challenging commute had worn off, and it was time to play ball. The setting sun shone brightly on us. The breeze smelled fresh, of cool cut grass. Newly painted green benches sat comfortably behind the old steel backstop. The tall maples shaded each line where the crowd could gather. The beautiful topography set the field front and center, laminated by the shadows of the setting sun. The grass was the best-kept lawn in the county, clean as the living room floor on which you practiced the Mickey Mantle hook slide your dad taught you.

The squeal of a power saw from a nearby woodworking business echoed over the complex. The distraction bothered Vern, and he muttered under his breath. The field, filled with the colors of spring, was now filled with motion. Players were warming up. Vern counted us—we had all shown.

Vern assembled this year's roster months before, stretching back to August and September of 2004. Competing against the other league coaches for the same thin piece of the local talent pool, Vern couldn't afford to wait until spring for half-hearted declarations of commitment and bottom-of-the-barrel talent. He didn't have the luxury of penciling in one of the countless great staples of past Bud teams like Jimmy or Johnny Wahlig, Neil Fiala, Carl Braun, Mike Wirth, Mark Ludwig, Jim Anderson, Lonnie Fulte, Todd McClure, Mike Roy, Dick Dillinger, Rick Keefe, Roger Ferguson, Scott Haberl, Tony Musso, or even recently retired Buck Riva or Vern's son Clay Moehrs — Clay retired abruptly at the end of last season. It was rumored Vern didn't want him to miss a weekend of baseball to take a family vacation. Father and son disagreed.

In the fall, on the white-lined paper, the team had looked strong. Vern created his ideal balance of young and old, right- and left-handed, leaders and followers, and, most important of all, a deep pitching staff. Looking at his work in front of him, Vern saw zero weaknesses. Except maybe Kaiser up the middle. Kaiser was the wild card. At 38, Kaiser had lost a step or two in the past few years. He had just come off a previous summer where he hit an all-time worst .258 in limited time in the infield. With Clay gone, Kaiser needed to step up.

Vern saw a group of dedicated, skilled, hungry ballplayers. He believed in building a roster of loyal and committed men. And just like jockeys in horse racing, Vern planned to ride his thoroughbreds across the finish line in August regardless of the ride's turbulence. Vern's balanced roster relied on youth and experience, a hallmark of winning teams.

The three coaches mulled several possible batting orders before finally agreeing. The lineup was set. It read:

Player	Position	Age	College
Friederich, Jake	2B	23	St. Louis University
Thompson, Aaron	LF	21	Butler
Ohlau, Craig	1B	23	SIUE
Queern, Jim	CF	23	Mckendree
Caby, Eric	C	22	Quincy
Hardin, Pat	3B	22	Truman State
Blackwell, Corey	P	27	SIUE
Wigger, Chas	DH	22	Missouri St. Louis
Kaiser, Jeff	SS	38	Missouri State
Hurst, Jake	FR	25	SWIC/Daytona State

Reserves: Thompson, Jordan 18, Baxmeyer, John 38, Bergheger, Jeremiah 27
Pitchers: Musso, Brandon 27, Mueller, Mark 23, Smith, Brian 29,
Waeltz, Brandon 23, Buck, Peter 28, Schlecht, Jim 38

"My strategy in putting together a roster was simple. Although the league permits 22 players per team, I carried only the number I thought I could use—an active player is a happy player, and an inactive one is not. The competition is on the field—not the bench. Most of my players were kept happy. I was always an excellent coach—all I ever had to do was write out the lineup."

Woodies

In the early days of baseball, wood bats ruled every level of baseball. Ash, the robust and light wood, had emerged as the popular bat of choice. Despite the light wood, batters of the old dead-ball era (1900-1919) still swung heavy, long bats. Babe Ruth wielded a 47 ouncer when he belted sixty home runs in 1927. Roger Maris started a revolution of sorts when he broke the Babe's record in 1961, using a bat of 33 ounces. Lighter models were becoming more and more popular as hitters were beginning to understand the importance of bat speed. The lighter, thin-handled bats favored stars of the era like Ted Williams and Henry Aaron. Players began taking notice.

Heavier models sank into the depths of history by the later years of the twentieth century. In the 1980s, however, as athletes became bigger and stronger, some hitters began switching back to a denser wood. Wood, heavy or not, has a significant draw-back—its durability. Depending on the hitter, a Major Leaguer could break 200 bats in a single season. Some hitters chose the more durable ash. Ash bats that don't break deteriorate after a few hundred hacks. Even with the more durable ash as an option, replacement costs are high when it comes to wood bats. This can be easily taken care of by pro teams, whereas leagues like the Mon-Clair had to consider alternatives. In 1970 Hellerich and Bradsby, a big maker of wood bats, collaborated with Alcoa, a metals giant, on its first generation of a new kind of bat, one made of aluminum. The original idea to produce a long-lasting alternative to wood may have been supported by prudence, but aluminum bat makers soon conquered wood's performance. Not constrained by the ratio handicaps present in solid timber, engineers toyed with the balances of metal. Within a decade, lightweight thin-walled aluminum had replaced wood at every youth and amateur level. The Mon-Clair league made the switch in 1980. The first bats were awkward feeling. But as the technology improved, they got better and better and better. Wood quickly became an afterthought and the "ping" quickly replaced the "crack."

I was used to swinging the wood. It was part, along with a certain girl, of what appealed to me at the small University in Southern Illinois. SIUE was part of one of the only wood bat conferences in college baseball at the time, the Great Lakes Valley Conference. Using wood seemed cool. I could play college ball and, at the same time, prepare for my future pro career. With my short and smooth natural swing, I managed a semi-successful college career swinging the woodie. Sam Bats and X Bats were my bats of choice. They were made from maple— the hardwood. I didn't pick them because of their hardness. Similar to youngsters emulating Ted Williams and Hank Aaron with their thin handles, I mirrored the modern-day sluggers Barry Bonds and Sammy Sosa on their preference of bat brands. My thought process was simple and more than naive. "If I use the same bats they are using; then I'm bound to hit more home runs." If only I'd been privy to their real secret.

With that being said, after blasting twelve home runs the preceding summer ('04) with my favorite juiced up

TPX, I was eager as heck to step into the box for the Buds and grip the thin handle of my beloved Tournament Players Extra-Light Baseball Bat once again.

My first two at-bats in the opener with the Spikes netted a lineout to short and a hard single through the right side. It was only a matter of time for me to center one up in the air. I adopted a more patient approach in my third at-bat.

The air was growing cool as nighttime approached— it was now the 5th inning. I took the first pitch of at-bat #3, an off-speed hammer down and away. I watched the second, a fastball, miss, inside. With the count 2-0, it was time to change my approach. Patience was now an afterthought. I geared up for a swing.

Hisss. It was a boiler down and in.

I loved 'em down and in. Most lefties do. Why? You ask. Well...it's a question that has perplexed baseball minds for years. My kinesiological take on it is this: *Physiologically left-handed people tend to have more muscular non-dominant arms relative to right-handers—they are more often ambidextrous. You see this all the time, as many natural lefties can throw, bat, and swing golf clubs effectively right-handed. The reverse is rarely true. A low pitch requires power from the front (non-dominant) arm to drive with less force needed from the back (dominant) arm. High pitches are reversed. They require more power from the back (dominant) arm. If you don't believe me, try it. Swing a bat and feel where most of the energy is generated.*

My left-handed low-ball uppercut sent the low-inside fastball flying into the dark, crisp right-center field air. I felt the concussion in the palm of my hand.

The ball lifted high in the summer air toward the fence. With the maple X-bat woodie I was used to swinging at the University, the ball may have flown 350 feet and one-hopped the wall. But this wasn't college ball. Mike Tallis, the Spikes star centerfielder, raced for the gap until running out of room at the base of the chain length wall. The three-run blast cleared the 360 sign by twenty feet—our lead increased to six—the game was all but over. We added a run in the eighth as our pitching platoon topped off a nine-inning, six-hit, one-run Mona Lisa.

We hopped out of the dugout after the last out was recorded, lined up to shake hands, high-fived, low-fived, and told the Spikes good game—our post-win ritual—our major-league ritual—our first win of '05.

Chapter 6
"Red Gold"

Cruising the reconditioned Chick Magnet into my summer place of employment at the Metro St. Louis waste remediation facility a few minutes before 7:00 a.m., now $400 poorer, I felt the twinge of a bum knee and the seed of a dull ache growing in my neck. "Are you kidding me; this is how old man Kaiser is supposed to feel," I groaned to myself and fellow part-time temp, local high schooler and nephew of one of the owners, Keaton Flood.

"Let's go sleep in the new break room I made. I threw a couch into the truck driver's closet in the warehouse. It's pretty chill," Keaton remarked. "It is way too damn early to do any work."

I laughed at his adolescent statement as we had just started the day.

Although I had been passed over "talented," more "experienced," or more "connected" applicants for the summer gig I most desired, I was offered a summer job of a little less prestige. I was to be a warehouse floozy—my duties ranged from sweeping the fume-saddened warehouse to power-vacuuming deadly chemicals from buried pipes deep in the ground to transporting scrap to the Brooklyn auto shredder and leftover trash to the local landfill. The job was offered to me by one of the owners, Paul Bonde—former Army sergeant turned cut-throat environmental sanitation worker. But, more notably, he was the father of my current love interest. I accepted the work for two reasons: one, I desperately needed the cash, and two, it seemed in more ways than one that I had to. I enjoyed the freedom and the physical work the job offered. I asked for extra hours to help pay off the busted water pump, the stolen hubcaps, and a police citation I received for rolling through a campus stop sign. I was able to work from 7:00 a.m. to 4:00 p.m.—this allowed me to get my hours in, get home, work out, eat, recreate—which often meant playing poker online—and be ready for anything else the summer nights would allow.

In the sizeable organized office, Bonde had toiled for an hour already, preparing the day. "Get in here!" he directed his two summer apprentices. "The manifests for the drums in need of pick up are in the folder," he said, handing us the manila envelope holding the day's manifests. "Take the truck. You'll need a dolly and an extra ring for the drum you pick up from Casey's. It's missing a ring, and trust me on that one—you will need the ring, or the oil will spill. Get the directions to the other sites. Take the scrap in the truck to the shredder before you do any of the pick-ups. Make sure they give you payment. If you need anything, call." The retired Master Sergeant was always direct with his orders.

We sauntered over to the adjacent office where truck drivers Tim, a 6 '5'' sturdy-looking Viking of a man, and Chuck, a 50-year-old shaggy-haired goofball gomer prankster socialized with the office staff. "Hey, boys!" I boomed to the duo of truckers. For days we had been going back and forth with how much shit we could throw in each other's direction.

Chuck took the honors. "So, Ofer, how'd you guys do Wednesday night?" Referring to our game against the Spikes. "Were you an ofer? Ofer. Or were you a homer?" Chuck's compunctious sense of humor was evident as he laughed loudly at his own words.

"Chuckles," I responded with arrogant sarcasm, "we won, baby, and I dropped a bomb that hasn't even landed yet."

Looking over the two rough men, Keaton chimed in. "Damn, you guys must work out. You're lookin' good in those jeans," Keaton sarcastically stated as he walked by, slapping the backsides of their form-fitted Wranglers.

Tim snarled as he chased the young apprentice down the hall. "I'm gonna beat your little ass!"

"We got to get to work," Keaton yelled, running away laughing.

We got to work. After reading the manifests, we loaded the white F-150. Tyvek suits, CHECK. Gloves,

CHECK. Masks, CHECK. Where's the dolly? The dull cement floors crackled, and the air smelled of chemical gasoline as I retrieved the drum dolly and put it on the back of the truck. The radio from our newly transformed breakroom droned classic hits as we readied the Ford. Whitesnake was quickly drowned out by the heavy beeping of a reversing forklift loading barrels of oil, gasoline, and sulfates into the waiting trailer. I grabbed some extra rings for the drums, and we were off.

The stops listed on the work order went as planned as we unloaded hundreds of pounds of scrap metal at the East St. Louis shredder—a place where old Tempos like mine go to die. We witnessed a few tragic deaths as we skittishly threw our stainless steel overboard under the crashing claw of the crane. As we exited the Eastside, we waved to a soliciting hooker working the corner, almost breaking the law in the process. We passed by the baseball field we would be visiting in a few weeks, the home of the East St. Louis Colt 45s–the 45s had a long history in the Mon-Clair League dating back to the '70s with stars such as Louis Cochran, Art Fields, and Don Stovall representing through the years. With the now empty bed, we ventured to a Wood River Phillips 66 where a single 500-pound dirt/oil barrel awaited. The hydraulic lift gate on our Ford made it less hard to load. We drove to a Casey's General Store in South City to pick up the two grease barrels we were warned of, and one indeed was missing a ring. We headed Next to Barnes Hospital for a mystery drum, and to the cafeteria grease pits of the Fenton Chrysler plant for more oil, this time of the vegetable variety. We successfully finished in record time—if you minus the 20 gallons of grease spilled in Casey's parking lot. We returned to the shop, conquering heroes. Two temp environmental garbage men navigating a city, kicking ass, and taking names.

To the truck drivers at the shop, we were entitled. Privileged. The boss's nephew and the boyfriend of the boss's daughter. I forgave them for their miscalculation. I couldn't speak for Keaton, but privileged or not, they couldn't fault me for my hard-working attitude. Bonde said I was the hardest-working summer help he had ever hired. He never called me the smartest. He also mentioned I was the only floozy with a college degree. I wasn't sure how I should take that compliment. He ordered me one last job of the day. "Ohlau cut up those six drums. Use the good Sawzall this time, and when you're done cutting, toss all the pieces into the dumpster. Put your suit on, wear the gloves and the glasses. You never know what the hell is in those things. Even when the manifest says Non-Haz, it could very well be hazardous—this is a dirty business. Whatever is in there, you don't want it on you, and you sure as hell don't want it in you. Get that done and you can take off early. Be careful."

Damn, he told me to be careful. He must be starting to like me, I thought. "Fine by me, sir," I said, halfway smiling, knowing what I had left to do. I grabbed the saw, my glasses, and my gloves, shrugged off the idea of wearing my suit—It was 110 degrees in the warehouse—I didn't want to die of heatstroke. I got to work, making my $7.35/hour. At about the same time Bonde was walking away, my Sawzall was reaching climax. Over the loud growl of the saw, a loud explosion rang out just outside the warehouse doors. Bonde scurried quickly in the direction of the bang. I looked straight at Keaton through the blurred lenses of my red, sweat-stained goggles.

"What in the hell are we doing here?" I asked my young co-worker, my arms vibrating as the saw shredded the plastic.

"We are getting rich," Keaton answered. "Just look at that," he said, pointing to the vibrating plastic being torn into pieces propelling red liquid solution into the air and onto my exposed arms and face. "You struck gold...Red Gold!"

CHAPTER 7
BIG JUICY

"To me, playing for the Buds was everything. Every year I got older, and you know, anything could have happened that ended things for me. A knee, my back...I wanted to play every game and play as long as I could. Baseball was everything to me."
— *Ironman Jake Hurst*

A dozen spectators showed up early for the first Sunday doubleheader of the summer season. The opposing team was Millstadt VFW. The typical 1:30 p.m. Sunday afternoon start allowed fans to go to church, attend brunch, and then relax for a day of baseball in the town's backyard. In the Monroe division of the Mon-Clair league, four teams played home games within an eight-mile radius.

The pregame hitting practice gave the few fans present an opportunity to witness things they might not get a chance to see in any one game. We felt the eyes watching as we swung.

The batting practice, like most summer batting practices, had a laid back, comforting rhythm. Buds flowed freely in and out of the batter's box and on-deck circle. We angled bunts down each baseline and sprayed line drives into the gaps. Fly balls floated to the warning track and occasionally found their way out — disappearing beyond the outfield fence. We searched for rhythm, worked on our flaws, and attempted to shake off any rust. It was easy to do our work against Coach Vogel, arguably the best BP hurler in the eight-county region. Vogel, throwing three-quarter speed, put the pitches right where the hitter wanted them.

Eric Caby showed once again why he was one of our main power guys. Caby shattered the rhythm. He made people look up from their conversations with his Wahligian power. The pings of the aluminum rang out, echoing through the long arcs of air. He'd hit them high, piercing the leafy canopy of the trees protecting the neighborhood beyond the left-field wall. He homered on four, five, six consecutive swings. Even the casual observers could sense a different fury in the contact he made.

Only one other player on the team, right-fielder Jake Hurst, could rival Caby's BP home run show. Like many of the different Buds, Hurst grew up in a small, southern Illinois town. He'd played at tiny New Athens High School, had been recruited by a few junior colleges, and washed out of making it in the pro game after finishing college — a common theme amongst his fellow Buds.

"I'm going to play with a harder nonchalance this year," Hurst facetiously replied as Vern commanded him to hurry into the box to begin his round.

He stood six feet tall, possessed a beer drinker's core and long arms that quickly extended against Vogel's slow cock high pitches. Scientifically, Hurst created a long lever and generated large amounts of energy when cutting his swing loose. He cocked his bat back by moving his hands as he transitioned into his rhythm. By doing this, he had to start his swing early to get his power.

"A long swing," analyzed Vern—a weakness that is amplified when facing better, faster pitching. This swing feature earned him the title of the Buds' best twelve-o'clock hitter.

Hurst was known on the team as "Big Punisher"—Punisher for short—or sometimes even "Big Juicy"—referencing his burly stature and the signature 62 oz. sno-cone he sold at his hometown shaved ice stand. His outgoing attitude, lumberjack physique, and reluctance to cut down and shorten up his swing lent credence to his nicknames. Vern quipped, often sarcastically, "Swing harder, Jake! Damn it...for Chrissake, just shorten up and put it in play!" Punisher rarely listened.

The game started slow but ran swiftly. At the top of the fourth inning, Caby led off against Millstadt's hard-throwing right-hander Andy Galle. Galle, a local boy from the nearby town of Columbia and a current Indiana

State Sycamore—known for his fastball that peaked at 90 mph—was aggressive and liked to work fast. A confident hurler, he believed in getting ahead with first-pitch strikes and challenging hitters. Caby cut loose on such a fastball and laced a bullet to the power alley in left for a two-bagger. After a few quick outs, Punisher followed. He quickly fell behind in the count, no balls, two strikes. Punisher stepped out of the box contemplating his approach while tightening the Velcro on his gloves. He wore eye black that spread throughout his entire face — similar to that of the Ultimate Warrior of professional wrestling — wrist bands on both arms, tape on his wrists, and Oakley sunglasses on his eyes. A loud, direct command came screaming from the third base coach's box. "Shorten up and hit the damn ball!" Punisher glared toward the barking Vern. Shaking his head in disgust, he re-entered the box.

Galle had averaged better than a strikeout per inning in his first two outings of the summer and knew full well the mentality of his present rival. Punisher took a vicious cut at the 88mph fastball in his eyes. Luckily for him, he was able to tip it just barely as his bat entered the zone.

"Put the damn ball in play!" Vern yelled again. "For Chrissake!"

Punisher gripped the bat with a juicy vigor. He had grown more confident with each pitch. After all, he had gone 5-5 with three doubles in the previous game vs. the Spikes. He was in what athletes would call "the zone" — the feeling of enhanced focus and clarity that comes on suddenly and unpredictably that enables one to perform at a very high level. He was riding the feeling. Hitters yearn for it. As much as drug addicts crave their next fixation or high, athletes ache for their next experience in "the zone."

Punisher had no way of knowing how long he'd stay hot — he could stay in the zone for an at-bat, a game, a string of games, or a month. And then lose it just as suddenly or mysteriously.

The ever-confident Galle was worn with the idea of blowing the fastball by the aggressive Punisher. However, he knew the weakness his opponent possessed. He opted for the pitch with a little more finesse—the slider. Galle whittled the snapper at a perfect location down and away as Punisher exited "the zone." Anticipating a heater, Punisher swung early, over the top of the tumbling brick. The strikeout ended the inning.

In the sixth, with the score tied 1-1, Punisher got a second chance. He returned to the box and remarkably re-entered "the zone." Learning from Caby in the fourth, he took advantage of the first pitch from Galle. The 0-0 pitch from the now laboring Galle floated into Punisher's honey hole—up in the zone and over the plate. The perfect ball position for the Bud slugger to extend his hands and apply maximum bat acceleration. The small sphere exploded from the "ping," rising high and deep into left field. In the majors a ball hit with that kind of trajectory and height is called a major league fly ball. Most balls contacted in such a manner, a fraction below the sweet spot with most of the bat's energy working towards the ball's upward motion, don't make it over the fence. This one, however, kept going and going and going. Fans behind home gasped at the moon shot as it floated further and further toward the trees. Watching from the top step of the dugout, I laughed. I wasn't watching the ball. I was watching Punisher's bat flip and his Cadillac trot around the bases. I mimicked his uppercut, pretended to stand for a moment watching the blast, flip the bat, then slowly walk to first, still admiring.

"Damn Pun, Lucy could've made it around the bases faster than that," Jordy said, laughing.

"I got that one...didn't I Vernie?!" Punisher broadcast rounding third as everyone was now having a good time.

"Oh, now that you finally got one, you decided to talk again? It's good to have you back, Pun. You were starting to act like Franchise," Jordy added with a grin, referencing Franchise's pouty nature during struggling times at the plate. "That's just great. Now Galle is prolly gonna plunk poor Franchise." Franchise, looking anxious in the on-deck circle, was next up. Jordy's humor seemed to restore a little of the natural balance usually present in the dugout.

The Millstadt players, always seeming thin-skinned when it came to a batter supposedly showing up a pitcher, had taken offense to Punisher's shenanigans. Neither manager nor club wanted a repeat of last year's beanball war that took place from similar transgressions that led to a bench-clearing brawl—a brawl which saw two Millstadt players getting bruised and bloodied and numerous Buds players getting ejected.

Cooler heads prevailed and Franchise did not get plunked.

A few batters later in the same inning, after Galle exited, designated hitter Chas Wigger stood in against a glass-armed Millstadt fireman and crushed a 2-0 fastball into the trees—the ball almost identically following the same travel plan as Punishers.

"This is Buds baseball!" yelled Vern as he shook hands with his smiling Bud during his home-run trot around third base.

"Big Juicies for everybody!"

CHAPTER 8
THE BALL PLAYER

"There ain't much to being a ballplayer
if you're a ballplayer."
— Honus Wagner

"The most unfortunate thing is that money and television
has changed the game. It has transformed most of the nation
into spectators and pretenders instead of actual participants."
— Lon Fulte

We were fresh off doubleheader sweeps of Millstadt, East St. Louis, Fairview Heights, Marissa, and Valmeyer, and single-game wins vs. the Spikes, Cape Girardeau, and the St. Louis Printers. Our only loss was to Columbia in Game 2 of our home series—our record stood at 14-1. We were rolling in the good times.

The morning sun diffused through the crooked blinds of my one-bedroom apartment window. Another Sunday had arrived — I headed south.

At Ss. Peter and Paul Field, on June 19, the Young Guns of Marissa, came to town to close out our season series. Mueller was set to start. The slender right-hander had given up only one hit and struck out nine the previous Sunday as he shut down arch-rival Valmeyer on their home turf. In doing so, he stretched his league-winning streak to seven dating back to last summer. Years later, Mark would recall his one-hitter and 2005 state of mind vividly:

"It was the Summer of 2005. I remember a lot from back then, although frankly, I'm not so sure how I can recall much of anything from that time period. One of my favorites from that season was the day I pitched a one-hitter with no underwear. Valmeyer's famous Twyla Luhr Field is well-known for its sweltering heat and humidity, and this Sunday was no exception. 98+ humidity at 1:30 game time, with plenty of humidity to spare. The opposing pitcher was a young fella by the name of Floarke. The big red-headed right-hander ended up the Monroe division ERA champion. I remembered that he had a bit of a reputation for being a hot head while pitching at

SWIC, and I hoped to bring that out in full force this afternoon and get him out of his game. The previous night a friend of mine had one of his locally famous ragers that featured massive amounts of beer kegs, beer bongs, 75+college age guys and girls who thought that this would be way better than going to a local bar on a Saturday night. They were correct in that respect. This was not my first rodeo, so I packed my baseball bag and uniform in my car, anticipating that I'd stay at my friend's house and head straight to the ball field and arrive just in time for the 1:30 start time. The party was insane! There was a pool house close to the deep end of the pool that if you could make the dangerous climb up a retaining wall, balance on a light post, then leap onto the roof of the pool house, you could make an epic run and jump into the pool. "And the crowd went wild" is what the voice in your head is saying while you mustered up the courage to do it. So, I'm a bold guy, but not bold enough to drop my drawers in front of 75 people and jump off a 15-ft. roof. Plus, you needed to wear shoes if you were going to make this epic climb and leap. And there's nothing cool about a naked guy with just a pair of Nikes on. So, I cannon-balled into the pool—my shorts and underwear on—and continued raging into the late hours of the night. The next morning when it came time to get ready for the game, my boxers were still ridiculously soaked. I had coach Neil Fiala's voice in my head, saying, 'Hell, baby, just go commando.' In Neil I trusted, so I did just that. Solid preparation goes a long way toward achieving consistently good performances in baseball. With that being said, sometimes you prepare all week just like you should, and on game day, your stuff is very average. Other times you just have "it" for no good reason at *all. That day I had it. I was throwing hard all seven innings. My fastball in my prime sat upper 80s, touching 90 mph with deceptive arm motion and late movement. I remember hearing Kaiser at shortstop early in the game, saying to Jake Friederich, 'He's throwing pretty hard today.' And like most of my best outings over my career, I had an effective changeup that day, even to right-handers. I knew after one time through the lineup Valmeyer wasn't going to get many hits. But what I wasn't sure of was whether or not I'd have a heat stroke and pass out. But I had an old trick I learned in the Khoury League. I put ice cubes in my hat when I went out to pitch before each inning. They managed one single that day, but because I can't hold runners on worth a shit, he stole 2nd, advanced again and scored on a fielder's choice. There's a reason why all of us are in the county league—it's because we have holes in our game. So, it's a 1-1 game late, and I'm really banking on getting in Floarke's head with some off-the-wall shit that I'm going to yell at him while he's on the mound. 'He's throwing turkey burgers up there, sit on it.' Or 'Grip it and rip it, slap a gap, choke and poke, hit it right off his shoe-tops like Tris Speaker.' Ball one... 'He's rattled, he doesn't know what to do.' Ball two in the dirt...'He's killing worms, he's choking his brains out.' Ball three...'Freakin' gosh darn, show some gumption out there, show some moxie.' 'Back door, screen door.' 'Chocolate Thunder, Chocolate Paradise.' Ball four... 'We got to keep our composure; we've come too far.' And the chants just get more ridiculous as the trouble on the mound brews. It builds into a crescendo until the guy on the mound is thinking more about walking off the field and trying to kick your ass than he's thinking about throwing strikes and holding runners on. You* see him start to break out there and the dugout takes the momentum. The next thing you hope for is for the umpire to not give him a borderline pitch. Naturally, the choking, pissed off pitcher shows up the umpire, disputes the call from the mound, looks like an ass, and the wheels keep falling off. Floarke is looking in our dugout, trying to snuff out the nut job hollering nonsensical baseball references, abstract commentary, and popular movie quotes at the top of his lungs. That would be none other than the opposing pitcher trying to eke out another victory in this heated rivalry game while pitching with no underpants and a soaking wet, crooked baseball cap. We did it. We scored our second run of the game, and I pitched them out in dominant fashion the rest of the way. Time to ice the arm, run some poles, and have a few beers and bask in the glory of a complete-game victory against the hated rivals in their own ballpark.

2005 was the last summer I got to play catch with my brother Kurt Mueller. It was also the last summer I played catch with my good friend Ben. Kurt would die suddenly of a drug overdose while I was playing in Adelaide, South Australia, December 17, 2005. Ben's candle was more of a slow burn. He overdosed in April 2008, but the summer of 2005 was the last time I recognized the person who I loved like a brother and understood me better than any other friend or teammate I had ever had. How could I have known those things then? I was riding this minor local celebrity thing telling people stories of the dreams of my future.

At 23, and lucky enough to have a regular job, I had saved up a bit of money from September to May, working at Mueller Furniture with my dad. In Early 2005 I received a letter in the mail with a contract to report to Spring training with the Mid-Missouri Mavericks. Baseball in the previous summer of 2004 was a step in the right direction. I was invited to Spring training with the defending Frontier League champions, the Gateway Grizzlies. They averaged 5,000 fans a night, and even though only 500 intently watched the game, it felt like real professional baseball. Busch Stadium is right across the muddy Mississippi River in St Louis. You can see Busch Stadium every time you enter or leave the park; it was like seeing your dreams so close to being fulfilled, but in reality, it's a hell of a long way from the Frontier League to the big Leagues. It's not impossible, though; people have done it, and many of us truly believed that with improvement and a little luck, we could still make it. That brand of ball is not like college where you go to school, make grades, and the coaches yell and scream and all you do is practice. We played every night at 7 pm in front of paying fans and kids that asked for your autograph while I watched and dissected the game pitch by pitch in the bullpen. I'd wake up in the morning and choose whether I should lift weights or recover from a hangover. I'd be back at the park by 3 o'clock to start pre-game stretching, running, throwing, and more running. You condition your body to play ball every night. It gave me perspective on just how good the big Leaguers are. I always thought that I had a major-league fastball. It's true, I could throw ONE. But a REAL big leaguer throws that fastball every time, day after day, game after game. If I threw a 7-inning game of 110 pitches, probably 80 fastballs, only 20 would be legit big-league pitches. Upper 80s to 90, downhill trajectory, late and hard sink, down in the zone with an arm-side run. The ability to repeat it is the challenge. That's why you get the running done, that's why you kill yourself on the leg press, jump squats, and with the medicine ball so you build the physique that allows you to repeat a powerful delivery under the duress of a baseball game. I made the team and pitched so well in inter-squad and preseason they had me as their number 4 starter. I thought to myself, Holy shit, I finally actually got good. It was the first time since 6th grade tryouts that I really had to bust my ass to make a team. After a subpar start and a bad relief outing, I was cut. By noon the next day, I was on my way to the Gas Mart in Millstadt to sign a contract to play for the Waterloo Buds. I was dominant in my month with the Buds that summer. I continued to call the Grizzlies Coach Fiala and Danny Cox, even bringing in a video of one of my starts, trying to show them I deserved another shot. Gateway didn't want me, but they did get me a tryout with the Mid-Missouri Mavericks while they were visiting for a 3-game set. I showed up, threw every pitch I had as hard as I could and impressed them enough for them to sign me. Now if I could only make it until August 11th, then there's no more roster moves, and I'm guaranteed to be on the team the rest of the year. I was given the role of middle relief, which meant I had to be ready to pitch every single night instead of just one out of every five days. I enjoyed it and did well. I thought I established myself as an above-average relief pitcher. I went into camp in 2005 with the Mavericks with the full intention of making the club and staying with them the entire season. Or if by chance I get cut somewhere along the line, I would have enough of a reputation to catch on with another club. That's how professional baseball (and come to find out professional life) works out. You know a guy on another team well enough that he can put a word in for you to the manager. Someone on their team struggles, you get a tryout and your baseball career has life again. When I arrived at camp, the first thing I noticed was we had a different pitching coach. Same manager. "Diamond" Jim Gentile was an old school baseball-type that reminded me of my grandfather's era of ballplayers. At every bit of 6 ft 4 and 275 pounds, he was still a mountain of a man at 71 years old. I pitched well in two inter-squad games, getting out in succession our 3,4, 5 hitters on 7 pitches. Looking back, it happened too quickly, not any strikeouts. In an exhibition game in Evansville, Indiana, in the same stadium they shot the movie A League of Their Own, I gave up 2 runs on a 2-out, 2-strike shitter of a fastball up and out over the plate to a left-handed batter. Banking on my previous summer success and reliability, I still thought I had done enough to show the new coaches. But they kept 2 guys that were real raw talents. 6 ft 5 230-240 pounds throwing low to mid 90s. They sure as shit had no idea where it was going, and most of the time the slider was buried in the dirt or the fastball was a straight cock-shot. They got hit hard, too. I understood keeping the Dominican guy, he had real talent, but the other was complete garbage. Neither of them lasted the year. Since I was cut on the last day of spring training, the other teams had already set their rosters. My last chance was the River City Rascals in O'Fallon, Missouri, or one possible last crack to get back with the Grizzlies. I was desperate at this point, holding on to hope. Neither panned out. I was the kind of athlete that was right on the cusp of real professional talent. What it would have taken for me to make it would have been nothing short of a psychotic dedication to the game and complete discipline and maturity towards life off the field. I worked and trained hard, harder than 90% of guys on the teams I played on. But the going out, not sleeping enough, not eating right truly affected my physical development and my mental health. It is why I never made it further than the Frontier League. 2004's momentum was curtailed when I was unable to make the right connections and got sent off to play winter ball in Australia. So, I stayed at home and worked full-time at the family business, Mueller Furniture Company in Belleville, IL. A blessing for my life, a curse for my baseball career. I loved the whole, I wake up every day and try to make myself a better baseball player aspect of professional baseball. There's nothing else but baseball and training for baseball. My plan was not to work or find a job at a gym or somewhere that would hire a history major with no work experience besides delivering furniture. That way I could keep part-time hours, make enough money to go out occasionally and mainly focus on transforming my body into a machine that could crank out fastballs at 90 mph one after the other by May 2005. Dad meant well by offering me the job, but the unintended consequences were that I now had enough money to go out any time I wanted and spend twice as much as ever. $500/week for a kid living at home with no bills, no car payment and very familiar with which clubs and bars had drink specials on which nights was a dangerous thing for a guy of my temperament. I had a great one-liner for the inevitable question, 'So what do you do?' I'm a professional baseball pitcher, and I'm also studying to get into law school. I remember the return line! 'Oh, well. . . How impressive.' I became neither."

—email, Mark Mueller, March 1, 2020

The *Clarion Journal* recognized Mueller's one-hitter by naming him their player of the week. The paper and its sports reporters covered the Buds as if the team were in the Majors—the paper carried recaps of games, standings, line scores, and featured articles. They even allowed Jordy and me our own column. We called it "A Strange Brew," after *The Adventures of Bob & Doug McKenzie: Strange Brew*, a 1983 Canadian comedy film starring Rick Moranis and Dave Thomas. Now, Jordy and I had no idea what the film was or what it stood for, but the name was recommended by our good friend and *Clarion* journalist covering the team—Rick Broome—and the combination of words fit us perfectly. "Strange" was true; "Brew" was cool. The column survived five weeks before upper management at the paper deemed it too biased and controversial for print.

"HOMICIDE UNIT," "WATERLOO RIDES AGAIN," "MURDERERS ROW GETS IT DONE," and "IT FEELS SO GOOD" were just some of the headlines boldly captioned on some of the local sports pages during the summer of '05. As players, though, we were too young and oblivious to pay any attention or understand our place in the local history. You see, baseball players rarely leave the here and now, with our principal faults and our skills coming out in the instinctive actions of the present, most always typically mirroring the man. We recall our stats with an almost unbelievable recognition. We remember photographically specific at-bats and crucial pitches that remarkably endure for years. The history of local baseball brewed around us regularly and unknowingly. Those on the periphery of the game, newspaper reporters from the *Clarion Journal*, The *Waterloo Republic-Times*, The *Belleville News-Democrat*, The *Alton Telegraph*, The *St. Louis Post Dispatch*, longtime coaches, volunteers, fans, and the veteran players carry along with them the fraternal memory of all games and summers past. It is these people, the true heroes and lifers that keep this blue-collar brand of baseball alive.

The first sprinkles fell just after 11:30. Temperatures fell ten degrees in a matter of minutes, and dark clouds took over the sky. Harry tried tracking the storm on his new Blackberry. "Boys, we are getting this game in. The storm's following the river south."

The players had arrived early for batting practice at noon to the darkening sky. The wind howled out of the southwest across Ss. Peter and Paul Field. Chas and Punisher put on a show as they launched seven or eight into the jet stream in left field. Three of the bp blasts collided with houses beyond the trees. This frustrated Garrett Schlecht, the team's 12-year-old ball-hound, who had to retrieve them. Garrett was the son of Jim, longtime pitcher and tourist in the Clair and current iceman reliever for the Buds.

At 1:07, after a quick infield outfield, the sky now fully gray, the full team gathered in the dugout. The few fans in early attendance packed up their coolers and lawn chairs and headed straight to their cars, sensing the impending doom. The sky opened seconds later. The storm didn't go south, as Harry predicted.

Kevin Hayes, part-time exotic dancer turned full-time chromatic county league umpire — known to the players as "Hollywood Hayes" for his prowess on the dance stage and his charisma on the baseball field — was the chief ump scheduled on the game. Five minutes after looking out into the hard rain, he stepped out from the cover of the visitor dugout, yelled over to Vern, waved his hand, and called the game. Hollywood walked the twenty paces through the downpour to Lucy behind the backstop protected under the canopy of the maples. He wasn't seeking refuge; he was seeking payment.

In the Mon-Clair, game day rain could wash out games quickly. Midwestern storms popped up without warning, with the potential to dump massive amounts of precipitation in a short period of time. Without the use of tarps, infields were at the mercy of Mother Nature—oftentimes, Mother Nature won. This phenomenon not only wreaked havoc on the summer schedules but caused some clubs to begin questioning the motives of certain managers who called an early rainout. Fish was infamous for making these types of allegations—Were they lining up their pitching? Was the "A" team on vacation? Did they not have enough players?

In Vern's early days of coaching, things were a little different. When the weather hit, after stopping play, plate umpires on occasion asked each team's manager, an infielder, and a fungo hitter out to the field. After watching each infielder try to field ground balls and maneuver around on the wet dirt, the umpire made the call as to whether or not they could continue the game. "It was comical," Vern said. "If the team was winning, you could see it in the fungo demonstration. The hitter would try like hell to make it as easy as possible for his teammate to field the ball. If the team was losing, the fielder would look just absolutely ridiculous, immediately slipping, falling to the ground. Umpires eventually just came to rely on their judgment." The longtime manager of Millstadt VFW Syl "Tuffy" Mueth had his personal preference on field care. "We'd get up on a Sunday morning before we'd play and then go out to Bill Seib's farm and hook up a team of mules. We'd bring the mules in and hook a mower up, mow the grass and then put the plow on and drag the diamond with the same mules. Then we'd go home and change into our uniforms and play ball."

The Waterloo storm raged as the players clustered in the tiny area the grounded dugout offered that was protected from the pelting rain. The Prince, next to Vern on the far end, was harassed by Franchise and Chas, who sat close. The guys joked, "Imagine that. Vern down sittin' by his little Prince. Figures...Prince will be captaining this ship when you kick the bucket anyway, right Vern? After all, he is your little pet."

Caby and I sat near the middle of the bench, while Mueller, Jimmy Schlecht, and Harry sat together on the other end. We sat with our bags next to us on the green, paint-chipped wooden platform, making sure the bags didn't fall onto the dugout's flooded muddy floor. At

1:45, the rain was still falling. By this time, we were in our street clothes. The game had long been called. Caby distributed Budweisers from his iced-down Coleman cooler.

The rain poured, and the beer flowed. And the stories followed.

Stories are as old as the game is played. Stories need to be told, or they die, and if they die, we are left lost in a purgatory of nonexistence struggling to remember who we are or why we're even here. There is the one of 19-year-old Mickey Mantle hitting a 656 ft. home run against USC in Bovard Field while he attended the University of Oklahoma. Babe Ruth ran through a concrete wall in 1924, chasing a fly ball—he held onto the ball. Honus Wagner, "The Greatest Shortstop of all-time," is fabled for holding his hands apart on the bat to allow for the pulling of hits to the foul line—this style won him seven batting titles. Are the legends true? You bet they are. Storytelling is our obligation to the next generation lending truth to memory. And if we are talking legends of County League baseball, it is true what they say about the King of Beers—every Bud has a story.

Mueller brought up the time I slapped a double during an intentional walk attempt. He also thought it funny to add that in the same game, he played dumb after intentionally plunking a guy in the back for pimping a home run.

There was the time I forgot my pants for Valmeyer. "Don't give him any pants!" Vern told his reserves. A 44-

year-old Jimmy (Wahlig) started instead —he played left field—went 4-4. It was the last time Jimmy suited up.

I brought up the game(s) Schlecht pitched against Farmington. He single-handedly saved us twice by getting out of bases-loaded, no-out jams in the seventh of game one—the same inning Randy Wells got ejected arguing balls and strikes—and if his game one heroics weren't enough, Schlecht did it again in game two—we won both games by one run. "Jim, you are a legend," Mueller sugared with a hint of sarcasm. Jim loved it when you told him how good he was.

"I saw the Wahligs, Jimmy, and Johnny, hit three home runs in a game on more than one occasion," Schlecht added.

"Jimmy makin' shit up again," Jordy joked. . . He wasn't.

"Ohlau did that last year off three different pitchers," Mueller interjected.

Jordy mentioned Chas's six-for-six day in Millstadt. All six hits coming in the form of "Chazzy Specials," Texas Leaguers—looping line drives or fly balls that sneakily fall just outside the reach of diving defenders.

There was the time a disgruntled Franchise left his jersey on a fence post after a game. Vern left it. "Call him," the Prince commanded to the old skipper. The Prince wanted Franchise back on the team. "No! If you want him to come back, you call him!" Vern shot back. "I'm not calling that Son of a B—!" Franchise returned for it the following day, asking facetiously, "Did I leave my jersey here last night?"

Chas brought up Harry's tirade, where he verbally attacked an opposing coach for barbering too much in the third-base coach's box. "He was whining about why he didn't have his 'A' team—about all the guys that didn't show—making excuses about why his team was so pathetic," Harry recalled. "Paul Bearer just wouldn't shut up."

We talked on and on about the good, the bad, and the ugly. Vern's stories, however, provided a different perspective, a perspective long gone in the sandlot circles. He talked of matters decades ago. He spoke of players he considered the best semi-pro players he's ever known, "baseball players" who were defined by the game. And moments eternally remembered. He covered six decades in a little over twenty minutes. He told more of the Mon-Clair's "Bash Brothers" Jimmy and Johnny Wahlig in the 90s.

"We were playing Jacob, IL," he said. "There was a softball tournament going on nearby, and I had to go to the Jaycees diamond 10 minutes before game time to get John out of that damn slow-pitch softball game. 'Two more outs and I'll be over,' John said. When he finally gets to the field, he comes strolling across the infield and hands me a wood fungo bat. On the handle, it says: 'To Crab Ass.' It was a gift from Rich Hacker of the Cardinals. I was not particularly happy about the situation, but John made up for it. He leads off the game and hits a home run and asks me while he's trotting around third, 'How's that?' "Still not forgiven," I told him. Next at-bat, he hits another one and says, 'Am I forgiven?' I forgave him.

His older brother Jimmy, a former Blue Jays farmhand, was the most clutch player I ever managed. We're playing at Valmeyer on the last day of the season. We are tied with them for the division lead. Both teams 22-3, bottom of the last inning, tie game, two on, no outs. I called to Jimmy and gave him the sign to bunt. He looked at me like I was crazy. 'Give me one swing,' he yelled down the line. The first pitch he hits over the fence, and just like that we are division champions. I'd tell our guys all the time, 'There are two sets of rules on this team. One for all of you and one for Jimmy.'"

He mentioned one of his best arms of all time. "Jon Adamson. He won 127 games for me. Jon pitched two 14-inning doubleheaders. As a team with only three pitchers, we were able to win 101 games in two seasons. According to Jon, no one ever got a hit off him. He'd religiously yell at Carl Braun in right field and tell him where to play each hitter. A guy then hits a home run high over the right-field fence. Carl yells to him, "Where the hell do you want me to play now?"

He told of Dick Dillinger in the '60s. "With the bases loaded Dick decided to steal third. I asked Dick what the hell was he thinking. 'I got a great jump!' he told me."

Vern kept on hurling.

"We'd go down and play the Menard Maximum Security Correctional Center prison team every year. What an experience! The inmates would take a liking to some of our bambis—man, they were sure fond of ole

Dennis [Gentsch]. Gentsch had nice hair— long and blonde with a few curls—they liked blondies. There was the time he slid into second on a steal. Cons were umping each base, four in total—the con, called him out. Gentsch argued. The con just stood there—didn't say a word— didn't even react. I turned to their bench, looking confused. 'He can't hear! He's deaf,' the bench of inmates colorfully responded.

"There were guards with sniper rifles up in the towers, and just underneath we were playing baseball. It was surreal. They treated us like Big Leaguers, though. We got fed, had hot showers, and the prisoners gave us balls. Not sure where they got 'em. 'We can't get in trouble for stealing in here,' they said."

He rambled on about "The Sundown Kid" Danny Thomas—"the most talented player to ever put on a Bud uniform." Thomas was a high school standout from Dupo, IL. He became one of the most highly regarded amateur players in the country at the time. "He played for me in 1970 and Southern Illinois University in Carbondale the year after. In the June 1972 amateur draft, the Brewers drafted him sixth overall." Danny was an atypical ballplayer in more ways than one. He stood 6'3" tall, weighed 190 pounds, and could run a 4.4 40-yd. dash. "His speed came from his size 7 feet," Vern claimed. "Those are some small feet for such a large man. He glided across the diamond."

Danny's story is an interesting one. He bounced around a lot as a kid, from Birmingham to Mobile to southern Illinois and to the rough outskirts of East St.

Louis. "My mother is a religious fanatic," Danny would tell reporters. "She tried all kinds of faiths before settling with the World-Wide Church of God," a sect of Fundamentalist Christianity that had been founded in the 1930s as an over-the-air radio church. Danny joined his mother in the church, but only for a short time. He left when its decree that no member shall work between sundown Friday and sundown Saturday interfered with his baseball schedule. Thomas' rise and fall ranged from mental hospitals, drug addictions, the minor leagues to the big leagues, the WWCG, a horrific rape allegation, and his eventual suicide—all which made national headlines. Vern never forgot about him. "His story was Horatio Alger," wrote *Mobile Press* scribe Chris Hall after his death, "but written by Edgar Allen Poe." The old man paused for a moment after talking of The Sundown Kid—the rain still splashing the field. "That's truly a sad story. The best talent we ever had," he continued after another pause. "And we've had some good ones."

Vern continued lobbing tales around the dugout. He mentioned a typical day in the Clair.

Bon-Air, Waterloo battle ends in doubleheader split

By JEFF ALLSMAN
For The Telegraph

EAST ALTON — The Bon-Air Silver Bullets and Waterloo Buds both flexed their muscles Sunday afternoon at Van Preter Park.

The result was a double header split with Bon-Air winning the first game 6-0 and Waterloo winning the nightcap 8-2.

Bon-Air ran its record to 3-7 in the Mon-Clair League. The Silver Bullets are 6-9 overall.

In the first game, Bon-Air banged out 10 hits off Waterloo losing pitcher Jason Kemper, who struck out two but walked seven.

Todd Kunz and Randy Martz were each 2 for 4 with two runs scored. Brian Kasting added two doubles.

But Bon-Air manager Jim Blackledge said good defense earned the victory for the Silver Bullets.

"We've struggled early this season defensively," he said. "It looks like we're starting to put something together now. We're catching the ball better which really helps us."

Doug Fox picked up the shutout going seven innings while allowing only three hits. He struck out two and walked three in what was probably his final performance of the season.

Blackledge said Fox is leaving for the Jayhawk League in Kansas.

"He probably won't be back the rest of the summer," Blackledge said. "But we think we have some other pitchers that can do the job."

The second game turned out to be more a slugfest, literally.

One player from each team was ejected following a bench-clearing brawl in the fourth inning. The home plate umpire's glasses were broken in the struggle and the game was held up for about 20 minutes while the umpires changed equipment and switched duties.

A Waterloo player was cut during the scrap but the Buds got even on the scoreboard off losing pitcher Matt Buhs. Bon-Air miscues in the fifth inning aided the Waterloo victory.

Left-hander Jason Vogel kept the Silver Bullet batters off balance with off-speed pitches and picked up the win for Waterloo.

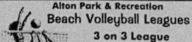
Alton Telegraph June 14, 1993

John Markert and Todd McClure in '94,

Markert Magic Pulls Out A Win For Buds

By Mike Eisenbath
Of the Post-Dispatch Staff

A pleasant Friday night at Fairview Heights' Longacre Park — save for the occasional bug bite — turned into a regular Maalox Moment.

The Waterloo Buds, as mighty a dynasty in the Mon-Clair League as the New York Yankees ever were in the American League, went into the bottom of the final inning trailing East Alton 7-2. The Buds crawled back . . . 7-3 . . . 7-4 . . . 7-6 . . . East Alton brought in a relief pitcher.

Josh Markert will be a junior at Bradley University in the fall, but Friday, the Dupo strongman carried the prayers of Waterloo baseball fans.

Two on, two out. Full count.

Then Markert unloaded — a booming three-run homer and a 9-7 victory. His teammates mobbed him. The team's 60-plus fans gave him a standing ovation. Had Markert hit the home run in a big-league uniform, his smile couldn't have stretched his face any wider.

"That was awesome!" a fan screamed.

"Put the stuff away!" a coach screamed.

On the other side, a tall and muscular East Alton catcher slowly pulled off his equipment and stowed it in a bag. Shaun Watson knows what it's like to lose; the New York Mets released him from their minor-league system after three surgeries rendered his pitching arm unable to earn a paycheck.

Watson appreciates the sentiment behind the big-league players strike; he has friends hoping to be big-leaguers. But Watson can't imagine not playing the game.

"I just love the game," Watson said. "Even though we lost, games like this one keep me going. I tried softball, but there wasn't enough action."

Games like this one . . . On the other side of the horseshoe pits and picnic pavilions, with power-walkers working up their heartbeats beyond the outfield fence, where a lawn chair is the best seat, with kids returning foul balls, where all 100 fans can hear every bench jockey's tease, with a father and 6-year-old son playing catch behind one bench.

"My day starts when I get home from work and he says, 'Come on, Daddy, let's go play ball,'" said John Adamson, a former minor-league and Buds pitcher. "I saw two Cardinals games this year. I'd rather play with him, or watch Waterloo."

Waterloo includes Neil Fiala playing third base and batting leadoff. (Yes, he's the Neil Fiala who got into five big-league games with the Cardinals in 1981.)

"It's still a challenge to keep swinging the bat," said Fiala, 37. "It's always fun to go out on a field."

"That baseball strike . . . ." Waterloo's Todd McClure mentioned to no one in particular during the game. (Yes, he's the same Todd McClure once traded for current San Francisco pitcher Mark Portugal but who never made it to the bigs himself.)

McClure, a proud new papa, looked along the bench and out onto the field, then shook his head.

"Can you believe that stuff?"

Jerry Naunheim Jr./Post-Dispatch

At a Mon-Clair League game, Todd McClure passes out cigars to celebrate his new son's arrival.

St. Louis Post-Dispatch, St. Louis, Missouri, Sun, Aug 14, 1994 – Page 4

Mike Roy in '85,

Page 5 Booming Bats

The Waterloo Buds of the Mon-Clair Baseball League are beating down the fences with their aluminum bats.

St. Louis Post-Dispatch, St. Louis, Missouri, Mon, Jul 22, 1985 – Page 54

Carl Braun and Lon Fulte in the "glory days,"

'Grand Old Man'
Waterloo's Lon Fulte Just Keeps Rolling Along

Baseball

By Steve Overbey

The year was 1967. The Cardinals were well on their way towards the National League pennant and world championship.

And Lon Fulte, of the Waterloo Buds, was playing in his first Mon-Clair League all-star game.

The Cardinals may be struggling this summer, but Fulte is still rolling right along.

At age 39, the grand old man of the league is set for his 17th all-star appearance tonight, when his Monroe Division squad takes on the best from the St. Clair Division in the mid-summer classic, played this year in Sauget.

Fulte is a legend in Metro East baseball circles. He has captured three league batting titles and is one of the reasons the Waterloo club has been the league's most successful team the past two decades. He has hit over .300 in 21 of his 22 seasons in the league and reached a lofty .453 in winning the batting crown in 1972.

Fulte's age has forced him into the designated hitter role, but he still pounds the ball with authority. He carried a .429 average into play last weekend. Last summer, he hit .375 and helped the Buds to the league title.

Naturally, Fulte can't remember all his all-star appearances. But he does know that he has not been too successful in past games.

"I guess it's because there are too many good players out there," he kidded.

Fulte credits much of his longevity to his job as high school baseball coach at Waterloo High. He has compiled a 289-133 record in 15 years at the school and feels coaching is what has kept him young.

"I'm a pretty active coach; I get out there and hit with the guys," he said. "I'm right there at batting practice getting my strokes in."

Working out with his team helps Fulte stay competitive in a league that is dominated by younger players. Despite his age, he is able to hold his own against pitchers college-aged and younger.

Fulte says he is considering retiring after this season. He played his first game in the summer of 1965. Two years later, he was selected to the all-star team. He has missed just three all-star contests since that first appearance.

"I want people to remember me as a good player, not some old guy just hanging on," he said. "I've got this fantasy about hitting a home run in my last game. I want to be playing well enough that it might happen."

So this all-star game could be the last for Fulte.

"I'd really like to have a good one," he said.

□□□

The Monroe Division appears to have a strong hitting team, while pitching is the strength of the St. Clair squad.

Shortstop Neil Fiala, of Sauget, leads all the stars with a .536 average. He is a former major leaguer with the Cardinals and Reds. Fiala is one of four players from Sauget in the Monroe starting lineup. Bob Hughes (third base), Jeff Junker (catcher) and Robert Giegling (center field) will also be playing in front of the home crowd. The rest of the lineup includes first baseman Dave Dallenberger, Waterloo; second baseman Gary Floarke, Valmeyer; left fielder Al Rohlfing, Valmeyer; right fielder Jim Wahlig, Waterloo; and designated

See FULTE, Page 4l

Fulte

From page 51
hitter Fulte.

Waterloo's Warren Fehrenz (5-1 2.53), from McKendree College, is the starting pitcher. Valmeyer manager Dennis Pieper will lead the squad.

The St. Clair roster has three starters from Belleville: Brian Barton (first base), Dave Kassebaum (second base) and Ron Feher (shortstop). Feher leads the team in hitting with a .457 average. The rest of the lineup includes third baseman Andy Walker, East St. Louis; left fielder Jeff Schulte, Highland-Pierron; center fielder Mike Harrawood, O'Fallon; right fielder Jim Brown, East Alton; catcher Charlie Jarvis, Millstadt; and designated hitter Tony Duenas, Millstadt.

East Alton's Joe Silkwood (6-1 2.33)

is the starting pitcher. The team will be managed by East Alton's Jim Blackledge.

□□□

If the all-star game is anything like the divisional races, it could go extra innings. Waterloo and Valmeyer are tied for the top spot in the Monroe Division with 15-3 marks. Valmeyer has beaten Waterloo twice this year. The teams will meet on the last weekend of the season in a game that could decide the regular-season title.

East Alton and Millstadt are tied for the first in the St. Clair Division with 12-6 records.

(Steve Overbey is a free-lance writer.)

St. Louis Post-Dispatch, Thu, Jul 17, 1986 – Page 73 and 74

Carl Braun
Mon-Clair Batting Champ
1964
Batting Average .475

Carl Braun 1964

L-R: Lon Fulte, Carl Braun, Vern Moehrs, John Wahlig, Jimmy Wahlig

managing his son Clay,

Vern and Clay 1970

Clay Moehrs 1974

*"Baseball is played with love. It is definitely played with fear.
The fear of getting hit, making an error, of striking out. Kids
play the game for many reasons but always against the same
ole backdrop."*

1990

"*My fondest memories of Buds baseball was riding with dad to the games.*"
—*Clay Moehrs*

and his playing days in the 60s and 70s.

Waterloo Buds 1971

Vern 1960

Vern rambled on and on but could only scratch the surface on the long history of his club. We sat intently hanging on almost every word. The rain refused to end. None of the players went home early that day—even though the game was called close to two hours earlier. Rainout sessions of reminiscence tugged at the heart of everything the game of baseball had to offer. Baseball has the wondrous ability to stop time. There has never been a clock in baseball. The county league legends Vern portrayed in his engaging dugout epics were all twenty years old, just as they were last year, five years ago, ten, twenty, fifty, sixty. Nothing had changed—that was the illusion—his big, beautiful, illustrious illusion.

"It's not what you look at that matters, it's what you see."
— *Henry David Thoreau*

CHAPTER 9
FAR EAST

"Youth is Wasted on the Young"
— *Oscar Wilde*

On June 27th our record now stood at sixteen wins and two losses—four games up in the Mon-Clair's five-team Monroe division. Our latest victory in the previous night's game had been Vern's 1600th as manager of the club, and fifth all-time among coaches in the entire world of semi-pro baseball—wins that meant more to him than any other achievement in his non-family life. His heart continued beating steadily with his club and the league.

Vern had come into the league as a player in the beginning. He never possessed the power, speed, or arm strength needed for advancement up the baseball ladder. "I knew I would never play in the majors—too small, too slow, no poppie poppie. I've never hit a home run over the fence."

In November of 1984, at a ceremony in the basement of the Millstadt VFW, the powers of the league presented

Vern as one of the eight inaugural members of the league's hall of fame. His acceptance speech said it all.

"This is my Cooperstown."

Ballplayers Honored — Inducted into the Mon-Clair Baseball League Hall of Fame as charter members at a recent post-season awards banquet held at Millstadt VFW Post 7980 were, from left, Vernell Moehrs, Carl Braun, Joseph Jorn, Mel Patton, Barney Elser, Norm Rutter, Sylvester "Tully" Mueth and Bill Mohr.

1984 Charter class of the Mon-Clair League Hall of Fame (Photo courtesy of the *Republic-Times*)

Vern turned down lucrative umpiring jobs that would have netted him thousands of dollars every summer, boycotted many family gatherings and vacations, missing only three Sundays of baseball in 60 years. Instead, he chose the more glamorous route, "working" year-round with his Buds for an annual stipend of $0.

His work provided him more than any money could give. The Buds gave him stature and prominence that he thoroughly enjoyed in the form of virtual tokens to be used anywhere in town. He liked having locals come up and buy him a drink at the local club. He loved being treated like a "big deal" at Papa Vito's and Waterloo

Hardware. He relished getting free coffee at McDonald's, free sundaes at the Dairy Queen, and free golf at The Ridge.

He was tickled when he was chosen to throw out the first pitch at a St. Louis Cardinals' game. And when he was honored for induction into the St. Louis Amateur and Missouri Hall of Fames and given the Metro St. Louis Legend Award for prestigious accomplishments in St. Louis sports. These awards put him in the same breath as St. Louis greats Jackie Joyner Kersey, Brett Hull, Kurt Warner, Lou Brock, and Stan Musial. Coaching the club the last sixty years placed Vern on a national stage on more than one occasion. He was a finalist for the United States Baseball Federation National Volunteer Coach of the Year Award in 1988 and enshrined into the National Semi-pro Baseball Hall of Fame in 2006. He mentions these honors often.

Being somebody is hard to achieve in any realm— business, politics, theatre, academia. Vern's stature in amateur baseball made him a somebody.

Winning. It is what matters to the man. He knows it matters to his players. He knows if his team wins, the players will come, and the players know that if they win, Vern will let them stay. "It's easy to get players when you're winning. They hear about it, and they come to us looking for a place to play. They want to win. They want to be part of something special."

Vern seldom teaches the fundamentals of the game. His players arrive in Waterloo drained from a long college season or a real-life work season. They come with mandates for fun, beer, and baseball—not for an old man teaching fundamentals. He keeps things simple, especially when it comes to his signs. He swipes two fingers across his chest in a gesture as religious as Saturday evening mass at Ss. Peter and Paul. Steal, Bunt, Hit and Run. He's made the same sign for 80 years. His players never consider him close to a braille man in the third base coach's box. Banjo eyes are never needed to steal a Moehrs' sign. What Vern lacks in his ability to give signs and his motivation for teaching the fundamentals, he makes up for in his lessons on life's most important factor. Winning, of course, but, more importantly, how to win. "Talk never makes a play or hits a home run," he drills into his students. "Work hard and get the job done" is his mantra, and winning is his anthem.

• • • • •

Waterloo, Illinois, June 30, 2005, a Thursday night, the setting for a non-league game against the Printers of St. Louis; the Prince would be starting on the bump. This night, the plan was simple: use the game and its innings to platoon pitchers every couple of innings to save and condition the pitchers' arms for the league games on Sunday.

The fans were sparse at Ss. Peter and Paul Field. Only about 25 turned out for the 6:30 start, mostly diehards— moms, dads, and a few girlfriends. The game dragged early—the sun was setting, hovering slowly to the horizon and impeded by nothing. Jordy and Mueller halfway stretched their hamstrings, killing time in the bullpen before the call to put in Mueller. The Prince started strong as he made quick work of the Printers in the 1st two frames. As he toed the mound to deliver in the third, which was going to be his last—his pitch count sat at a mere eighteen pitches. In any usual contest, 100 pitches in a game was considered low for the Prince's standards. He was willing to go double that if needed. The Prince had been money all summer. He was currently leading the entire league with a 1.35 earned run average and was second to Moose in wins with 4. We led 2-0.

The anchorman for the Printers in the third was 45-year-old "Cubby" Bryan. Once considered a real stroker, at his current age, he was looking more like a caddie. The old baseball phrase "He can't hit a bull in the ass with a bass fiddle," applied to Cubby during the twilight of his career. It didn't, however, totally apply to his next at-bat.

He waved his magic wand and slapped the Prince fastball in the direction of Hardin at third. The ant killer never made it to Hardin as the infield grass ate it up. The swinging bunt allowed Bryan to beat out his first infield hit of the new millennium.

The second batter of the inning, the real anchorman of the Printers, a nineteen-year-old loud-mouthed bearded wonder, dropped an intentional bunt directly in front of an unsuspecting Prince. Aggressively the Prince accelerated from his trench on the mound, forked the ball, turned, and chucked it hurriedly to second. It was a throw the Prince had made a thousand times. He had thrown it to his dad in the yard—he had thrown it on the playground in Freeburg. The Real Deal saw him throw it at SWIC. Bo Collins saw it at SIUE. Vern trusted in his arm more than anyone else's on the team. But the throw in the direction of shortstop Kaiser at second sailed errantly wide.

He rarely made such errors, and his anger flared. "Give me the damn ball!" he yelled to Kaiser. Kaiser quickly obliged.

Every player at every level of ball has had to learn how to act in those excruciating seconds following an error before the next pitch could drown it away.

A moon-shot sac-fly by longtime Printer slugger Rick Monday followed a hard bingle by the two-hitter. The game had suddenly changed.

After a fly ball can of corn recorded the second out, the Prince fingered the ball in preparation for what was likely going to be his last batter of the evening. He gripped the red, tightly wound laces across the horseshoe as he let go of the four-seam heater—it wasn't his best. 83 mph read Fish's gun. The nuthin' ball held steady in the middle of the plate. The six-foot-two inch 230-pound ex-Crimson Tide star who was hugging the plate ate the greasy puck for supper. He'd never seen a better-looking room service cheeseburger. High into the darkening sky, it went—a real tater.

"Damn, that was a bomb. You think I should go get it?" Jordy asked Mueller as the two progressed to playing catch down the line.

"Nah, I wouldn't, let little Schlecht have it. Lucy will have a couple of quarters for him. Hell, you wouldn't want to chase after that, it went over the houses."

"Corey's fastball looks dead as a doornail."

"Yeah, he is toast," replied Mueller, beginning to throw full speed.

The Prince was finished.

"Son of a b— you old f—, how long is it gonna take you to get out here?" the Prince mumbled loudly to himself as Vern blindly staggered his way to the mound for his official removal. There was no wasted energy in Vern's walk to the mound. The Prince waited for no one, especially in moments like these. He paced quickly towards the old man, meeting him halfway between the chalked lines and the repose of the mound. The Prince slammed his newly gifted pearl into Vern's open hand, wasting no time leaving the site of his cataclysmic debacle.

Every player at every level has had to learn how to act during those excruciating seconds.

Ten-year-old kids sometimes cry. High schoolers swear at umpires, trying to deflect blame. Grown men do it differently. They find more creative, open, and direct ways of venting frustrations.

The Prince let his inner caveman take over as he started old-fashioned with his words. "This is nothing but dogshit! That piece of shit mound! All those bullshit f—ing hits! Piece of shit umpire! Shit hitters can't even get more than one run off this shit ass bum?!" He directed his anger to the hitters on the bench—though there were none. James Powell, a newly signed relief pitcher, took the brunt of the lashing.

After cursing everyone under the setting sun, the Prince turned to a more conventional form of stress relief by heaving the half-filled water cooler off its perch on the bench. And lastly, the grand finale. He set his sights on the rake leaning against the fence next to the beer cooler. Gripping the handle of the six-foot-long giant field rake, he raised it above his head. Ax-like, he forced the four-foot-wide head into the ground. Not once or twice, but three times, bending the shaft and busting the head. Upon completion of his destructive therapy, the Prince disappeared into the tree-soaked shadows behind the dugout. Waiting on the mound, a nearly front-row seat to the tragedy taking place, Kaiser and I could barely keep it together—observing the entertaining outburst of emotions by our designated Team Captain. With a cunning smirk, Vern looked over at his fuming Prince amongst the trees, glanced back at Mueller, now warming up on the mound, and voiced concern. "I sure hope Corey is going to be ok. Mueller, just throw 'em that Far East shit." And with those words of encouragement, Mueller went to work.

The eclectic moundsman settled in promptly with his unique Asian style—with his pumping delivery and his constant fingerings of the ball, Mueller supplied hen fruit over the next four innings. He was the bullpen ace on this night. What started as a game filled with muffery evolved into a classic come-from-behind Buds victory. Vern's Buds were known for that.

We partied that night. A cooler packed with Buds was supplied by our sponsor—one of the few lucky times we were privy to such comped refreshment. After all, this was semi-pro baseball, and this seemed to be a special occasion.

Park policy was made clear to us by Buds management that "No alcohol was to be allowed on park grounds. NO EXCEPTIONS." Exceptions, however, were frequently raised.

Vern—a self-proclaimed non-drinker and abider of rules—stuck to his routine and shot gunned his one conventional non-drinker post-game brew. He was first to hightail it home after cutting the lights. "Take all the cans with you. We got it too damn good here for you guys to be screwing things up," he said as he rolled up the window on his red Ford. It was three hours past his bedtime.

At night the park seemed to fall from the heavens into blackness. Only a few streetlights luminesced in front of our faces. It didn't stop the fun. On the contrary, it seemed to facilitate it.

Punisher had stripped down. His spandex sliding shorts hugged tightly his full base, which accented the sagging Budweiser cutoff that exposed his comely core. He was the one passing out the lager. For some, these parties had become almost a weekly ritual. Punisher, with his dad "Shifter" and Waeltz, the ringleaders, sprang for the beer when the sponsor failed, and policed the cans when they piled up. The affairs would drag long into the comfy nights and early mornings, out of view from the main drag and away from any Waterloo cop who might have stopped at the sight of cars parked after midnight in the park.

By a young man's definition of fun, some of the after-game amusements had been a blast, lots of girls—well, a few—beer—craziness—one night, two girls, maybe three, streaked around the bases. And friends. But this night was quieter. The Prince and Chas sat on the open bench spittin' *Red Man* and conversing with Caby's girlfriends who were visiting from nearby Edwardsville. Katie Wahlig, Jimmy's daughter and Waeltz's high school sweetheart, sat with Punisher's sister on the backed-up tailgate of Punisher's Chevy Silverado. Periods of soft conversations were broken up by recurrent loud voices and laughter. We frolicked in the times, the summer, and the fellowship. We were discovering if we hadn't already, the real reason why the game we loved was so inviting, why all of us were still here in this empty parking lot at 1 a.m.

CHAPTER 10
AMERICAN GRAFFITI

"The Midsummer Classic means a lot. It's baseball, and I'm a baseball fan. I love baseball. I don't think I've missed one game every year I've been down here."
— *Sylvester "Tuffy" Mueth*

It all started in 1971. The Valmeyer Lakers and East Alton Stags ventured North to the small central state, Illinois town of Riverton. Enticed by a baseball tournament that attracted amateur/semi-pro teams from central to southern Illinois as well as Chicagoland, the two teams traveled with the hope of Independence Day glory. The Stags were vets of this tourney. The rookie small town Lakers, however, were there to fill a last-minute vacancy. The group of talented Monroe County hayseeds (Allen Goldschmitt, John Asselmeier, John Belk, Gary Pieper, Mike Degener, Chip Bieber, Allyn Rohlfing, Willis Bundy, Ron Rohlfing, Lou Sondag, Tom Vogt, Don Rains, Dennis Pieper)—lowly ranked and hardly thought of— scrapped their way through the winner's bracket and advanced all the way to the title game. The only team that stood in their way was a team from Chicago dubbed a "powerhouse." Fans from all over southern and central Illinois were present to cheer on the underdog Lakers. Valmeyer proceeded to dish out an exciting late-inning come-from-behind victory and take home the ultimate prize. The players, coaches, and fans enjoyed the weekend festivities so much—they had to create something of this caliber as their own. Blessings were given, and the annual "Valmeyer Mid-Summer Baseball Classic" was born.

Looking for America?

In the first week of July, Valmeyer's Borsch Memorial Park is considered baseball heaven. The park's mature trees, which were planted at its conception, take you back in time to the beginning, when the Park was just a fraction of what it is now. "It began with a small checkerboard tent rented from Ralston Purina, a few picnic tables and eight hungry ball clubs eager to fight for No. 1 bragging rights. There wasn't even a grass infield for the first several years. I slept on top of the dugout most of the time, so I could get up early enough in the morning to water the diamond because there was no grass," Dennis Pieper, longtime Valmeyer coach, said with a laugh when being interviewed by a local paper. "It's unbelievable," said Pieper, who 'til this day continues to organize the event with his brother Gary. "It gives the kids a chance to play in front of a crowd." Pieper would know; he started in the league when he was just fourteen, playing with his dad on the team in Fults. "It has also given players a chance to show off their skills to Major League scouts. MLB ball clubs have drafted more than 30 Mon-Clair players over the years, many from the tournament."

Those involved with the tournament will tell you there is a divine power at play in Valmeyer. During the horrendous flood of 1993, when the town of Valmeyer was utterly overwhelmed, the waters approached the outfield perimeter and stopped, leaving the field undisturbed. "Even God loves amateur baseball in southern Illinois." It is a tournament that has withstood the test of time, in a town that has endured the wrath of Mother Nature.

A lot of baseball fans will offer you a laundry list of what is wrong with the game today. They will tell you how the pro players are arrogant businessmen who are unresponsive to the fans. They will tell you the game is too expensive for families and that the ballpark atmosphere has become too commercialized. They will say the same for youth sports. They will tell you big money, pay-to-play tournaments, and gate fees rule the amateur game. They will lament that the game has gotten away from its pastoral roots. These people have never been to the 4th of July tournament in Valmeyer—Admission $0.

The stage was set for a revival—a grand revival. By the dawn of July 2nd, the beer tents were up, coolers iced, potatoes curly cut, burgers pressed, batter mixed, and fryers hot. Country music blared from the grandstand loudspeakers.

Well, beat the drum and hold the phone
- the sun came out today!
We're born again, there's new grass on the field.
A-roundin' third, and headed for home, it's a brown-eyed handsome man;
Anyone can understand the way I feel.
Oh, put me in, Coach - I'm ready to play today;

Look at me, I can be centerfield.

Our opponent was the St. Louis Printers. Not Valmeyer. The organizers didn't want to take away from the evening's fireworks. As the sunlight filtered through the trees, the sun slowly ascended over the Mississippi's horizon to the west, raising the last beaming cool on a morning heavy with heat and expectation. It was the kind of day that lived in the mind's eye. All those earlier 4ths of July opening round 9 a.m. morning games Vern liked to schedule, blurring together into this so that the day played out as if it had already happened.

We gathered in the dugout at 8:00, one hour before game time. Vern chose the third-base cave as he always did. We never asked or ever understood why. He was wearing "his suit," Vern's vernacular for a uniform, the black ball cap, the mesh royal red button-down, and dull gray pants, which bunched just below the knees, giving way to knee-high black socks. On his feet were a pair of 1980s molded low top cleats.

"For all the young people," Art Voellinger, public announcer, interrupted the music, "foul balls are 50 cents a ball." A 100% raise from what Lucy paid out at home games. A waft of burnt hot dog and funnel cake floated by—if summer were a fragrance, that would be it. Old Glory waved behind the center field fence. Sweat started showing up in kinky places. It was now 8:30.

We sat putting on our "suits" in the intensifying cinder block sauna that was the third-base dugout. Cleats clattered on the portable rubber floor amidst the discord of the dugout. Hurling and hocking and chucking and plucking and cupping and picking and farting and spitting. A baseball dugout is no place for the faint of heart. Our favorite pastime, it ain't always pretty.

"Damn, Punisher, what the hell happened to you?" the Prince asked Punisher, who was slumped over the bench half-naked as if he ran out of energy midway through getting dressed. "You look like a guy with the seven-year itch for the second time."

"Damn, Pun, you gotta lose those love handles, baby!" Mueller jeered as he walked past, eyeing Pun's midriff. "I have a workout you should try."

"Guys, I think we should lay off Big Pun. He had a rough one last night," Waeltz told the dugout laughing. "I believe he and Jaime spent the night in the caboose!"

A survey of Borsch Park showed its grandstands, concrete dugouts, hundreds of lawn chairs lined up on each baseline, blankets, chairs, and pavilion beyond the short 300-foot right-field porch, the major league style scoreboard in right-center, the campers, and tents in left-center, and the playground and old-time caboose behind the fence in center. Stories of players, fans, and the caboose go back decades. Late night and early morning parties, weekend shack ups, first and last dates, marriage proposals, and divorces. The caboose is legendary.

"You and Jaime spent the night in the caboose!!?" asked Jordy as interest spiked. "No way she stayed the night with you in that thing, she's so out of your league!"

"That train was chugging all night long!" Vern quipped. "Choo-Choo!" The entire dugout laughed hysterically as Vern usually stayed out of such matters.

"Hey, assholes, I'm still drunk, shut up," Punisher mumbled as he leaned over the nearest trash barrel.

"Hell, it doesn't matter anyway. We play the Printers. We could all be drunk and beat those guys." Jordy was right.

We made quick work of the storied St. Louis Union Printers. Albeit early and a Saturday morning, most of us, except for Punisher, were fresh and coherent in the 10-0 Schneider drubbing. A perfect win to avenge the close bang-up contest we had with them a few weeks prior.

· · · · ·

In the semifinals the following day, we were matched against the team from Alton. The As were currently tied atop the St. Clair side of the division with Fairview Heights. Alton was stacked with top-of-the-pyramid local talent. They were primed and ready to play spoiler to Vern's storied Buds. A local paper summed up the game in one sentence. *"The Waterloo Buds' domination of the Alton A's at the Valmeyer Mid-Summer Classic continued Sunday at Borsch Park. But just barely."*

It was a dogfight throughout. With the score tied 1-1 with one out in the 11th inning, A.T. singled off the aspirin-throwing A's closer Derek Stratman. A.T., the rabbit that he was, carried the mail quickly to second. Stratman struck out Hardin with a fastball clocking 87 mph on the radar gun of a local scout. With two outs, an open base at first, and a lengthy visit with Stratman, A's manager Scott Harper and his young pitcher decided it was in their best interest to challenge the Bud three-hitter.

I was familiar with Stratman. I was his college teammate, both in junior college and at the University. I knew what he was packing, and I was confident I could handle it.

All the pressure of a game-changing moment quickly turned into pleasure when I blazed a line drive up the box, scoring A.T. with the go-ahead run. Queern followed with a frozen rope of his own, doubling me in for the insurance tally. The Prince hurled a scoreless bottom of the inning, securing our advancement to Monday's title game.

• • • • •

Monday, July 4, 2005, Independence Day, the championship set. By 3:00, the consolation games had finished, and the temperature had risen to a sticky ninety-seven degrees. Brooks and Dunn echoed through the complex.

One kid dreams of fame and fortune
One kid helps pay the rent
One could end up going to prison
One just might be president
Only in America

Just beyond the ballfield, a train roared by; it was no holiday for rail freight. Fans sat under fans in the grandstand. A couple of kids threw firecrackers on the sidewalk. Red, white, and blue banners draped the length of the grandstand; the big red caboose sparkled in the summer sun, baseballites and drunk bleacher critics sat socializing, sweating, and fanning themselves with tournament programs. In the humid air close to 200 people packed into the greenback chairs of the newly built grandstand, with more arriving, filling the sidelines and outfield grassy areas with lawn chairs, blankets, and coolers—300, 400, 500—adolescent boys and girls, old-timers living in the surrounding bluff hills, farmers, players in uniform from other teams, well-heeled women—Borsch Park on the 4th of July was as much a social as an athletic setting, like the boxing venues of Las Vegas. Only here, in the humid river valley, the girls came not in fur and diamonds, but nipple-tented summer blouses and short jean shorts whose soft fringe tickled the peek of their ass pressed on the hot metal of a lawn chair. Young kids filled the playground in centerfield, their parents, siblings, or sitters keeping one eye on them. Teenage boys roamed in packs on the outskirts of the fence looking for girls, beer, firecrackers, or anything that might spark their kid-like interest. Moms and dads looked on with parental pride. Sons and daughters did the same. Girlfriends watched with admiring eyes on their man in suit. Some of the older admirers looked out and recalled Fourth of July's past. Could it be? Gary Gaetti, Nelson or T.J. Mathews, Neil

Fiala, "The Sundown Kid," Cal Neeman, Ray Ripplemeyer, Rich Hacker, Larry Stahl? "Could it already be 25 years since Gaetti played down here, 360 Major League home runs ago?" Was everyone gathered for the evening's fireworks display or the baseball? We didn't care. We were playing ball.

Sitting next to Rich Hacker, a former Major League player, manager, and current MLB scout for the Cardinals, Lucy was too nervous to sit.

This year's pre-game featured a local high school gal attempting a world record. "Chelsey Kipping sets a new world record for completing thirty-two consecutive back handsprings," Voellinger bragged over the PA. Everybody cheered.

Wearing our trademark red, we jogged to the third-base line while lineups were announced. We took off our hats and placed our hands over our hearts, facing the flag in center. The guessers stood shoulder to shoulder, Ouija boards in hand near home plate, drenched in their own sweat, easily showing through their umpire blues. The visiting Granite City Steelers, named honorifically for the steel plant that sponsored them, stood at attention on the first baseline in freshly washed white tops with red trim. Red, white, and blue shown everywhere on the field of Borsch Park green. Members of the Bud Light Brigade, an area-based group of musicians, played the national anthem. The smell of grass, Mississippi mud, chewing tobacco, sunscreen, beer, funnel cakes, pine tar, and sweat wafted with the dust in the sultry breeze. The scene was pure baseball, the essence of summer.

Moose would be handling the pitching duties. Moose was a real baseball gamer who pitched with a mean focus only the Prince could rival. He went from mean to meaner after giving up a bloop single to the third man he faced.

Caby quickly put a stop to any hope of a first-inning rally for the Steelers as he popped out of his crouched position and rocketed a strike to Franchise covering second on a would-be steal attempt. As we ran to the dugout pumping our fists, longtime commentators Voellinger and Patton tuned up the PA with a song that seemed fitting for this special bush-league extravaganza.

I said girls, I ain't as good as I once was,
I got a few years on me now,
But there was a time, back in my prime,
When I could really lay it down,
If you need some love tonight,
Then I might have just enough,
I ain't as good as I once was,
But I'm as good once, as I ever was.

Franchise led off the bottom half pulling a pitch sharply in the hole between short and third. We found out quickly that the defending tourney champions had come to play. Jeff Stephens, a former standout at Southern Illinois in Edwardsville, ranged to his right with ease, backhanded the liner on a one-hop, and threw to first, getting the speedy Franchise. Steeler starting pitcher Adam Tyler, an Indiana State product, and a real

Edison on the mound struck out A.T. on a wicked pitch that resembled the motions of a Cuban forkball. Tyler lured Queern into flying out to shallow left on a whittling changeup, and our emotions quickly settled.

Moose quickly established a loose and comfortable groove. He mowed Granite City down in the second, in the third, and again in the fourth.

In the fifth, and hitting cleanup, I dug in, as close to the plate as I could. I wasn't scared of Tyler's fastball—its top was generously around 85 mph. It possessed some cut but not enough for concern. Tyler, however, didn't get outs with his fastball. He was a fox. He tried to outsmart his opponents by mixing things up and pulling the string.

As I inched my way up in the box, I anticipated such a pitch, and unlike Vern's hold on his dip can, I saw the circle in his grip.

Resembling the spin of a fastball and thrown with an identical arm motion, a stellar changeup is unrecognizable until it is too late. Unless, however, you know it's coming.

Keeping my weight balanced and my hands loaded, I patiently waited for the ball. And in a split second and at the perfect moment, I released the stored energy in my beloved TPX. My bat did ideal work on the Tyler watermelon and unloaded an atom ball off the top of the "Twyla Luhr" scoreboard in right-center. The ball ricocheted directly into the lap of an innocent picnicker, "Throw it back, throw it back, throw it back," the debauchees yelled from beyond the field's boundaries as the ball came hurling back onto the field of play.

Under the hot sun in the river bottom, we were glistening. Our hands were soft; we glided, we dove, and we whipped the ball around the infield. Voellinger and Patton were still having fun on the PA playing baseball trivia with the crowd and pounding choruses from Springsteen, Adkins, and Keith.

In the sixth Moose got an out on a grounder, another on a weak fly, then struck out a batter on a tailing fastball. The sacred 4th of July was turning into a duel of arms. In the seventh, the Steelers finally opened a can on Moose after two consecutive worm burners made it through our airtight infield.

Moose slumped his shoulders, gave the ball a flip, and stood to wait. He had reached the 100-pitch count and was beginning to wilt. The game, now 3-1 Steelers, turned tense. Vern sauntered to the mound. Surprisingly, the skipper left his pack animal in for one more hitter.

"You got it, Brandon, go after him," Moose heard his dad say, but he wasn't sure whether it was in his head, he heard it or from the other side of the fence. Tony, who had been at every one of his son's games since Tee-ball, never shied away from giving his son advice, even in adulthood.

Moose went back to work. He seemed to thrive at the sound of his real name. The veins in his bull neck bulged each time he reared back to fire a pitch at Caby's demanding mitt. He caught a little luck as the Steeler six-hitter aggressively attacked the first pitch. Moose doctored the pitch just enough to create a little sink. The sinking motion of the ball and the hitter's inability to adjust produced a bleeding ground ball that was easily picked up by Hardin at third and heaved across the diamond for the third out. In the stands, Moose's mother Beverly, a baseball lifer herself and daughter of Barney Elser — Clair legend and Hall of Famer in his own right — relaxed her clenched hands. Her son's day was done.

Tyler, it seemed, was aiming to go all nine. A.T. was set to lead off against the Granite ace. Vern knew if he and Hardin could reach base, we would be in great shape with me and Queern to follow. Down by two in the bottom of the eighth, A.T. provided support to his earlier claim that he was the best stroking lefty on the team. He slashed a lead-off single, going with a 1-1 fastball to left field. Hardin followed with a sharp single of his own. And with no outs, everything Vern had hoped for in the birth of the inning was coming true.

Mueller, standing at the base of the dugout, screamed at me walking to the plate and alternately began heckling Tyler.

"Chocolate Thunder! Chocolate Paradise! Tyler, you got nuthin! Throw it harder! Throw him the chicken sandwich!"

Now standing closer to the on-deck circle, Mueller wanted to remind the Division-I pitcher that this was the Mon-Clair League.

"Tywer's getting tired! Tywer's getting tired!"

There is no sport short of debate where communication is more a weapon. In basketball, of course, the home crowd goes insane as the opposing guard tries to sink a one-and-one free throw with no time remaining. In a race, there is no eloquence in the single one-syllable word "Go!" You could just imagine a golfer trying to sink a putt on the 18th hole with the crowd jeering. But in baseball, there is time for narrative. Personal accounts are to be expected. A girlfriend's name was not off-limits, though one's mother was. Mispronouncing names is one form of acceptable defamation.

"Tywer's getting tired! Tywer's getting tired."

I strolled into the chalked rectangle, the championship on the line. I surveyed strike one. Whether it was the weather, the pressure, or the comment about his girlfriend, the Steeler moundsman located his next pitch so fat that I couldn't believe its location. It was a big, juicy honeydew. I went for broke—the ball connected to the center barrel of my hollowed out TPX. But in my overanxious swing, I had crushed it slightly too much on the left side, suffering it to spin sideways as it shot to second base. Running on down angle contact, Hardin sprinted to second, looking to beat the bang-bang play, but more realistically to break up a double play. He slid late with his break-up slide, hindering the would-be turn. It was now up to Queern.

Like many of the other Buds on this year's club, Queern had come through in big spots before. In high school and college, he'd been a money player, as cool as a player could be. The tenser the situation, the less he seemed to care. A defense mechanism— maybe. Whatever the stimulus, it looked cool to his teammates. And he always seemed to come through.

To an ordinary baseball fan, Queern's 0-3 stat line told of a struggling hitter. His .000 game batting average was in no way indicative of the game Queern was having. Unlucky missiles hit at gardeners can do that to a player. On the bench, Mueller was up to his old tricks. His voice cut through the crowd noise like bench jockeys at a circus.

"Freakin' gosh darn, show some gumption out there, show some moxie! We got to keep our composure! We've come too far! Hit the turkey burger! Come on Q babay!"

Queern focused amongst the heckles and worked the count to full. His balance. His hands. The ball. He smashed the Tyler action pitch with perfect backspin as it carried well over the centerfielder's head. I scored easily from first. The game was tied. Queern, heads- up, took the extra base as he belly-whoppered into third on the missed cut home. It was the biggest smash of the summer.

A go-ahead sac-fly by Jordy followed. With the Buds up 4-3, Tyler was finished.

Waeltz replaced Moose and quickly closed the door on the conquered Steelers. He dominated the ninth by striking out Stephens with a caving forkball and soliciting power man cleanup hitter Brian Harshany to soldier a fastball with mustard on the plate's black.

We celebrated on the field through the setting evening sun, Korbel and Budweiser washing off the sweat from a long day, a long week of play. It was the best life had to offer. Three days of baseball...three days of summer...and fireworks!! Genuine American graffiti.

"I sure do miss celebrating those championships drinking champagne and shooting bottle rockets out of Brandon's (Waeltz) ass crack!"
— Corey "The Prince" Blackwell

CHAPTER 11
SAINTS

After the champagne dried and the fireworks fizzled, the summer carried on. The trip to Columbia's "Field of Dreams" on Sunday, July 10, was special. The field, constructed by Gary Kleinschmidt, a rural Columbia farmer and loving father of two boys, Doc and Tyler, was built in 1993. "We had trouble finding a diamond to play on in Columbia when we were kids, so Dad built one for us," said Doc. "The main requirement for us to get into the league was that our field had to have a fence. Dad took care of it. He had to work the farm when he was a kid and never had a chance to play, but he lived out his baseball dreams with us," Doc said of his dad. The field is positioned only feet from their front door and stood in the middle of a cornfield. Sound familiar?

Across Monroe and St. Clair counties on Sundays, players drove with a narrow focus, windows down, and radios rattling. We drove in sporadic caravans to away games. Vern and Harry rode together. Harry Thompson was in his second summer with Vern, long enough to know the challenges faced in Columbia. The Saints were always a team that was overlooked. Homefield advantage was huge at "The Field of Dreams." With an absence of a proper hitting background — an open-chain length fence bordering a cornfield — deciphering a pitch from the pitcher's hand was nearly impossible. Of Vern's six losses the last two seasons, three had come at the hands of the Saints. "We just need everybody to show and not get anybody hurt," Harry said to Vern as he shifted his truck to park. "This field is a pasture!"

Originally designed with precision, "The Field of Dreams" was aging. Mother Nature was eroding the unevenly graded infield composed of loamy topsoil. The Kentucky bluegrass that grew on the pasture was thin and sparse. Dusty lines connected the bases. The batter's box was trenched, and with a non-existing watering system, the infield dirt had the consistency of baby powder. The air filled with dust as the Saints completed field prep. With no mature trees for shade and a cornfield surrounding it, the field was an oven, and you baked along with the crop. The heat was the worst of the summer. 102 degrees. The only positive thing Harry had to say on this day. "It has nice dugouts."

Vern complained of nothing. He knew how good this generation had it. The field his team played on this day eclipsed all the sandlots he played on as a youngster. He knew what mattered, and it wasn't the weather or the condition of the field.

Only a few Buds showed up for the optional 12:30 batting practice. Chas's hands swished in his leather batting gloves; he could barely swing without his bat slipping, the dust from the box hanging low to the ground, clinging to his cleats. One swing caused his bat to leave his hands altogether. He walked back to the dugout, smiling, with his bat under one of his arms, took off the batting gloves, and wrung them out like a sponge. Punisher's gray Daytona State cut-off had darkened with sweat even before his first round of swings. Caby took BP shirtless, drawing the envious attention of the misshapen Saint players.

Several things crystallized on that hot afternoon on the farm in Columbia. The Prince pitched another gem. Some said he had more to pitch for on this day due to the fact his current love interest used to date the Saint first baseman. The Prince didn't allow that trivial fact to bother him. He threw a complete-game shutout. Just as the Prince did in his father's living room, his balls were whistling. He had only given up two runs in his last three starts. His earned-run average had remained steady throughout his eight season appearances and was sitting at a robust 1.06.

The heat was relentless, and the summer drought blistered on as game two of the doubleheader began. It was the second week in July, and the clocks read 3:30 p.m. when Brandon Waeltz baptized the game ball and made his way up the ash heap mound. The grass around him had burned in patches. The wind whipped across the field of dreams out of the south from right field, swirling mini cyclones of what was left of the infield dirt.

In the wind and swirling dust, the Marissa farm boy kept the ball low and got the first three batters on ground balls. Only one of the pitches was stung—to Hardin at third, who stayed down and picked it off the pasture soft as cotton. Waeltz threw all fastballs that inning. In the second, he fell behind on a couple of batters and walked the elder Kleinschmidt brother, Doc. Inconsistency was uncharacteristic of Waeltz. Waeltz was broad-shouldered with thick legs on a tall frame. His arm typically followed his legs in the simple progression of the pitching motion. Today, however, his arm wasn't loose or springy like it was a week prior when he, along with his buddies, the Prince, Moose, and Peter Buck won MVP honors at Valmeyer. Today, it was out of sequence. There was a slight hitch, maybe fatigue, interrupting the natural flow of his motion. It stopped his arm from getting a full, smooth extension.

With Kleinschmidt on first, Waeltz threw a fastball from the stretch position. Even without the whip of a full windup, Waeltz was still producing good velocity.

Waeltz finished the inning without giving up a hit. In the second, his inconsistency continued. He struck out the Saint nine-hitter. But hit the next one and walked another. With the bases full and two outs, he fell behind three balls, and no strikes to Columbia's beefy five-hitter, a six-feet-three-inch 230-pound free-swinging elementary school teacher named Bridgewater. Waeltz fired a strike, then another, and then got Bridgewater to sky one into the dry, muggy outfield air. On any other given Sunday, the rainbow fly would have been a can of corn. The waning four-o'clock sun and the sweeping south breeze played fits with the ball. Punisher never saw it; Queern saw it leave the bat and lost it in the glaze. The glaring camouflaged sky protected the white ball and prevented any hope of Punisher running it down in the gap. Queern was our only hope. Jimmy raced to where he calculated landing. Seconds later, the ball returned to view. A last-ditch dive came up inches short. The full house emptied its Saints on Bridgewater's buffalo triple.

A Bud hit famine followed the blow-up inning, and the Saints continued their upset dominance over our distinctly superior club. They had beaten us for the 5th time in the last eight league meetings. The game-two defeat dropped our overall record to 24-4 heading into All-Star week.

Leaving Columbia, something was up. There was more to my 0-9 day at the plate than the obscure cornfield-hitting background, the trench in the left-handed batter's box, and the impatient yard barker behind the plate. I wasn't right. Physically. Mentally. Was it burn out? Exhaustion? Or was there more to my uneasy feeling?

• • • • •

AIDS, Acquired Immunodeficiency Syndrome, was first clinically reported on June 5, 1981, with five cases in the United States. The initial cases were a cluster of injecting drug users and homosexual men with no known cause of impaired immunity who showed symptoms of pneumonia, a rare opportunistic infection that was known to occur in people with very compromised immune systems. The initial period following the contraction of the virus that causes AIDS, HIV, is called acute HIV. Many individuals develop an influenza-like illness or a mononucleosis-like illness 2–6 weeks after exposure. In contrast, others have symptoms that most commonly include fever, large tender lymph nodes, throat inflammation, a rash, headache, tiredness, and possibly sores of the mouth and genitals.

I read over the list of symptoms as I sat in the town library vexing on my irresponsible decisions and researching whether I needed to see a doctor for my lingering problems. HIV is some serious stuff. No freakin' way that Barnes Hospital drum was tainted! Why didn't I listen to Bonde? How could I have been so stupid!? All I had to do is wear the freakin' suit!

I sat in the cold reclining plastic reading through the most popular source of health information on the World Wide Web: the ever reliable and trustworthy WebMD. Check Your Symptoms. I clicked the link. Fatigue, Nausea, Fever, Sore Throat, Swollen Glands — Enter — I waited ten seconds for the list of possible illnesses. Mononucleosis, Hay Fever, Adenovirus Infection, Tonsillitis, Strep Throat, Human Immunodeficiency Virus. No freakin 'way...It can't be! HIV? WebMD is the most trusted name in internet diagnoses. It can't be wrong. Can it? I needed to know for sure.

The long walk to the cold exam table seemed like it took longer than a Punisher Cadillac pimp job—the longest twenty steps of my life. I saw every crack in the tile.

I was for sure dying—I had to be—I had every symptom—well, almost every symptom. And I was 0 for my previous 9...against Columbia. A million thoughts raced through my head as I nervously awaited the Doc's arrival.

"Son. Why are you here?" was his first question as he stared into my anxious eyes.

It felt like he was looking into my soul while slowly gutting me. "Why do you think you need to be tested for HIV?" — A serious question posed by a serious person in what seemed at the time a somewhat rhetorical tone.

I told him the whole sad unsuspecting story. The noxious warehouse. The summer heat. The Tyvek suit— or lack thereof. The boss's order. The Red Gold. And most notably the 0-9. I must have intentionally left out any other concern about how I could have possibly contracted such a terrible disease. "I need to know if I'm dying, sir."

Chapter 12
Lucky Charm

1969 Monroe Division All-Stars (photo courtesy of the *Republic Times*)

A day after the most forgettable day of the summer, possibly my life, I needed a distraction. The Mon-Clair All-Star Break, which dates back decades, has been a long time Mon-Clair distraction ever since the Mon-Clair battled the Greater County league in the inaugural game in 1966. The break from seasonal games was a welcomed respite from a summer seeming longer by the day as the midsummer temperatures continued to climb. This year's All-Stars were chosen by a vote of the league's managers to form a Monroe side and a St. Clair side—Moose, the Prince, Franchise, A.T., and I were chosen to represent the Buds. We never found much meaning in a game where we were forced to be teamed up with our rivals in the division. We hated most of them. No Bud wanted to share winning with a contender.

The current event wasn't anything like the spectacle it had been in decades past when it featured a home run derby and various sideshows—cow milking contests were common in the 90s.

Photo by PAUL BARLARGEON

Cow town — East Alton's Tony Stoecklin gives the art of cow-milking a try during the preliminaries of the Mon-Clair League All-Star game last week in Waterloo.

Holy cow!

Fans get to view stars, milky way

By Tony Panozzo
Staff writer

Sauget designated hitter Jim Greenwald was the first player to arrive last Thursday at Waterloo Park District Field for the Mon-Clair Baseball League All-Star Game.

He didn't take the cow-milking contest too lightly, either.

GREENWALD, who was informed of the all-star agenda last week, asked his father for a hands-on lesson before Thursday.

The experience must have helped. Not only did Greenwald's cow-milking team win, he also slugged a three-run homer in the fourth inning of the game.

Contestants for the cow-milking event were rounded up by Lucille Moehrs, the wife of Waterloo Buds manager Vern Moehrs. Vern had heard about cow-milking contests held at baseball games in the minor leagues.

"We had to come up with some originals, don't you think?" Vern said.

"Since this is a farm community," Lucille said, "we thought it would be a good idea. I'm a farm girl."

GREENWALD ACCEPTED the idea in earnest.

"I'd been out of town for a couple of days," Greenwald said. "There was a message on my answering machine. It was Mrs. Moehrs that called. I took a few lessons, believe it or not, from my father. He grew up on a farm.

"Vern told me he picked me, Wayne Rohlfing and Mike Roy, who are like the oldest players in the league. It was for novelty reasons, I guess."

When Greenwald and Rohlfing

(See COW, Page 3D)

•Cow

(Continued from Page 1D)

— the last two Monroe competitors — finished, Monroe's pail contained more milk than St. Clair's. Before the contest, Greenwald said, "I don't know how much farm activity he's had."

ROHLFING, WHO plays for Valmeyer, said he didn't necessarily need a lesson in cow-milking.

"I was raised on a farm, and my dad had a milking cow named Daisy," Rohlfing said. "If I've done any milking, it was very minimal. I have a sense for animals. There was a comfort level there."

This year's game was absent sideshows. It was the Monroe division vs. the St. Clair division in one nine-inning game at Longacre Park in Fairview Heights, IL. The game was uneventful for league standards with our side winning 9-3, marking the 25th time in league history Monroe beat St. Clair. The Millstadt duo of catcher Ryan Switzer and Jay Francois led the way with two hits apiece, driving in four of the nine Monroe runs. They were named the game's most valuable players. The two would only need to earn five more MVP awards to surpass Jimmy Wahlig's league record of six. After the game, we had only a few days 'til our final meeting of the season with our second-most-hated rival, the Capahas of Cape Girardeau, Missouri.

• • • • •

Vern had seen it every summer. July 4th, the apex of the summer until playoff time was over, and as the days began melting into the rest of the month, the players started looking at the calendar—energies wilted with the midsummer heat. Players lost their fervor for getting to the ballpark. It was Midwestern hot! Some guys only had a couple of weeks left of summer vacation before school started up again. Vern had witnessed late-summer struggles mostly in the teams we opposed. His Buds had won the division championship 21 years in a row and the league championship six of the last ten years. His late-summer runs were that of league legend. Guys competed hard, buying into the idea that the championships meant something. Vern didn't take vacations, and neither did his players. Vern checked the calendar and looked at his roster of players—reaffirming his position on the character of his club. With only a few games left until playoffs, we caravanned the two hours south into southeast Missouri.

The games against Cape always mattered. Vern took great pleasure in conquering Jes Bolen's Capahas, a sibling rivalry of sorts, never schadenfreude. The Capahas are the oldest amateur baseball team in the country, dating back to 1894. Jess Bolen managed the Cape Girardeau club nearly as long as his chief rival has with the Buds. In 50 years of managing, Bolen amassed an incredible 1,516 wins against only 409 losses. His teams won 17 state and regional tournaments and have participated in the National Baseball Congress tournament for 35 straight years. Bolen's approach was similar to his combatant to the north. Bolen's ability to promote his club and attract sponsors allowed him a rare freedom shared with his good friend Vern—managing and recruiting with one thing in mind—winning. Bolen, not constrained by the competition between the city and college leagues of the big city, was able to pull in players from Cape and the entire surrounding southeast Missouri and southern Illinois regions. Bolen sought his club's recognition as a premier semi-pro club throughout the region. He did just that. Scheduling Waterloo for an annual home and away was not merely to fill his schedule with games. "To be the best, we have to beat the best," Bolen told reporters covering the contests. "And Vern's Buds are the best."

We rode into Cape that Friday evening excited with what lay before us. The two-hour drive down Interstate 55 hadn't dampened our energy. We loved coming to Cape for Friday night games. Capaha Park was beautiful—the manicured grass, the stadium feel. Fresh and clean after a college season supporting the Southeast Missouri baseball team, it was ready to impress. City leaders understood that when the Buds came to town, good baseball would follow. Gatherings at the park seemed to correspond with the game frequently. To accompany the annual evening game, the Boy Scouts of America regularly held their group picnic. Fans filled the stands—adding to the game's allure.

The game itself was a seesaw battle. The Capahas scored a run in the first and another in the second. We struck back with two in the fifth to tie it. The Caps then scored another run in the seventh. We got it back in the eighth. Waeltz had thrown a hundred pitches by the sixth inning which typically was around his limit. A blister had developed on the middle finger of his pitching hand and was bleeding. At the end of the seventh, his pitch count at 127, Vern pulled the plug. Bolen had lifted his comer after six innings. A battle of the bullpens would decide the contest.

In the top half of the eighth, on the bench, things started getting weird. Jordy absentmindedly began toying around with a few items in his baseball bag. He was searching for the barbecue flavored sunflower seeds he stashed an inning prior. Before Jordy could find his bag of *Bigz,* he discovered something else of size—his Size Large jockstrap encompassing his Size Large cup. Simultaneously as he primed the athletic supporter, on the field, Queern pulled a Chinese blow through the right side of the Cap infield for a base hit. As Franchise raced across home, scoring the tying run, we all looked at each other in superstitious disbelief. We quickly dubbed Jordy's supporter as "the lucky jockstrap" and determined one thing. He was going to have to hold it for the remainder of the game.

Baseball is a sport with a long history of superstition. Anything that happens before something good or bad in baseball can give birth to a new superstition. Many baseball players—batters, pitchers, and fielders alike—perform elaborate, repetitive routines before pitches and at-bats due to their beliefs in superstition. The desire to keep a number the player has been successful with, purposely stepping on or avoiding stepping on the foul line when taking the field, not talking about a no-hitter or perfect game while it is in progress are examples of such notions. Big Leaguer Justin Verlander is superstitious with the foods he eats on game day. Verlander has a specific meal—three Crunchy Taco Supremes (no tomato), a Cheesy Gordita Crunch and a Mexican Pizza (no tomato) from Taco Bell. Jason Giambi wore a gold thong. Moises Alou peed on his hands.

On this day, Jordy had his lucky jock.

I don't know if our decision to have Jordy hold his jock was based on a superstitious inkling of it aiding us in victory or only for it to be a vessel in our own dirty game of amusement. But seeing him sit there with his holy jock in his hands—in a game seeming to last forever—we stood confidently by the notion.

At the end of eight, the game was still tied 3-3. One run could win the game and secure a season sweep of Bolen's Caps. Every pitch was now filled with tension.

Franchise was set to lead off the top half of the ninth. A year earlier, we had been down to our last strike when the leggy hitter beat out a bunt to spark a winning rally. Bolen must have remembered Franchise's former act when he yodeled from his spot in the dugout for his corners to cheat in and look for the bunt. Bolen's foresight didn't deter the masterful bunter. Franchise laid down a beauty that trickled ever so softly between the pitcher, third baseman, and catcher—smack dab in the middle of the Bermuda Triangle.

Jordy held tight to his lucky supporter.

Caps pitcher Ryan Forsythe struck out the next two Buds in the order. It came down to Hardin.

Hardin— who had been steady all summer along, connected on a dilly to the gap in right. Franchise ran on contact without any hesitation from first. Bolen watched in disbelief as his deer-like centerfielder cut off the sharply hit ball. As the ball shot from the deer's bazooka, something happened. Franchise stumbled as he rounded third. The stumble cost him three steps and the momentum of a perfect turn. The throw carried over the outstretched arms of the extended first baseman and two-hopped perfectly into the catcher's readied mitt. Using the Mickey Mantle hook slide he learned as a youngster, Franchise threw his body toward the rear of the batter's box, reaching his hand behind as he slid. He was late. "You got the ball?" questioned the umpire to the Cap catcher. As the catcher showed the glove, the ump confirmed the call. "He's out!"

I was beginning to think the lucky jock wasn't so lucky at all.

Capaha fans—albeit only a few still in attendance— and players couldn't hide their joy. They were going nuts.

The Caps came up for their licks at the bottom of the inning. Mueller was now hurling for us.

The first batter flew out to left field. Lance Seasor, a Morehead State University star and the Caps' best hitter, flew to Queern in deep center—he threw down his helmet in disgust. The third hitter of the inning had no chance. Mueller dropped in a Lord Charles helicopter for strike three—inning over.

Vern's watch read 11:49 as we readied for the tenth — the midnight diehards sat in a sleepy haze. Queern swung the doughnut in the on-deck circle — he was to lead off.

After working the count to full, Queern whiffed on a boiler for the first out. Caby was next. Caby skied one into the darkness. Jordy, still holding tightly to his good luck charm, quickly stood, admiring the hit. The dugout was going crazy. The left fielder scampered toward the left-field wall. "Come on, baby! Come on, baby! Get out of this dump!" Punisher yelled as the ball carried to the warning track. "Go...Go...Go." The Cap left fielder jumped as high as he could, banging against the wooden Plaza Tire advertisement showcasing itself on the wall. From our vantage point nearly 360 feet away, the outcome was up in the air. Our question was answered only moments later when the outfielder forked the ball in his glove and held it high above his head. "Are you kidding me? He caught that?" Caby growled, stopping as he rounded first. Stomping heavily back into the shocked and exhausted dugout—Caby had one thing on his mind. "Give me that damn thing," he snarled as he ripped the now unlucky jockstrap from Jordy's tightly gripped hands. We all laughed as Caby tossed the stained piece of cotton into an overflowing trash barrel.

With two outs, we still had a chance—Chas was up. The first pitch—a fastball up and in—he let it go—the next one—a slider low and away. The cagey Chas was fooled by the pitch but managed to throw the bat head just enough to poke a single into right—a Chazzy special!

After throwing the next two balls well out of the zone to Punisher, the Caps' pitcher was beginning to look a little nervous—or maybe a bit tired. After all, it was now after midnight.

Bolen walked to the mound to settle nerves. It seemed to work as his hurler came back with two quick strikes. Punisher was pushed into a corner. We were down to our last strike of the inning, maybe even the game. With the count even at two, the Caps' stopper threw what he sought to be a fastball on the hands of the long swinging Punisher. Instead, it hummed right down Broadway. Punisher's late swing contacted the ball medially and laced it over the second baseman's head. From his chair in the dugout, Vern watched as Harry waved Chas to third. Harry had replaced Vern the previous inning. It was past Vern's bedtime.

The go-ahead run was 90 feet away. The few Capaha fans still in attendance began to experience a familiar sinking feeling in the pits of their stomachs as the Caps had come up short many times before in the late innings to the Buds. Vern called on his last remaining player on the bench—he needed a pinch hitter—Jordy was his man.

One problem, Jordy was nearly naked on the bench—his shorts being the only garment gracing his bony carcass. He threw on his uniform top as fast as he could then went for his pants. "Hey, slow down kid," the veteran Kaiser motioned to the eighteen-year-old rookie. "Aren't you forgetting something?"

"What are you talking about?" Jordy asked. What??

"Prince...get it out of the trash," Kaiser commanded the Captain. "And Jordy...put it on." The dugout looked on with complete hilarity as the scene played out like a Hollywood movie. This wasn't Roy Hobbs in *The Natural*..."Pick me out a winner Bobby." This was Jeff Kaiser telling Jordy Thompson to put on his lucky jockstrap and win us a game. "Chocolate Thunder...Chocolate Paradise," Mueller jived as the Prince threw Jordy his lucky charm. Jordy slipped on the jock and hurried to the box. On his way, Kaiser whispered some advice. "Don't swing at anything out of the zone. Make him come to you." It seemed Kaiser had his doubts with Jordy in this clutch situation—doubting the power of the lucky charm. What followed was the most gripping at-bat of the game, maybe the season.

Baseball superstition lying in the balance, like two boxers slugging it out, Jordy was the one with his back against the ropes, fending off thunderous blows that could've knocked him out at any moment. The benches were screaming with each delivery. The pitch sequence:

1. The first delivery climbed the ladder, but Jordy was a free swinger and took a real cut at it. 0-1.

2. Ball one. Low. 1-1.

3. Ball two. Outside. 2-1.

4. Bolen wanted to get Jordy. Franchise stood on deck—foul ball. Strike two—2-2 count. Again, we were down to our last strike. The Capaha players were poised— with one foot in the dugout and the other on the field—ready to fire up the hitters for a rally.

5. Jordy fouled off a cutey. 2-2. Vern was screaming for him to stay alive.

6. Jordy defensively fought off another breaking ball. 2-2. Tensions were mounting with each pitch. Jordy skittishly called timeout and stepped out of the box. Taking a deep breath in and out, he adjusted himself fully, cupping the lucky jockstrap.

7. The Cap decided on an inside fastball with the intent of handcuffing the unsuspecting Bud. There was just one problem—the pitch tailed too far inside. The ball hummed towards Jordy's rib cage—he jackknifed out of the way. The ball etched the mitt of the lunging catcher and bounded away. "Go, Go, Go," everyone yelled. Chas scored from third standing up. Punisher moved up to second on the wild pitch. Jordy, smiling and relieved, looked down at his crotch like he had seen an apparition. We mobbed Chas as he pranced gleefully into our arms.

8. The count was full. Jordy, no longer in a position to solely knock in the go-ahead run, relaxed at the plate. No matter how he swung or what pitch he waved at, his

bat seemed to only have foul balls in it. He fouled another one. 3-2.

9. Foul down the first-base line. Late again. 3-2.

10. Another fastball. Jordy swung late, slicing one weakly in the air toward the garden in shallow right. It turned into a real gorker as the ball floated just over the outstretched glove of the Cap second baseman. The ten-pitch at-bat was over—after Punisher jaked home—the score turned 5-3.

Maybe the pitcher gripped the ball too tight. Perhaps the catcher lost it as Jordy jackknifed out of the way. Or we were just the more resilient team. In any case, we won. On the way home, Vern beamed ear to ear as he had just gotten the best of his good friend, Jess. Jordy, sitting snug in the back seat, held tight to his lucky charm.

CHAPTER 13
THE HUSTLER

"Mon-Clair Playoffs Kickoff Today," the *Belleville News-Democrat* announced anew the morning of Wednesday, August 3. "Top-seeded Monroe Division Champion Buds (33-4) take on eighth-seeded Columbia (10-16)."

We cruised into Fairview Heights on yet another hot and sticky dog day evening for our single game first-round matchup seeking revenge. The Saints were a dangerous Round 1 opponent in the single-elimination eight-team tourney—two of our four losses came at the hands of Gary Kleinschmidt's Saints. We were not going to lose a third—or so we predicted.

Thirty-eight-year-old shortstop Jeff Kaiser had two weeks left in a baseball career that spanned more than three decades. Kaiser would be retiring at the end of the summer for reasons many would understand. It wasn't because his body was soapy, and his skills were fleeting—even though it was, and they were. His decision to hang 'em up was based solely on his eight-year-old son and eleven-year-old daughter. Mon-Clair league veterans are famous for their willingness to play past their prime. "Once you quit, there is no going back," is a well-known phrase used by most lifers. So, what do they do? They keep playing—Don Stovall of East St. Louis played at a high level until he was 60, Bud legends Lon Fulte and Jimmy Wahlig won championships until they were 47 and 45, Cubby Bryan of St. Louis slapped poopers 'til age 50. Vern himself tore both hamstrings attempting to stretch a single to a double at the ripe old age of 64. Kaiser had no intention of experiencing such ageless glory.

Just like in his old "cornball" days, old man Kaiser led off the second inning by chopping one off one of the high limbs and sending it through the third base hole. Kaiser, nicknamed Will Ferrell by us younger teammates, streaked to first amidst cheers of "Atta boy, Kaiser! We are going streaking! Through the quad and into the gymnasium!"— quoting and referencing the Will Ferrell classic, *Old School*. Kaiser was "old school." He was a "hard ninety" guy, and at 38, habits stayed the habit as Kaiser always looked to take the extra base. He slid headfirst at second base on steals and dove for any ball in the field he might have a chance at reaching. His uniform always seemed to be dirty. Vern referred to Kaiser as a classic, old-fashioned shortstop, referring to his fundamentals of fielding a baseball. Kaiser's style allowed him to lay back slightly on most ground balls as he turned most hops into Hollywood hops. Good players possess this rare ability as they can slide into position late, field it out front between the legs, then set and throw a hard one to first. At his age, he was nowhere near as quick as he was twenty years ago, but he still possessed the soft hands and arm to make it work. His body ached, but he was tough, and he knew how to make things better—he popped three Advil before every game.

Lucy sat in the stands next to her lifelong friend, 84-year-old Celie Fulte, who was the mother of Bud great Lon Fulte. Both women accompanied each other to most games which they attended. This game had been marked "special" on the calendar for Lucy and warranted an inviting pre-game call to Celie to assure attendance. It was Vern's birthday. Vern was turning 71, and Lucy, with her plans for a family dinner at JVs Sports Bar after the game, turns out, wasn't the only one with a surprise for the birthday boy.

Jordy, long the inveterate joker and team jester—still wearing his lucky jock from the weekend prior—he hadn't taken it off, even to shower—pulled his Honda Civic into its parking spot. Jordy may have relied on his lucky charm to assist him in sport but when it came to his natural game—talking to girls—he advanced on his authentic charm. Girls loved his boyish good looks—looks that came from his mother. He acquired something much more valuable from his father Harry. What Harry, the old railroad worker, couldn't provide in his lectures on charm and wit, Jordy made up for in his self-education through women's "literature." Jordy studied the opposite sex in the only way he knew how. By reading. Jordy became a connoisseur of periodicals geared towards the inner and outer workings of the female mind and body. His Honda Civic was packed full of those academic necessities—along with the other life essentials required for the move out of his parent's house—clothes, baseball gear, a case of Mountain Dew, Doritos, Ramen noodles, oatmeal creme pies, a basket of clothes. His new college apartment was to be adequately furnished.

Luckily for us—the Prince, Caby, and myself—we arrived at the same moment Jordy was opening the butt of his car in search of his baseball gear. As Jordy tossed around his goods and retrieved his suit, spikes, and glove from the packed trunk, we caught a glimpse of something extraordinary peeking through the covers from under his Levi's. Lifting the gym shorts and dish rack uncovered a lifetime collection of Hustler magazines. There they lay, exposed and unclad throughout the filthy ass of the 90s Hatchback. Fat in the right places, they laid goddess-like on the pages. We squinted at them briefly with the mesmerized curiosity of an astronomer spying a new planet. The same beauties that provided the young Thompson a childhood of sexual education were now going to provide us with some "clean" fun of our own. "Dude, why in the hell are you carrying around a stash of Hustlers?" Caby asked as we laughed hysterically. Slightly embarrassed, well, not embarrassed at all, really—Jordy explained in the simplest way he could. "I'm moving out and going to college. What was I supposed to do with them? Leave them all with Harry?" Jordy had a way of explaining things to make perfect sense. Realizing an opportunity for some great fun, we conjured up a plan. We chose the blonde. Vern liked blondes.

As for the game, Vern calmly watched as we built a quick 8-0 lead against the overmatched Saints on the back of our old shortstop. He observed Kaiser glove a ball in the top half of the fourth inning and gun it across the diamond. "You know, he has been damn good for us all season; I had no idea he would hold up the way he has," Vern mumbled to Harry.

"I wouldn't be surprised if after the season he tells you he wants to play another year," Harry joked.

"I hope not," Vern replied. "I already have his replacement."

In the bottom of the fifth, we scratched across two more runs, embarrassing the Saints and enacting some sweet revenge in the five-inning short game, preserving the skunk win for Moose. This game was Moose's last scheduled start of the summer, potentially ending a season where he had won 10 games versus only one loss and had an earned run average of 1.37.

After the customary shaking of hands, Vern made his short speech and returned to his spot on the bench next to his beloved and time-tested attaché briefcase. As he had done almost 2,000 times before after games concluded, he reached over to the case, unlocking the metal push buttons to lift open the top as if the curtains were being peeled away on a burlesque peep show. The attaché exposed its inner secret. There she was, straddling the top of the lined paper that listed Waeltz, Buck, and the Prince as probable starters for game two.

Jenna Jameson, in all her glory—the most famous Hustler Honey of a generation—cuddled up next to Vern's black book. Vern liked blondes. She was Jordy's favorite too. Shocked and speechless, he held a stoic pose—as he would a ball four—eyeing curiously the inside of the box. One second...two seconds...three seconds...Five seconds...Seven seconds...Ten seconds. Calmly, after what seemed an eternity, he closed the case, ending the sultry scene. The blonde, busty vixen disappeared into the darkness, never to be seen again. With a slow and methodical turn of his head, he picked up the Gatorade bottle flanking his left thigh. Taking a sip of the blue tasty water, he eyeballed the culprits of the sleazy dugout peep show smiling at the end of the bench. "Happy birthday, Old Man!" announced the Buds. "Don't let Lucy in on our little secret."

CHAPTER 14
JUICED

Marred with many fights and controversies over the decades between 1960 and present-day, Waterloo-Valmeyer, the bitter rivalry, climaxed in the year 2000 when then shortstop, Neil Fiala attempted a tag on a would-be Laker base stealer. The Valmeyer bad boy slid cleats high, tearing into Fiala. Fiala recalls the ordeal distinctly 20 years later.

"When I first started playing in the Mon-Clair league, the Waterloo Buds and Vern Moehrs were at the top and the team to beat every year. Our Sauget Wizards team put together back-to-back championships in 1988 and 1989, which was a tremendous feat, given the quality of the Buds. After playing part-time due to job constraints from '90-'92, I was able to play full time again in '93, and the opportunity to join the Buds came about.

During seven years with a veteran group of players and some key younger players, we were able to put together four championship teams, including a 47-1 undefeated league team in 1998. There very well should have been a 5th championship.

In 1999 we were flying high and in the championship series once again. We were up one game to none and had to be beaten twice by the Valmeyer Lakers to lose the series. Waterloo and Valmeyer were always fierce rivals over the years. It all came to a head in the championship that year.

Valmeyer had a good group of veteran players and were playing well. They had one player whose nickname by the teams in the league was "Hothead." While we were leading in the middle of the game, it looked like another championship was in sight. "Hothead" ended up on first. Our shortstop Jeff Kaiser and I both looked at each other and warned each other to be careful as "Hothead" was on first and was notorious for hard slides.

On the next pitch, he took off for second base on either a steal or a hit and run. I was covering 2nd on the throw. As I went in front of the bag preparing for the throw, I noticed that he started running inside the baseline. As I caught the ball, I tried to make a quick tag and get out of the way. Luckily, I was able to get parts of me out of the way as he jumped in the air with his spikes high. If I had not, his high slide very well could have broken my leg. His spikes ended up tearing my pants and splitting my leg open with a 6- inch gash that went down to my leg muscle.

A resulting brawl ended up with both benches clearing and the police being called to the field as tensions were very high, and the large crowd feared something bigger could happen. I ended up in an ambulance and needed 63 stitches to fix the wound. Ten people were arrested, and the tournament was called, never finished, and no champion was declared for the season. Thus, we did not capture our 5th crown in 7 years."

— email, Neil Fiala, January 8, 2020

The historically intense Waterloo-Valmeyer rivalry got injected with another classic dash of fury on August 4, 2005, in the semifinals of the Mon-Clair playoff at Ss. Peter and Paul Field.

6'3" 215-pound Erik "Big Red" Floarke—the fire head ace of the Laker pitching staff—infamous for his intensity and competitive desire on the mound, was mulling potential Division-I offers after a successful junior college sophomore season where he compiled school records in wins-14, complete games-11, strikeouts-100, and innings pitched-114. He possessed one of the few power arms in the league with a dominant fastball capable of reaching 92 mph with an equally good slider and a bulldog mentality to match. He entered the game with a 7-1 record, with one of his wins already coming against us in a dominant complete-game fashion. He had pitched his club's first-ever perfect game three weeks prior and was psyched at the opportunity to duplicate his past success against the most potent lineup in the league in the most meaningful game of the summer. We sought the one thing we could deliver— revenge.

Franchise wasted no time proving Big Red's imperfection, introducing himself immediately to the infamous chucker— after all, he was our batting champion. Franchise confidently stepped in and ripped a first-pitch scorcher to the left-center gap for a double. Our bench went ballistic! "We're going streaking!" "You got nuthin' Flunky!"

A passed ball allowed Franchise third base two pitches later. A sac-fly by A.T., and we quickly led 1-0.

I entered the box.

I was in the middle of the biggest slump of my life—zero for my last eighteen. Fuming from the Franchise double and subsequent run, Floarke got nasty. He chucked a slider. Stee-rike one! Hollywood yelled. Maybe it was the shadows? The 87 mph? The HIV? I didn't even see it. I was lost. I swung at the next one, a radio ball on my hands. It, too, was a blur. I got only a slight piece as the 90-mile-per-hour pitch grazed the thin handle of the shaved metal. A high spinner put the count at one ball and two strikes. The next buzzer did me in as it nicked the inside black with me standing motionless—zero for my last nineteen. I slammed my bat and helmet into the decades' old wooden bat rack, reverberating my frustrations throughout the entire park. Elevated cheers and heckles from the Laker wolves displayed all the emotions of past duels between the two clubs.

A few innings passed with little action. It was the bottom of the third.

I prepped waywardly in the on-deck circle, hoping to find something...anything before my second chance.

Just then, a loud voice rang out from the end of the dugout.

"You need to forget about that last bullshit at-bat and you sure as hell ain't dying of AIDS! Get up there, quit being a p— and do something!" It was the Prince, at the top of his lungs. The Prince was ready for a fight. "Do something!"

"You need a beer? Ooooor...maybe...my lucky jock?" Jordy added, looking amused from all of the yellings. Good friends are always there when you need them the most.

"There is a cooler full of Bud over there, and my lucky jock's right here!" Jordy remarked again while grabbing his manhood and pointing to the cooler of comped Koerber Budweiser—indeed a special occasion.

I stopped swinging and thought for a moment—a brief moment. "Hell, I'll try anything at this point," I said to the team jester, staring back at me. Jordy snapped out the top button, releasing the tension at his waist, creating a divergent boundary in the elastic of his pants.

"I'm not talking about your jock, dumbass! Throw me a beer."

The iced cold dripping Budweiser achieved four revolutions before I snagged it flush and buried it Stone Cold style—white foam dripping from my chin.

Something happened the moment I downed that golden Budweiser in the batter's box before the biggest at-bat of my season. My 0-19 didn't matter anymore. Whatever vexed my sick mind and body exited as quickly as the golden lager flowed down my thirsty gullet. I had a feeling of enhanced focus and clarity—I was focused and free.

Was I entering "the zone"? If spinach was Popeye's magic elixir...Was Budweiser mine? I didn't even drink.

A calm warmth overtook my body. I knew what I had to do.

It was the top of the third, a slight breeze blowing out to right with the blackness of night encompassing the sky. A.T. led off and was hitting. I stood on-deck waiting. A.T., confused by a first-pitch Floarke changeup, swung hard, capping it to third. As the third baseman charged quickly, he fielded the ball out of his natural rhythm. He took his time. The throw to first sailed high, pulling the first baseman from the bag. Our bench roared.

"Ohlau, you're up." My hard metal cleats forced through the delicate grassroots as I strolled to the lonely batter's box. My brain free and clear, I began visualizing what I was aspiring to do — "Sweet vindication. Sweet vindication. Sweet vindication!"

Floarke didn't give a damn who was stepping in. That wasn't him—he was The Big Red Monster! He demanded respect—he knew my zero for nineteen.

I dug in. Here it comes—fastball. "Stee-rike 1!" Hollywood called. I stood in a looker-like daze taking the Big Red heat.

Nope, I thought, I'm not in the zone.

Next pitch—slider. "Stee-rike 2!" Like a statue, I stood. "No balls, two strikes," shouted Hollywood again from behind the plate.

I stepped out of the box, adjusted the brace, supporting my leg and shin guard protecting a blue-black welt. I tried blocking out the previous two pitch results, the hooters in the stands, and the monster eyeing me from the mound. I took a deep breath and swallowed — I could still taste the Budweiser. I tightened my Franklins, dug once again into the carved-out box, and expected his best—the slider. I got fully naked. No, not that kind of naked.

Total surprise! You know of fastballs so hard and heavy that if they ever nip your elbow, you'll fear the pain for the rest of the summer. Let a third strike by or swing errant, and you'll feel the pain for the rest of your life. You hear the pitch as briefly as a bug. You have one fraction of a moment to make a decision.

Total surprise! For whatever reason, Floarke offered up a hummer. It was a grooved one hissing and sinking in. I loved 'em down and in. I had a fraction of a second to make the decision. I cut the barrel loose and let it fly. I dropped the scandium barrel with precise acceleration. I squared the pint-sized piece of leather directly off the enlarged sweet spot of the perfectly altered juiced up metal TPX.

Swinging with metal, the physics of collisions worked well for hitters of this generation. Struck along its length, a wooden bat vibrates like a guitar string — anyone who has ever hit with wood has experienced the stinging that comes from such vibrations. If one is skilled enough, a "sweet" spot exists in wood—albeit a little one—on the bat's barrel. If a ball is centered directly on the "sweet" spot, the bat will almost flatten the ball completely, silencing the vibrations, allowing the decompression to apply a maximum reaction force to the ball, sending it flying. That's why with a wooden bat, only balls hit off the sweet spot result in home runs. However, swinging with metal is different. Metal bats have a much larger sweet spot, giving the hitter a much larger margin for error. A juiced-up hollow metal bat transfers energy to a pitched ball much more efficiently than wood, resulting in almost no vibration of the handle (less energy loss), fewer stinging hands, and more dingers. With the absence of compression and the presence of straightening during impact, the metal bat creates a catapulting effect, launching the ball into the field of play. According to engineers, this "trampoline effect" allows metal bats to achieve a hit distance an astounding 100 feet further than wood. In other words, a 380-foot bomb in the Clair was a 280-foot flyout in the pros.

Waterloo becomes Waterloo for opposing Napoleons.

Grace is power at perfect acceleration. God made the human eye to see the swinging of a bat at perfect acceleration as the most graceful of things a man can do without a woman. The bat catches the ball and lifts it skyward. There's an optimal angle, a trajectory that is so fulfilling you can't believe it came from your bat that is so much of an extension of you.

I stood watching, pimping it. The accelerated motion of the Floarke hummer magnified the reaction force as the ball beautifully exited the "ping" at a near-perfect thirty-seven-degree angle. The square-up was monstrous—an arching shot. The home run ball rose over the right-field fence and disappeared before it started its downward arc. The roar of the crowd turned to silence. All 200 fans remained on their feet. But where was the ball?

"Daaamn, it should be illegal to hit a ball that far," base umpire Carl Thomas quoted as I trotted around second base.

It was picked up two batters later by the ball-hounds—100 paces from the fence in the right-center alleyway, an estimated 500 feet from home plate. The bomb was the most ridiculous hit of my life. Legend is told it is the longest ever hit at Ss. Peter and Paul.

Floarke paced circles as he fumed.

Meanwhile, the Prince was paralyzing the Laker lineup. He gave the 200 fans in attendance another reason to stay standing. He put on a show of complete command. In between fighting for foul balls, which paid a quarter a piece if returned, the young kids stood close to the backstop, hands clasped in the chain fence, attentively watching the Prince dissect every Laker who entered the box. It was easy for him. He had done this before.

With one out in the fifth, I came to the plate for my encore. I wanted more. The Laker ace had other ideas.

Floarke sought to set the record straight the only way he knew how. I could see it in his vindictive expression— the glare of a man seeking revenge.

Baseball contains elements of intimidation and retribution. But it is also a sport with traditions and acceptable limits. When a pitcher is getting pounded as hard as we were pounding him, and when a pitcher experiences the embarrassment of an admiring home run hitter, he can traditionally throw a brush-back pitch. Unless the batter freezes, no damage is done. The hitter ducks, avoiding the ball, but he does get to hear the humming whine as it blurs past him. Floarke, in his frustration and my very humble opinion, exceeded the acceptable limit. He would have told you differently.

He wasted no time avenging his earlier embarrassment. The sizzling tomato went alto queso, falling short of my neck and hitting me square in the meaty part of my back between my flexing shoulder blades. I didn't think this was any way to play the game or to enact repayment for my cherishing actions which occurred innings earlier. Heck, pitchers can yell and scream at hitters after strikeouts, so why the hell can't hitters capitalistically enjoy dingers? Floarke looked on in true spiteful Laker fashion through his shit-eating smirk. I looked the monster in the eyes. "You should probably throw it a little harder next time you chicken shit bastard," I said through the pain with a half-baked smile.

"F— you Ohlau and F— your team!" he replied, striding toward me. The benches raised and came to life. It was fierce; the old rivalry was back; the old Mon-Clair rancor returned.

Hollywood stepped in between us posturing idiots.

I walked to first, grinning—making sure I didn't show any pain or weakness—all the while mouthing my abuser as Hollywood mediated—it was just another night at the office for the part-time peeler.

I had won the battle, and our team was about to win the war.

The Prince's line was once again nearly flawless. Seven innings, twelve strikeouts, one walk. We had beaten our rival. The 5-2 victory cemented our spot in the weekend's finale.

"Having had the opportunity to play Mon-Clair ball for several years with success was an experience I will never forget. Vern and his Waterloo Buds were always the team to beat. They demanded the greatest respect when I was out on the mound. Vern had a knack for finding players and getting the most from them. His track record speaks for itself. You won't find many coaches that have had the continued success through the years as Vern has had. Win or Lose I always wanted to be on the mound against Vern and his Buds."

— *Erik Floarke, Valmeyer Lakers pitcher 2002-2009*

CHAPTER 15
LONG LIVE THE KINGS

Approaching the last days of the summer season, I had only one day left at Environmental Sanitation. Bonde and his partners were cleaning up. Or so it seemed. Barrels and tankers were entering and leaving the site at rapid rates. Although I was only part of the summer help, I liked to think that I played a significant role in the recent successes of the company. Teaming with Keaton, my skills behind the wheel of the pickup, and my navigating in the city were yielding ten drums/day. With a $75 profit per drum, we were valuable. The company needed us, and they liked us being around. Or so we told ourselves. I enjoyed the work—when the risk was not my life. I had $800 in my bank account. A high for the summer. More than enough to pay next month's rent. Life seemed good. The only thing was, this was my last day. I had nothing lined up for future employment and baseball...well...only one game remained. The few resumes I mailed out for teaching positions had turned up nothing, and my latest interview seemed futile at best. Five years of college and this was the state of my professional career? I didn't care. We were playing for the Triple Crown.

• • • • •

The day after the semi-final win, Vern and Harry nestled up to the bar next to the mantle with the old pictures and ancient trophies of past teams in the Moehrs' basement—they ate pizza—Vern drank Coke—Harry had Budweiser. Thompson opened the sports page of the *Belleville News-Democrat*. "Fairview Advances to Mon-Clair Finals" headlined the page. Fairview Heights, the third seed in the tournament and the youngest team in the league, held a 27-15 record. Managed by Ed Emge, a Belleville, Illinois, teacher, the Fairview team had a roster full of local college talent. They seemed poised to finally break through and win their first Mon-Clair title and avenge last year's championship round loss when we ended their season. Over the course of a baseball season, it was impossible to understand in the moment when a team had played a pivotal game—momentum was crucial but fickle. I can't speak for Fairview, but I knew one thing was for sure, we had it.

In the press box of Longacre Park—the designated league field to host the championship round of the tournament and Fairview's home field—on Saturday, August 6, 2005, Art Voellinger and Mel Patton were at it once again, ushering an end to yet another summer under the hot sun of the Clair. It felt strange to them both as the two close friends were celebrating another sudden end to a baseball season they had held so close to their hearts for a half-century. Over the many years of the league, these two were major contributors who provided lifeblood to the league. Voellinger, who was baptized into county league ball in 1954, was a batboy, scorekeeper, foul ball chaser, player for the old Shiloh, O'Fallon, and Millstadt teams, an announcer, and a league officer. Patton matched his buddy's love for the game. He served as league president from 1987-2001, was a three-time batting champion in the league (1969, '71, and '74), and a charter member of the league's Hall of Fame ('84). In just a few short hours, the 39th summer of the league's existence could end.

In search of the league's triple-crown and back-to-back championships, we looked loose and lively, talked it up, and seemed to carry momentum from Thursday night's win into Longacre. Vern penciled in his starting pitcher—Peter Buck.

Buck had been available and used sparingly throughout the summer of '05. He logged 27 innings, 25 strikeouts, and had a minuscule earned run average of 1.75. Vern always called him his "ace in the hole." Buck pitched as a man possessed. In his mind he had everything to prove—he wanted to go out on top. He, too, planned to retire at season's end.

Buck bluffed his way swiftly through the Redbird lineup. He dealt the Redbirds a horrible hand as he allowed just one hit, a double by Fairview center fielder Andrew Donovan in the third. Buck was masterful. "The best pitching performance of the season," fans were heard boasting. There was one problem, though. Fairview's ace, Kyle Rensing, equaled Buck's prowess. That is until a single error did him in.

Branders are typically unpredictable and rarely produce charity hops. Kaiser's third-inning hit was no different as the sure-handed Redbird shortstop booted the grounder. Two batters later, a Hardin single allowed Kaiser to trot home, the only run scored in the game by either team. The uncharacteristic 1-0 win put us one win away from our triple crown.

. . . . .

The eternal blue-black welt on my right shin had faded into yellow from my ankle to my middle shin. My lower tibia donned a calcified bump from the repeating traumas by foul balls. I continued to wear the ankle and shin guard when batting. My body was feeling strong, my mind at ease. I was not dying of AIDS—all tests negative. Thank God! I had lost ten pounds since summer began, mostly from scrimping on food and busting my ass at work. I still weighed in at 195 pounds and could push up 300, though. I was finished at Environmental Sanitation and was beginning my new part-time job at a downtown St. Louis UPS station. My first shift started in two days— the 2:00-10:00 a.m. one. I didn't even want to think about how desperate my life may become by the end of the summer minus baseball. I was a college graduate for Chrissake, working those hours for $8.50/hour. I couldn't fathom the thought if it came to me. It never did. I was still playing ball.

I had been in "the zone" for what felt like the last month...It was only a week. I was hitting the ball like I should, hard and consistent. My seven home runs and 40 runs batted in were tops in the league. My .436 batting average was lofty for baseball standards and put me close to tops in the league. High batting averages peppered the Mon-Clair League. .526 Jake Friederich (Waterloo), .452 Eric Walls (St. Louis), .438 Michael Adamson (Millstadt), .414 Jay Davis (St. Louis), .403 Chris Scoggins (Alton), .408 Aaron Thompson (Waterloo), .400 Brian Harshany (Granite City). Numbers always seem to be the measure of the man in the game of baseball.

Franchise was leading the league in hitting. A legit baseball grinder, he hung in there in times of failure and managed a steady climb from his once anemic .200 average in his first 20 at-bats of the summer. Franchise led the Buds and the league in stolen bases as well. His legs and short swing provided the engine for his impressive average and the spark that could jumpstart the team at any moment in a game. He was confident in his game again, looked forward to coming to the park, and wasn't worried about his failures. Nothing, including his current girlfriend, was clouding his mind. Franchise had played some of the best second base defense Vern had seen in his 50 years in the game.

He made a play in the title series that would have made any league's highlight reel. A hard grounder shot up the middle and kicked back towards the right as Franchise dove to his right. Unable to fight his inertia, he flashed his glove backward to snag the ball. Upon landing, he quickly sprang to his feet, jump-pivoted, and threw a strike to first, getting the runner by five steps. Vern saw a clear connection between Franchise's play and the Buds' success. He was a player who could carry a team with his all-around play. The good defense was appreciated by Vern and our pitching staff, specifically Brandon Waeltz, who was starting game two.

Waeltz grew up the son of a third-generation farmer. He starred in baseball and basketball at small Marissa High. It was on the basketball court that he caught the eye of a cute blonde cheerleader princess from the nearby town of New Athens. Her name was Katie Wahlig—true royalty—the daughter of a king. Waeltz sought to be her Prince on this day.

There were no charades at Longacre—no mascots running around pretending to dance, no concessions, no television cameras or radio stations, no pro scouts with radar guns. All we had were two old guys on the PA, two teams, two managers, a few fans, and the summer heat. It was baseball unadorned.

Waeltz warmed up quietly with Chas in the bullpen. He knew he had his good stuff going. His curve was breaking sharply, his fastball showing pinpoint accuracy. The seams of the ball felt familiar in his grip. He took his pre-game warmup seriously and then sat down. Sitting next to him, the Prince tried loosening him up. He spit *Red Man* juice on his cleats. "Go out there and bring home the crown, buddy." Without a response, Waeltz stood up, stepped out of the Prince's shadow, and walked to the mound as if he had built it himself. We hung the destiny of our championship, of our summer, on the arm of this one man.

Waeltz quickly went to work. He plowed through Fairview's leadoff man on three straight pitches—Fastball, Curve, Splitter. He didn't stop. Waeltz didn't possess blow away stuff, but what he lacked in Velo, he made up for in his moxie and his one special pitch, the butterfly splittie. Only men with lunch hooks possessed the ability to throw a butterfly splittie. He had them. Hands as big as pillows. Every generation of Waeltz had them. He outfoxed six of the first seven batters and looked as elegant as he had all year. The sharp leadoff double from the four-hitter in the second didn't shake him. He looked right at home, standing tall on his hill. Erecting from her chair down the first-base line, Katie clapped and cheered for her beloved prince.

Waeltz remained throughout his semi-pro baseball career, the focused, steady athlete his father trained him to be in tee-ball. A fan seeing him for the first time may have thought his concentration was limited to the pitching rubber, but they didn't know him. He was confident—confidence is a powerful trait—it makes players who they are, makes them look bigger, stronger, and more intense when adversity strikes; it makes them legendary. We sensed it more now in Waeltz—he knew his ability—he wasn't going to fail—his Buds weren't going to fail behind him.

With one out in the fourth, Fairview scratched Waeltz for two runs. The first scored on a weak pop-up down the line in right. The second scored on a feeble ground ball that skipped past Hardin on a bad hop. Things never change about the game of baseball—the gives and takes—both runs were charged to our right-hander. Waeltz came back and mowed the side down in the fourth and fifth. He was at the top of his game—he didn't have to be.

We managed all the runs we would need in the first inning off Fairview's second-tier starter Will Lawrence. Franchise singled, A.T. walked, I singled in Franchise, Queern singled in A.T., and Caby cleared the bases with a three-run double to the gap in right. Caby and I drove in three runs apiece, and as a team, we pounded out eighteen hits. We carried a 10-4 lead going into the seventh. Vern brought in Mueller to finish things off, just like in the days of yesteryear.

Waeltz's numbers on the day glistened—six innings, five hits, eight strikeouts, no walks. He finished his summer third on the team behind the Prince and Moose in innings pitched (52), wins (7), and strikeouts (40).

The win marked the twentieth time in the league's 40-year existence the Buds won the year-end championship. Earlier in the season, we had won the club's 32nd division title (24th straight) and 8th Midsummer Classic. It was our sixth League Triple Crown. Springsteen rang out over the loudspeakers into the sticky evening air as we gathered one last time in front of our dugout for a team huddle. The heedless party goers in the pavilion next door behind the covered wooden Longacre grandstand loaded their leftover barbeque into foil containers, drained their coolers, and cleaned the leftover trash. They had no idea of all that transpired on the battlefield only yards away; the championship that was won, the memories that were made. We huddled in a close circle while Vern addressed the team. We showered ourselves with Budweiser and champagne. Sons, daughters, and grandkids raced around the bases and hugged their loved ones. We stopped spraying the booze and progressed to drinking it. Bubbly and crisp, it quenched our indomitable thirsts. Each player removed his jersey and tossed it toward the middle of the circle—a standard tradition at the end of every summer—ending and starting anew.

We broke apart slowly after Vern said his piece; we mingled, shook hands with each other, and drank what was left in our coolers. The moment was ours. It was goodbye for some, as most would not see each other again until possibly the following summer, others even longer. Vern and Lucy were among the last to leave Longacre that evening. They lingered with the straggling fans and a few of the players downing their last beers. It's always hard to leave the atmosphere of such a win. You want to savor it, relive the stories of it, cement it in your memory. Vern did one last sweep of the dugout— the air was still hot. The two talked for a moment. Finally, they, too, ambled toward the parking lot. Vern stopped momentarily to adjust his grip on the attaché. He took the last sip of his one traditional Bud after the championship win. Never in his life had it gone down smoother. The lights at Longacre suddenly clicked off. Everything was dark.

Epilogue

"The Best Damn Game in the World"

"The trick is growing up without growing old."
— *Vern Moehrs*

For the graduates of the 2005 Waterloo Buds, there was no fairytale baseball ending to any of our stories. When the lights went out that evening at Longacre, there weren't calls from agents or big-league GMs. No bonuses were given out for winning the title, and no big contracts were looming. We were ordinary people again working our regular jobs and living our everyday lives.

Punisher went back to mowing lawns and selling Big Juicies, Chas landed a corporate gig crunching numbers for Panera Bread, Waeltz temporarily worked on the family farm until he found something more permanent. Caby, Hardin, and A.T. prepped for a return to school for their senior years, the Prince surveyed, Moose taught school, Kaiser coached his kids, Mueller moved furniture, Jordy entered into higher education, And I...Well, I had no idea what I was going to do.

With our summer over and our long-term futures up in the air, we knew one thing was sure. We were never going to forget what we did that summer in the sun as kings of the county league. None of us knew it at the time, but the summers we enjoyed balling, partying, and growing with the Buds ranked up with some of the best summers we ever experienced in our lives.

As the 21st century presses on, the unlimited leagues that used to pepper the landscape of America have mostly disappeared. Leagues that allow standout teenagers, college players, and former pros to combine their talents on one field are becoming rarer and rarer in the American landscape. The glory days of amateur baseball are long gone, barring a dramatic shift in the current American culture. Baseball has gotten away from its pastoral roots of being a priority in the lives of its participants. It's gotten away from being an outlet for a kid's imagination. Adults run the game. "The kids just don't play anymore," baseball lifers will tell you. "They are just busy with other things." Baseball is a kid's game that needs to be played to be loved. And with love comes wisdom.

Baseball calls on more wisdom than any other game. It's the pauses in the action. Times to think. The best thinking that is done at these times is in the form of clichés, the worn truths you rely on. You dig down to hold your ground. Wisdom is when a cliché suddenly rings personal. "Don't take your eyes off the ball." "Follow through." It was advice that won the war our grandpas fought in. It may have been football that prepared men for the attacks of battle, the sketching forethought on map paper and the charge and fusillade. The long waiting periods before, the concentration in the cockpit over enemy territory, the one-eye-clenched peering through crosshairs—it was baseball that conditioned the mentality of American boys from Brooklyn to San Francisco for WWII. Eisenhower was a football player, leading surges of one army against another, but Ted Williams (after batting .406) flew a fighter plane, long waits, and one moment to strike. Baseball was America's game.

The spirit of baseball lives. This spirit is best understood by understanding and appreciating the baseball lifers represented in this story. For some, the decades of memories blend like innings in a score book. As for all the Buds, our minds remain sharp and clear. Baseball players are like that. We recall single at-bats, crucial pitches, clutch hits, damning errors, and, of course, the unbelievable home runs. We remember the titles, the celebrations, the bonds. We remember each other.

Kaiser, years later, shows little traces of the sleek and smooth athlete he was in the early years. Now with smoky white hair and a belly constituted of pork and beer, he spends most of his time following his son Erik, former ball-hound for the Buds and current pitcher for Vanderbilt—a *Vandy Boy*.

The Prince pitched nine more seasons with Vern after the '05 summer. The stats he accumulated in his career in the county league were exceptional. He finished his Mon-Clair career with 147 wins. A team-record 129 came with his Buds. He was inducted into the league's Hall of Fame in 2016.

Moose followed the Prince into retirement in 2015 and followed his dad into the Hall of Fame in 2017.

Chas and Caby quit after three more successful seasons, retiring in '08. Chas earned MVP honors of the Midsummer Classic in '06 while Caby did it in '07 after smashing five homers in the four-game playoff series.

Punisher played eight more years with the club and, in true "ironman" fashion, never missed a game.

Mark Mueller continued pitching with the club for nine more seasons until leaving in 2014. A spat with Vern ended the decade-long relationship. You may, to this day, find Mark toeing a mound in the Clair, currently for Fairview Heights. He has pitched over 1,500 innings and counting in his amateur career and, just like his grandfather before him, runs the family furniture business.

It's been 80 years since Vern began his love affair with the game of baseball. Nearly 60 with his beloved Buds. To make the same journey in today's landscape of the times and the game would seem to many unthinkable or even impossible. The more he ponders and talks of his lifelong journey, the more confused and uncertain he appears to become. "Did I think I would do this for so long?" he asks himself. "I had no idea. It became part of me. It became who I was—who I am. I loved a lot of it."

Fathers and sons. The theme is as old as the dirt the game is played on. When asked of his standout memories of his near century in the game, his favorite comes to mind. "I got to manage my son Clay for 18 years." Clay is the all-time Waterloo stolen bases (230) leader. All you have to do is look through the decades-old handwritten ledgers.

"It's what has kept dad young, just being around the young players," says his daughter, Gina. "Dad is a very young-minded 84-year-old. Very sharp, too, with the whole strategy of the game and everything. He's so relatable to young men of all generations. It's a testament to him that they stop by his house. They'll just pop in."

These days Vern is an easy man to find. He spends much of his time as he always has. Coffee in the mornings with Lucy. A trip to McDonald's—then a quick three-minute drive to the field. A field tucked in against the age-old maples. A field positioned a long home run's distance from his front door.

The Moehrs' house is almost as easy to find as the man. Take the main drag through town and turn at the bank, another hundred or so feet, and you 're at the doorstep. "Look for the red truck!" he tells people interested in meeting him. When you arrive, you realize all the charming two-story brick homes look the same, but there, shining in the sun, is the red Ford pickup— Illinois license plate 2 A LGND. Lucy's Kia sits in the garage, license plate MRS MGR 2. "We sure have had a blessed many years," he says. "There were tough times," glancing towards Lucy. "But we wouldn't trade it for anything."

You will still find Vernell Moehrs under the Friday night lights or the scorching Sunday sun managing his beloved club. Life gives and takes many things from a man. It has never taken Vern's passion for baseball. His passion for winning.

It's 2019. The iconic Buds name has since been changed to reflect the team's current sponsor as increased internal demands on the team, and the club's choice of brew played major roles in the shift of power. A change of leadership at the top of the Budweiser beer giant and a few public marketing errors aided the move.

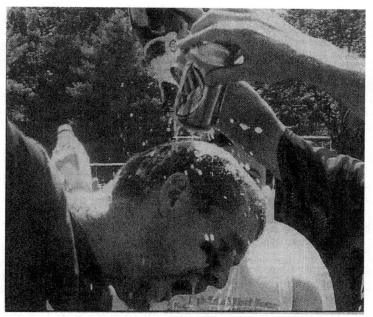

Waterloo Buds players celebrating their 2007 Mon-Clair League Championship. (*Kyle Eversgerd Photo*)
—"The King is Dead"—
Rumored photo that ended the Club's relationship with Anheuser-Busch. Vern had no choice but to complete the switch to the new Robert "Chick" Fritz beer distributor. The Buds became the Millers in '08. Rumor has it, Jordy brought the Miller Lite—the only Miller product in the entire park. It is true—the adage—choose your Buds wisely.

Vern won his 2,000th game in June. Stop reading for a moment and let that number sink in—2,000.

Southern Illinois has given rise to a few managerial legends. Whitey Herzog—New Athens—and Red Schoendienst—Germantown—grew up here, both World Series skippers for the St. Louis Cardinals. Legends. Cross the Mississippi to Monroe County, and you'll find another. This one is still managing.

It's the 4th of July.

"HEY, BURNS," Vern yells from the comfort of his folding chair at the edge of the dugout. It's the fifth inning, the loudest he's been all game. Kade Burns, a 20-year-old first-year middle infielder from Edwardsville, Illinois, scampers out as a courtesy runner for the catcher. Unable or should I say, unsafe for Vern to stand in the third-base coach's box, he is confined to the sideline in his temporary throne. It tears at him not being out there, front and center when his team needs him the most—when he needs his team the most. He screams for Burns as if he's making up for all the coaching he is no longer allowed to do. He pulls out a tin of long cut tobacco, and with an aggressive nonchalance, mischievously shoves some in his mouth. He holds the tin like he held the rocks on his grandpa's farm— prepping a skipper.

Lucy watches from the cool shade of the park's grandstands. She has watched thousands of games over the years—she still gets nervous.

"I'm his biggest fan," she says of Vern. "I've always been."

The game finishes. The Millers are 3-2 winners—Reid Hendrickson is the winning pitcher. Vern loves to show off the scorecard from win 2,000 a few weeks prior. Hendrickson won that game, too. Hendrickson's father is Darin Hendrickson, head coach of the St. Louis University baseball team. He played for Vern, too.

Reid Hendrickson (left) was the winning pitcher as Vern picked up win No. 2,000 as Waterloo manager on June 9, 2019 (Photo courtesy of the *Belleville News-Democrat*)

"It was 19 years ago. Darin (Hendrickson) was on our roster all year. But he didn't pitch until the championship game of the post-season tournament. I was out of pitchers, and so I called and asked him to

pitch. He pitched a one-hitter and we won the title. Nineteen years later his son pitches the game where I win my 2,000th game as Waterloo manager. Talk about your irony."

Win No. 2005. Using a cane, Vern stands up. "You need help with that?" Assistant coach Mark Vogel asks. Vern silently folds the chair. Lucy meets him at the extended tailgate of the red truck and softly kisses his cheek—Lucy and Vern married in 1958. "We had to have a dance because we were both great dancers," Lucy recalls the reception 61 years after the fact. "Now he walks with a cane." He gingerly gets into the driver's seat, the summer sun highlighting his timeworn complexion.

He's asked by a fan walking past, "Other people your age—what are they doing right now?"

"I hope they're enjoying life like I am," Vern says and then coughs twice.

"Do you still love the game?" the fan asks, smiling.

At the ripe age of 84, close to eighty years after his baptism into the game, Vern's mind wanders briefly before struggling for a response.

"Do I still love the game?" His voice catching with emotion, "It's the best damn game in the world."

THE END

NOTES

This is a work of nonfiction. It is based primarily on the accounts of those chronicled herein, particularly the main characters. Where archival information was available, I relied on it for information, quotes, and the foundation of parts of the narrative, in particular, the coverage by past and present reporters of the Waterloo Republic-Times, the Clarion Journal, the Belleville News-Democrat, the Alton Telegraph, and most notably Benjamin Hochman and others at the St. Louis Post-Dispatch.

While I relied upon a number of these sources, most of the research came from revisiting in memory those not-so-long-ago events. Distant memories at times are vague, and any mistakes herein are mine and mine alone. Some names have been changed to protect the—forgiven. THANK YOU to all who have made these memories and this book possible.

—Craig Ohlau

But there was one sport above all, one love, as a man loves one thing, one place, even one woman. Baseball.

APPENDIX A: 2005 WATERLOO BASEBALL CLUB

Corey "The Prince" Blackwell

Craig Ohlau

Jake "Franchise" Friederich

Eric Caby

Jeff Kaiser

Peter Buck

L-R: Aaron "A.T." Thompson, Pat Hardin, Peter Buck,
Brandon "Moose" Musso, Brian Smith

Brandon Waeltz

L-R: Pat Hardin, Chas Wigger, Jim Queern

L-R: Jake "Punisher" Hurst, Jordy Thompson, Brian Fuess (Bud Legend '06-'08)

Brandon "Moose" Musso

Mark Mueller

"I've had tendon and ligament tears, a torn rotator cuff, broken bones, and swollen joints. Coming back from all those injuries? No one else in the league would have ever done that. The moonlit nights on the track, running up and down the bleachers, doing reverse pull ups on the under-side, the begging and bribing of catchers and teammates to throw long or catch bullpens, the ability to still cheer from the sidelines and stay positive— the unique accomplishments of my career. I've gained a wealth of experience and perspective on what it means to have a baseball career. While mine did not reach the heights of the MLB, I played for 20 years at a collegiate/professional/semi-professional level. My career had a growth, a prime, and a tooth and nail fight to stay at a high level. I think to myself all the time, I don't know how good I got at this game at my peak, but I haven't gotten much worse. I'm pretty damn proud about that."

—*Mark Mueller on his 20 years in post high school baseball*

Vern Moehrs

2005 Waterloo Buds

Front Row L-R: Erik Kaiser, Chas Wigger, Aaron Thompson, Corey Blackwell

Middle Row L-R: Jeremiah Bergheger, Brian Smith, Jeff Kaiser, Jim Queern, Jordan Thompson, James Powell, Peter Buck

Back Row L-R: Harry Thompson, Vern Moehrs, Pat Hardin, Jake Friederich, Mark Mueller, Craig Ohlau, Brandon Waeltz, Brandon Musso, Eric Caby, Tony Musso

APPENDIX B: WATERLOO BASEBALL CLUB RECORDS

All Time National Wins Leaders in Semi-Pro Baseball

Manager------Team------# of Wins

*#1 Bill Rickenbach - Mechanicsburg, PA Cardinals - 2,674 ***
#2 Howie Minas - Midloathian, IL White Sox - 2,650
***#3 Vern Moehrs - Waterloo, IL Millers / Buds – 2,024 ***
#4 Henry "Harv" Tomter - Eau Claire, WI Cavaliers - 1,676
*#5 Jim Corte - Detroit, MI Jet Box - 1,508 ***
#6 Jess Bolen Sr. - Cape Girardeau, MO. Capahas - 1,482
*Still Active
Source: National Semi-Pro Baseball Hall of Fame

All-Time Home Run Leaders in Semi-Pro Baseball
#1 Jim Wahlig Waterloo, IL Buds 278
#2 Marty Watson Evansville, IN Outlaws 249 (53 in 2001)
#3 Keith Wentz, Mt. Wolf, PA, York Central League 225
Source: National Semi-Pro Baseball Hall of Fame

Waterloo Baseball Club Career Hitting Records

At-Bats	3451	Lon Fulte
Runs	1139	Jim Wahlig
Hits	1416	Jim Wahlig
Doubles	240	Jim Wahlig
Triples	45	Carl Braun
Home Runs	278	Jim Wahlig
RBIs	1142	Jim Wahlig
Walks	851	Lon Fulte
Strikeouts	398	Clay Moehrs
Stolen Bases	230	Clay Moehrs
Batting AVG.	.451	Jim Wahlig

"Last night I spoke to the first manager I ever played for, Vernie Moehrs of the Waterloo (Buds) Millers. Vernie signed me at 17 years old in 1998 to a team that was comprised of all former pro and college players, the likes of Neil Fiala, John Wahlig, Jimmy Wahlig, Jim Schlecht, Jim Anderson, Jon "Boxy" Baxmeyer, Clay Moehrs, Jeff Kaiser, Jeff Gansmann, Mike Wirth, Brian Unger, Chris Braun, Adam Pickett, Darin Hendrickson, and Mark Vogel to name a few. We won 48-straight games that year and lost the first game of the championship best of three series to Corey Blackwell who pitched for Sauget. We came back to beat him the next day and win the league. Vernie is about to begin his 59th season as Buds (Millers) manager and is 9 wins away from 2000. Several years ago, he was honored at Busch Stadium and threw out the first pitch before a Cardinals game. He recalled my first ever home run as a Buds player in Brighton, Illinois in 1998 but forgot what he ate for breakfast this morning. What a beautiful game, and fraternity it is!"

—*Social Media Post, April 5, 2019, Steve Haake, Waterloo Buds Outfielder 1998-2002*

Greatest Season

Waterloo Buds 1998 Season Results

Date	Record			R H E	Opponent	R H E	League
5/23	1-0	W	Waterloo	6-10-1	*@Valmeyer	1- 3-0	1-0
	2-0	W	Waterloo	12-18-2	*@Valmeyer	5- 9-1	2-0
5/24	3-0	W	Waterloo	9-14-2	*@Millstadt	2- 4-2	3-0
	4-0	W	Waterloo	5-10-0	*@Millstadt	4- 6-1	4-0
5/29	5-0	W	Waterloo	6-12-1	*Sauget	3- 4-0	5-0
5/31	6-0	W	Waterloo	10-12-0	Stl. Printers	9-12-0	
	7-0	W	Waterloo	9-11-0	Stl. Printers	4- 8-1	
6/3	8-0	W	Waterloo	10-12-1	Millstadt	0- 3-4	
6/6	9-0	W	Waterloo	Forfeit	*East Alton	Forfeit	6-0
	10-0	W	Waterloo	Forfeit	*East Alton	Forfeit	7-0
6/7	11-0	W	Waterloo	18-17-1	*@Brighton	4- 6-1	8-0
	12-0	W	Waterloo	10-16-1	*@Brighton	4- 4-1	9-0
6/10	13-0	W	Waterloo	18-17-0	Murphysboro	0- 3-3	
6/12	14-0	W	Waterloo	8-11-3	Stl. Printers	1- 5-1	
6/17	15-0	W	Waterloo	13-16-2	@Fairview Heights	9-15-1	
6/19	16-0	W	Waterloo	8-11-0	@Fairview Heights	2- 8-1	
6/24	17-0	W	Waterloo	15-18-4	*Sauget	10-14-3	10-0
6/28	18-0	W	Waterloo	7- 9-0	@(PSG)Westchester	0- 3-2	
	19-0	W	Waterloo	9-12-0	@(PSG)Westchester	1- 6-1	
6/29	20-0	W	Waterloo	15-14-0	@(PSG)Murphysboro	2- 6-3	
	21-0	W	Waterloo	14-15-0	@(PSG)East Alton	4- 9-2	
7/3	22-0	W	Waterloo	12-16-3	@(VT)Stl. Printers	8-15-2	
7/4	23-0	W	Waterloo	10-10-0	@(VT)East Alton	3- 5-3	
7/5	24-0	W	Waterloo	8-10-1	@(VT)Valmeyer	2-10-3	
7/10	25-0	W	Waterloo	12-12-0	Stl. Printers	6-10-6	
7/12	26-0	W	Waterloo	8- 9-3	*Valmeyer	5- 6-0	11-0
	27-0	W	Waterloo	14-16-1	*Valmeyer	2- 2-0	12-0
7/15	28-0	W	Waterloo	12-12-2	Fairview Heights	4- 8-2	
7/17	29-0	W	Waterloo	2- 5-0	*Granite City	1- 4-0	13-0
	30-0	W	Waterloo	11-16-2	*Granite City	4- 8-2	14-0
7/19	31-0	W	Waterloo	16-16-0	*Millstadt	9-12-2	15-0
	32-0	W	Waterloo	6-11-0	*Millstadt	5- 8-0	16-0
7/25	33-0	W	Waterloo	9-13-0	@Springfield	2- 5-3	
	34-0	W	Waterloo	9-13-2	@Springfield	4- 7-1	
7/26	35-0	W	Waterloo	15-16-2	@Springfield	10-16-4	
7/29	36-0	W	Waterloo	11-10-0	@*Sauget	5-10-2	17-0
	37-0	W	Waterloo	16-15-0	@*Sauget	4- 5-2	18-0
8/1	38-0	W	Waterloo	14-20-4	@*East Alton	3- 5-1	19-0
	39-0	W	Waterloo	15-18-0	@*East Alton	0- 1-4	20-0
8/2	40-0	W	Waterloo	8-11-0	*Brighton	2- 4-2	21-0
	41-0	W	Waterloo	9- 6-0	*Brighton	0- 6-2	22-0
8/9	42-0	W	Waterloo	9-13-1	@*Granite City	0- 3-0	23-0
	43-0	W	Waterloo	7-14-1	@*Granite City	2- 6-0	24-0
8/14	44-0	W	Waterloo	8-11-1	(P)Valmeyer	3- 8-1	
8/15	44-1	L	Waterloo	2- 5-1	(P)Sauget	6- 9-0	
	45-1	W	Waterloo	14-14-0	(P)Valmeyer	7- 9-0	
8/16	46-1	W	Waterloo	17-15-1	(P)Sauget	3- 7-4	
	47-1	W	Waterloo	8-10-2	(P)Sauget	7-12-1	

* - Mon-Clair League Games	1st place	24-0	
PSG - Prairie State Games	1st place	4-0	
VT - Valmeyer Tournament	1st place	3-0	
(P) - Mon-Clair Playoffs	1st place	4-1	

Facts about the Waterloo Buds 1998 season

- The average member of the starting lineup is 32 years old
- The oldest player is 41 (Neil Fiala) and youngest player is 17 (Chris Braun).
- 47 game winning streak (43 in 98) is the best in St. Louis area amateur baseball history
- 5 players played pro ball with one, Neil Fiala, playing for the Cardinals in 1981
- The hitters average nearly 2 homeruns a game and are hitting .401 for the season
- The pitching staff's ERA is 2.89 for the season
- Manager Vern Moehrs has been at the helm for over 30 years
- Won League title with a 24-0 record. First undefeated team in League history

Infielders

2b   Neil Fiala, 41, A former member of the St. Louis Cardinals in 1981, he is the teams starting second baseman and is leading the team in hitting and has hit in everyone of the teams games but one. He has been with the Buds for six years

ss   Jeff Kaiser, 32, A former San Francisco Giant farmhand, Jeff is an excellent defensive shortstop and has two grand slams on the year. He has been a Bud 11 years.

1b   Mike Wirth, 38, Played proball for the ~~Minnesota Twins~~ *Cardinals*, Mike has been the teams first baseman for over ten years.

3b   Clay Moehrs, 28, Played college ball for Southeast Missouri State and is the teams starting thirds baseman. This is his 13 year with the Buds

Catchers

Jim Anderson, 30, Played college ball for Clemson University and played in the College World Series. He is an outstanding defensive catcher. 4th year witht he Buds.

John Baxmeyer, 28, Played college ball for Kaskaskia College and is having an outstanding year at the plate. This is his 11th year with the Buds

Outfielders

Jim Wahlig, 39, has played for the Buds since he was 17 years old excluding 2 seasons of pro ball with the Toronto Blue Jays. He is the Buds all time hit leader.

John Wahling, 32, has played for the Buds for 16 seasons. He played proball for the Baltimore Orioles and three years ago hit 28 homeruns.

Steve Johnson, 22, just finished college baseball at the UMSL and is in his second season with the Buds. He runs well and is a good defensive outfielder.

Pitchers

Darin Hendrickson, 26, played at SIU Edwardsville and is the team's number one pitcher. He is the head coach at Fontbonne College. First year with the Buds.

Chris Hargan, 22, just finished playing at Northwestern University. He is the team's number two pitcher and possesses an outstanding fastball. 2nd year with the Buds.

Brandon Musso, 19, currently plays at Belleville Area College for Neil Fiala, he is the teams number three pitcher and is an up and coming star. 1st year with the Buds

Chris Braun, 17, The teams number four pitcher, he is recruited to play for the St. Louis University Basketball Billikins next year.

Jim Schlecht, 35, The teams ace reliever, he has 10 saves this year. 6th year Bud

Other players

Steve Haake, 17, will play for BAC next year, He is the teams 4th outhfielder.

Brian Unger, 17, will play for BAC next year, He is a lefthanded reliever.

Bill Phillips, 24, played at Coker College. He is a righthanded reliever.

Kevin Almond, 25, works at Scott Air force base. he is a lefthanded reliever.

Adam Pickett, 17, a utility infielder

Ben Margalski, 19, has filled in at catcher when needed. Drafted by Angels.

1998 WATERLOO BUDS PRESS RELEASE

Mon-Clair League Champions
Prairie State Gold Medallist
1998 Waterloo Buds 47-1

Back Row (L to R) Neil Fiala, Jeff Kaiser, Matt Miller, Kevin Almond, Brandon Musso, Darin Hendrickson, Mike Wirth, Jim Schlecht, Jim Wahlig, Vern Moehrs-Manager, Front Row (L to R) Mayor Gordon, Norm Mehnke-coach, Jim Anderson, Steve Johnson, John Wahlig, Cris hargan, Clay Moehrs, John Baxmeyer, Donnie Werth

WATERLOO BUDS ALL-TIME
RECORD/CHAMPIONSHIPS

CHAMPIONS

Year	Wins	Losses	Division	Playoff	Midsummer Classic
1961-					
1967	143	80	1 (1966)	1 (1966)	X
1968	41	6	1		X
1969	39	8	1	1	X
1970	24	12			X
1971	40	11	1	1	X
1972	42	9			
1973	40	10	1	1	
1974	51	5	1		1
1975	46	7	1	1	
1976	34	16		1	
1977	40	10	1		
1978	44	5	1		
1979	37	10			
1980	48	11	1	1	
1981	35	16			
1982	42	14	1		
1983	48	6	1	1	1
1984	46	5	1	1	
1985	42	8	1	1	
1986	44	5	1	1	1
1987	35	9	1		1
1988	35	8	1		
1989	35	11	1		
1990	36	14	1	1	
1991	38	12	1	1	1
1992	43	8	1		
1993	38	12	1		
1994	45	7	1		
1995	35	8	1		
1996	40	6	1	1	
1997	38	9	1	1	
1998	47	1	1	1	1
1999	36	6	1		

CHAMPIONS

Year	Wins	Losses	Division	Playoff	Midsummer Classic
2000	33	8	1	1	1
2001	30	5	1	1	
2002	34	8	1		
2003	31	8	1		
2004	35	6	1	1	
2006	37	2	1	1	1
2007	41	6	1	1	
2008	33	4	1		1
2009	22	12	1		X
2010	32	10	1		1
2011	20	15			
2012	25	10	1		
2013	30	10		1	1
2014	33	6	1		
2015	24	9	1		1
2016	23	9			1
2017	29	7	1		
2018	16	15			
2019	22	11			
2020	11	7			
Totals	2024	537	43	23	14

WATERLOO BASEBALL CLUB STATISTICS
(Source: handwritten ledgers provided by Vern Moehrs)

Individual Statistics: 1963

BATTERS	AVG	R	H	AB	2B	3B	HR	RBI	SB	BB	HP
Braun, Carl	0.417	22	40	96	3	4	2	19	15	5	1
Tucker, Tom	0.320	5	24	75	2	0	0	11	1	3	0
Leinicke, Jerry	0.316	21	25	79	7	2	1	10	4	7	0
Lutz, Dennis	0.294	18	25	85	5	2	1	20	4	13	1
Arns, Charles	0.280	15	26	93	4	2	0	12	4	4	1
Zaricor, Bob	0.288	7	17	59	4	0	0	10	2	5	0
Moehrs, Vern	0.261	14	24	92	3	0	0	13	7	13	1
Schatte, Dennis	0.246	9	15	61	0	0	0	11	0	3	0
Gentsch, Dennis	0.211	16	15	71	0	0	1	12	10	17	0
Scheibe, Jim	0.200	8	5	25	2	0	0	2	7	11	0
Hoffman, Walter	0.205	1	8	39	0	1	0	3	0	1	0
Harlin, Tim	0.167	3	5	30	0	2	0	1	2	4	0
Hustedde, Ed	0.333	5	6	18	1	0	0	0	1	1	0
Kaestner, Ronnie	0.167	1	1	6	0	0	0	0	0	1	1
Schneider, Robert	0.500	2	2	4	1	0	0	2	1	1	2
Klube, Bob	0.000	0	0	4	0	0	0	0	0	0	0
Schmidt, Bill	0.000	0	0	2	0	0	0	0	0	0	0
Niebrugge, Dave	0.333	1	1	3	0	0	0	0	0	1	0
Binder, Rich	0.000	0	0	0	0	0	0	0	0	1	0
McKinney, Mike	0.000	0	0	2	0	0	0	0	0	0	0
Totals	0.283	148	239	844	32	13	5	126	58	91	7

PITCHERS	IP	H	R	ER	BB	SO	ERA
Hoffman, Walter	56 1/3	52	28	20	13	51	3.20
Hustedde, Ed	29 1/3	23	13	7	7	42	2.15
Gentsch, Dennis	22 2/3	19	18	14	13	24	5.56
Niebruegge, Dave	3	5	7	1	3	3	3.00
Binder, Rich	3	4	5	4	4	4	12.00
Schatte, Dennis	90 2/3	75	31	24	31	63	2.38
Totals	205	178	102	70	71	187	3.07

Individual Statistics: 1965

BATTERS	AVG	R	H	AB	2B	3B	HR	RBI	SB	BB	SO	HP	SAC
Pitts, Jim	0.400	10	10	25	1	3	0	4	0	2	7	1	0
Schatte, Dennis	0.375	0	9	24	1	0	0	2	0	1	5	0	0
Fulte,Lon	0.370	11	17	46	3	0	0	10	1	8	13	1	0
Braun, Carl	0.364	27	40	110	7	2	0	17	10	10	13	0	2
Hoffman, Warren	0.359	7	14	39	0	0	1	4	5	1	6	0	0
Dillenger, Dick	0.319	25	43	135	9	2	2	28	2	22	10	0	0
Ray, Billie	0.292	4	7	24	1	0	1	9	1	2	7	0	0
Hoffman, Terry	0.275	13	25	91	2	0	0	6	3	7	23	2	4
Lutz, Dennis	0.275	14	25	91	1	0	1	14	3	18	22	1	0
Moehrs, Vern	0.274	21	32	117	9	1	0	15	10	20	14	0	0
Pelludant, Al	0.263	7	5	19	0	1	1	5	2	2	1	0	0
Hustedde, Ed	0.238	0	5	21	0	0	0	0	0	3	4	0	0
Rahn, Ken	0.224	22	22	98	4	0	0	11	10	19	17	2	2
Arns, Charlie	0.222	5	12	54	0	0	0	7	0	3	12	0	2
Toenjes, Tom	0.218	3	12	55	1	0	1	11	0	3	23	2	0
Hoffman, Roger	0.192	19	15	78	1	1	0	4	5	26	17	1	0
Studt, Alan	0.146	5	6	41	1	0	3	1	2	3	9	1	1
Binder, Rich	0.167	2	3	18	0	0	0	4	0	0	5	0	0
Hacker, Rich	0.167	1	1	6	0	0	0	1	0	0	0	0	0
Wiegard, Rich	0.071	4	1	14	0	0	0	0	0	4	6	0	0
Harlin, Tim	0.000	0	0	12	0	0	0	0	0	1	5	0	0
Kaestner, Ron	0.000	0	0	10	0	0	0	1	2	2	1	0	0
Totals	0.270	200	304	1128	41	10	10	154	56	157	220	11	11

PITCHERS	IP	H	R	ER	BB	SO	HP	ERA
Hustedde, Ed	44	35	13	11	16	39	0	2.25
Dillenger, Dick	98 2/3	103	48	30	29	103	4	2.74
Rahn, Ken	59 2/3	52	39	22	28	53	4	3.32
Binder, Rich	34 2/3	15	6	5	13	51	6	1.30
Niebruegge, Dave	18	8	4	3	4	19	0	1.50
Hankammer, John	2/3	1	0	0	0	0	0	0.00
Schatte, Dennis	27	21	7	4	5	16	2	1.33
Totals	282 2/3	235	117	75	95	281	16	2.39

Individual Statistics: 1966

BATTERS	AVG	R	H	AB	2B	3B	HR	RBI	SB	BB	SO	SAC
Braun, Carl	0.360	41	63	175	11	2	2	36	20	9	29	1
Moehrs, Vern	0.339	15	39	115	5	2	0	33	3	21	14	4
Fulte, Lon	0.333	49	48	144	11	2	2	33	9	28	16	2
Dillenger, Dick	0.327	31	48	147	9	1	3	33	7	24	9	6
Niebruegge, Dave	0.325	18	27	83	3	2	2	20	10	3	12	0
Studt, Alan	0.304	7	14	46	4	0	0	1	6	6	12	0
Rahn, Ken	0.286	33	36	126	9	1	1	14	10	22	25	0
Toenjes, Tom	0.245	7	13	53	2	0	0	6	0	8	13	0
Hoffman, Terry	0.245	20	35	143	4	2	0	11	8	8	29	1
Hoffman, Roger	0.188	13	15	80	1	0	0	6	3	16	13	3
Maurer, Robert	0.183	13	11	60	0	2	0	2	8	6	13	0
Binder, Rich	0.364	4	8	22	2	0	0	5	0	0	2	0
Mudd, Arnold	0.143	3	4	28	0	0	0	5	1	3	9	0
Hoffman, Randy	0.500	1	1	2	0	0	0	0	1	0	0	0
Pieper, Dennis	0.500	1	1	2	1	0	0	3	0	2	1	0
Hustedde, Ed	0.125	2	1	8	0	0	0	0	0	0	2	0
Toal, John	0.000	0	0	1	0	0	0	0	0	0	0	0
Hankhammer, John	0.158	3	3	19	0	0	0	2	0	0	1	1
Metzger, Bob	0.167	1	2	12	0	0	0	2	0	1	1	0
Musso, Tony	0.122	6	5	41	0	0	1	4	2	2	14	2
Fulte, Ray	0.333	1	1	3	0	0	0	0	0	0	0	0
Huedgel, Terry	0.280	15	21	75	3	0	1	10	1	7	19	0
Totals	0.286	284	396	1385	65	14	12	226	89	166	234	20

No Pitching Records Recorded

Individual Statistics: 1967

BATTERS	AVG	R	H	AB	2B	3B	HR	RBI	SB	BB	SO	HP	SAC
Gonzales, Kenny	0.667	1	2	3	0	3	0	0	0	1	1	0	0
Fulte, Ray	0.500	0	1	2	0	0	0	0	0	0	0	0	0
Braun, Carl	0.341	36	56	164	11	0	0	25	12	16	24	1	2
Musso, Tony	0.310	13	27	87	4	2	0	10	2	5	10	2	0
Dillenger, Dick	0.300	20	48	160	2	0	1	24	5	24	7	0	3
Fulte, Lon	0.291	33	41	141	4	2	2	24	5	33	14	2	2
Moehrs, Vern	0.258	17	24	93	3	0	1	23	2	30	8	2	8
Studt, Alan	0.256	14	22	86	2	0	0	12	7	9	9	1	2
Huegel, Terry	0.250	21	33	132	2	0	1	15	2	11	26	7	0
Rahn, Ken	0.200	13	18	90	9	1	0	12	3	12	14	1	0
Hoffman, Terry	0.193	15	22	114	0	1	1	12	4	18	23	0	2
Pieper, Dennis	0.183	12	15	82	3	0	0	6	2	10	28	3	1
Metzger, Bob	0.370	2	10	27	1	0	0	2	0	3	2	0	0
Pieper, Gary	0.224	8	11	49	1	0	0	9	1	6	12	0	0
Toenjes, Tom	0.267	3	4	15	0	0	1	1	0	0	4	0	0
Hankhammer, John	0.176	0	3	17	0	1	0	2	0	0	4	0	0
Niebruegge, Dave	0.263	4	10	38	2	0	0	2	3	0	9	0	0
Nicholson, Dave	0.250	2	2	8	1	0	0	1	0	3	2	0	0
Hustedde, Ed	0.333	1	3	9	0	0	0	0	0	1	2	0	0
Kuehn, Clyde	0.333	4	5	15	1	0	0	1	0	3	1	0	0
Paetzhold, Jerry	0.212	3	7	33	1	0	0	4	0	4	5	0	0
Lutz, Dennis	0.238	3	5	21	0	0	0	3	1	2	10	0	0
Totals	0.266	225	369	1386	47	10	7	188	49	191	215	19	20

PITCHERS	IP	H	R	ER	BB	SO	W	L	ERA
Dillinger, Dick	56	49	3	25	6	39	3	4	4.02
Hustedde, Ed	23	21	5	4	4	20	3	0	1.57
Musso, Tony	92	62	34	20	16	123	10	1	1.96
Hankammer, John	47	28	8	6	5	48	4	1	1.15
Metzger, Bob	35	23	7	4	9	29	2	2	1.03
Paetzhold, Jerry	92	52	15	6	16	83	7	4	0.59
Rahn, Ken	4	2	2	0	0	3	1	0	0.00
Totals	349	237	74	65	56	345	30	12	1.68

Individual Statistics: 1968

BATTERS	AVG	R	H	AB	2B	3B	HR	RBI	SB	BB	SO	SAC
Fulte, Lon	0.366	42	56	153	9	1	9	46	4	26	12	6
Dillenger, Dick	0.375	30	60	160	12	1	0	27	5	18	11	1
Moehrs, Vern	0.273	25	30	110	2	0	0	13	4	33	10	1
Braun, Carl	0.354	39	56	158	5	4	0	20	2	15	22	0
Degener, M.	0.317	16	26	82	0	1	1	14	3	10	22	2
Gonzales, Kenny	0.275	14	28	102	9	1	1	15	0	5	12	1
Rohr, Ray	0.302	20	35	116	6	2	1	18	0	7	12	0
Toenjes, Tom	0.158	2	9	57	1	0	0	4	0	4	19	0
Musso, Tony	0.312	16	44	141	2	0	0	21	6	8	10	6
Musso, Dave	0.214	2	3	14	0	0	0	2	0	0	7	0
Huegel, Terry	0.272	16	28	103	5	0	1	12	0	16	19	1
Hyatt, John	0.231	2	9	39	1	0	0	5	1	2	3	0
Studt, Alan	0.431	4	25	58	1	1	1	7	8	3	6	1
Nicholson, Dave	0.296	18	37	125	4	3	3	33	6	9	21	0
Neeman, Cal	0.250	22	4	16	2	0	0	2	0	0	3	0
Albrecht, Ed	0.246	2	14	57	2	0	1	9	0	3	6	0
Paetzhold, Jerry	0.265	14	9	34	2	0	2	10	0	9	6	0
Hankhammer, John	0.150	9	3	20	0	0	0	0	0	1	2	0
Pieper, Dennis	0.250	2	1	4	0	0	1	1	0	0	1	0
Rau, Gary	0.250	1	1	4	0	0	0	0	0	0	3	0
Fulte, Ray	0.000	0	0	1	0	0	0	0	0	0	0	0
Hustedde, Ed	0.000	0	0	4	0	0	0	0	0	0	0	0
Surber, Jim	0.000	0	0	0	0	0	0	0	0	1	0	0
Totals	0.307	296	478	1558	63	14	21	259	39	170	207	19

PITCHERS	IP	H	R	ER	BB	SO	W	L	ERA
Hankammer, John	46	42	10	9	7	51	7	0	1.76
Albrecht, Eddie	101	70	21	12	17	74	7	1	1.07
Paetzhold, Jerry	85	53	19	11	12	98	9	2	1.16
Musso, Tony	102	67	35	25	14	97	12	2	2.21
Dillinger, Dick	32	24	43	7	7	29	4	1	1.97
Hustedde, Ed	9	9	6	2	5	7	0	0	2.00
Rippelmeyer, Ray	7	5	0	0	0	7	1	0	0.00
Forfeit	0	0	0	0	0	0	1	0	0.00
Totals	382	270	134	66	62	363	41	6	1.55

Individual Statistics: 1969

BATTERS	AVG	R	H	AB	2B	3B	HR	RBI	SB	BB	SO
Braun, Carl	0.434	48	76	175	10	4	3	33	5	25	13
Fulte, Lon	0.355	43	61	172	9	2	2	26	2	26	11
Dillinger, Dick	0.348	33	57	164	10	1	2	25	4	24	14
Krueger, D.	0.289	27	35	121	3	0	1	15	14	16	22
Heugel, Terry	0.269	19	32	119	6	2	3	27	0	13	20
Degener, M.	0.179	12	21	117	5	0	0	12	0	13	27
Studt, Alan	0.286	8	10	35	0	1	0	2	2	3	3
Moehrs, Vern	0.274	9	23	84	3	0	0	11	0	25	6
Toal, John	0.310	17	31	100	3	0	2	7	9	13	39
Rohr, Ray	0.262	13	16	61	2	2	0	13	1	10	11
Jacobs, Art (Bucky)	0.472	8	17	36	5	0	2	15	0	2	2
Kreher, Dennis	0.271	17	26	96	4	1	0	9	7	6	6
Toenjes, Tom	0.267	4	4	15	2	0	1	2	0	1	1
Weinhoff, Don	0.067	1	1	15	2	0	0	0	0	5	9
Albrecht, Eddie	0.333	4	12	36	4	0	1	8	0	6	1
Hankhammer, John	0.400	0	2	5	0	0	0	3	0	0	0
Doughtrey, John	0.286	1	2	7	0	0	0	1	0	1	3
Pinion, Carl	0.375	3	3	8	0	0	0	1	0	2	1
Kuehn, Clyde	0.000	1	0	3	0	0	0	0	0	0	0
Gill, Rich	0.250	1	1	4	0	0	0	2	0	0	0
Nicholson, Dave	0.000	0	0	1	0	0	0	0	0	0	0
Conrad, John	0.200	1	2	10	0	0	0	1	2	0	1
Paetzhold, Jerry	0.316	7	12	38	5	0	1	7	0	9	9
Neidner, Fred	0.000	1	0	14	0	0	0	0	0	3	5
Werle, Dale	0.333	1	1	3	0	0	0	0	0	3	0
Neeman, Cal	0.400	5	10	25	0	0	0	7	0	7	2
Wyatt, John	0.167	1	1	6	1	0	0	0	0	0	2
Radison, Dan	0.167	1	1	6	0	0	0	0	0	3	1
Vogt, Jim	0.500	1	2	4	0	1	0	1	0	0	1
Totals	0.310	287	459	1480	74	14	18	228	46	216	210

PITCHERS	IP	H	R	ER	BB	SO	W	L	ERA
Dillinger, Dick	116	86	44	17	20	80	13	1	1.32
Weinhoff, Don	22 1/3	18	4	3	4	28	2	1	1.21
Paetzhold, Jerry	96	76	39	30	22	91	10	2	2.81
Albrecht, Eddie	88	85	24	23	9	51	6	4	2.35
Neidner, Fred	40	23	12	10	21	38	5	0	2.25
Hankammer, John	14	11	5	5	4	21	2	0	3.21
Doughtrey, John	10 1/3	10	0	0	4	10	1	0	0.00
Totals	386 2/3	309	128	88	84	319	39	8	2.05

Individual Statistics: 1970

BATTERS	AVG	R	H	AB	2B	3B	HR	RBI	SB	BB	SO
Dillinger, Dick	0.339	23	42	124	6	0	1	25	1	15	6
Fulte, Tim	0.328	31	38	116	9	2	4	23	1	28	12
Degener, M.	0.294	13	32	109	6	1	1	14	2	5	21
Adamson, Jon	0.373	10	22	59	6	0	4	18	3	3	10
Braun, Carl	0.366	24	34	93	7	1	1	19	12	10	11
Studt, Alan	0.218	28	29	133	7	0	2	14	12	17	25
Toal, John	0.221	18	21	95	2	0	1	10	8	16	26
Brenner, D.	0.250	6	14	56	5	0	0	2	1	12	16
Moehrs, Vern	0.250	4	8	32	0	0	0	5	0	5	5
Schmidt, Jim	0.313	11	10	32	3	0	1	12	5	7	4
Huegel, Terry	0.284	9	19	67	3	0	1	14	0	2	7
Thomas, Danny	0.381	13	16	42	6	0	3	10	0	6	5
Haberl, Chris	0.046	3	6	130	1	0	0	3	1	5	7
Wyatt, John	0.036	8	4	110	1	0	0	4	0	1	1
Jacobs, Bucky	0.333	6	8	24	0	0	1	8	0	4	1
Webb, J.	0.370	6	10	27	4	0	0	2	0	3	2
Westbrook, Todd	0.133	2	2	15	0	0	0	0	0	0	0
Albrecht, Eddie	0.250	1	1	4	0	0	0	0	0	0	0
Paezhold, Jerry	0.000	0	0	2	0	0	0	0	0	2	2
Luhr, Mike	0.500	1	1	2	1	0	1	0	0	0	0
Metzger, Bob	0.267	3	8	30	0	0	0	6	0	3	4
Griffin, Rich	0.083	0	1	12	0	0	0	0	0	0	0
Weinhoff, Don	0.231	2	6	26	0	0	0	4	0	5	5
Hankhammer, John	0.000	0	0	2	0	0	0	0	0	0	1
Radison, Dan	0.188	1	3	16	1	0	0	1	2	0	3
Totals	0.247	223	335	1358	68	4	21	194	48	149	174

PITCHERS	IP	H	R	ER	BB	SO	W	L	SV	ERA
Dillinger, Dick	95	67	31	25	21	62	8	3	0	2.37
Adamson, Jon	17	12	8	5	5	13	2	0	0	2.65
Griffin, Rich	20	31	16	13	9	15	1	2	0	5.85
Metzger, Bob	75	48	20	7	11	71	4	4	0	0.84
Weinhoff, Don	82	68	36	24	15	74	8	3	0	2.63
Hankhammer, John	7	7	4	12	0	13	1	0	0	15.43
Totals	296	233	115	86	61	248	24	12	0	2.61

Individual Statistics: 1971

BATTERS	AVG	R	H	AB	2B	3B	HR	RBI	SB	BB	SO
Jacobs, Bucky	0.241	9	13	54	5	0	0	5	0	5	5
Fulte, Lon	0.367	56	66	180	10	2	8	41	5	42	21
Braun, Carl	0.340	39	64	188	15	4	4	44	10	19	13
Dillinger, Dick	0.254	25	47	185	7	0	5	33	1	19	12
Studt, Alan	0.245	23	45	184	7	2	1	17	11	23	16
Moehrs, Vern	0.274	18	23	84	4	0	0	15	3	23	10
Adamson, Jon	0.325	20	38	117	11	1	1	26	2	13	17
Kreher, Dennis	0.341	18	28	82	5	2	0	11	3	8	5
Jackson, Jon	0.256	15	23	90	2	1	1	10	2	22	21
Radison, Dan	0.353	6	12	34	2	0	2	5	2	1	5
Douchant, Mike	0.243	11	25	103	6	1	2	14	3	9	16
Thomas, J.	0.235	4	8	34	1	0	2	4	2	1	9
Weinhoff, Don	0.208	5	5	24	0	0	0	0	0	3	9
Liskey, Bill	0.189	6	7	37	0	0	0	4	0	8	9
Metzger, Bob	0.143	4	5	35	1	0	0	5	0	4	5
Toal, John	0.409	10	9	22	2	0	0	3	1	12	9
Reichert, Bob	0.389	2	7	18	1	0	0	4	6	5	0
Mernick, Dennis	0.500	3	3	6	0	1	0	1	2	4	1
Totals	0.290	274	428	1477	79	14	26	242	53	221	183

PITCHERS	IP	H	R	ER	BB	HP	SO	W	L	ERA
Liskey, Bill	91 1/3	83	31	29	28	15	50	9	3	2.86
Dillinger, Dick	54	53	28	25	2	0	42	5	3	4.17
Adamson, Jon	85	57	15	10	9	1	57	6	1	1.06
Weinhoff, Don	69	66	35	29	25	4	66	6	2	3.78
Hankammer, John	25 2/3	22	20	15	17	2	25	3	1	5.26
Metzger, Bob	98 2/3	65	27	16	40	7	106	11	1	1.46
Totals	423 2/3	346	156	124	121	29	346	40	11	2.63

Individual Statistics: 1972

BATTERS	AVG	R	H	AB	2B	3B	HR	RBI	SB	BB	SO
Kreher, Dennis	0.402	38	49	122	8	1	7	43	12	17	11
Braun, Carl	0.380	49	73	192	15	3	5	62	16	19	13
Adamson, Jon	0.351	11	27	77	7	0	1	11	4	13	16
Dillinger, Dick	0.331	24	55	166	8	0	3	38	1	31	10
Fulte, Lon	0.320	48	48	150	10	1	8	40	2	60	25
Frech, Dennis	0.305	33	51	167	13	0	8	34	3	22	23
Studt, Alan	0.286	39	52	182	11	2	1	27	14	33	18
Mernick, Dennis	0.282	34	35	124	1	2	0	16	21	37	7
Kreher, Dennis	0.279	18	19	68	4	0	3	11	5	5	9
Douchant, Mike	0.263	24	30	114	7	1	1	15	14	15	25
Nicholson, Dave	0.259	8	7	27	1	0	1	3	2	6	2
Hirstein, Gary	0.257	5	9	35	2	0	3	6	1	4	9
Moehrs, Vern	0.246	10	15	61	1	0	0	6	3	12	5
Jacobs, Bucky	0.222	6	10	45	3	0	1	7	1	6	4
Weinhoff, Don	0.200	3	3	15	0	0	0	0	0	2	8
Doerr, Mark	0.200	1	2	10	0	0	0	0	2	2	2
Modglin, Don	0.100	3	1	10	0	0	0	1	0	0	1
Rohlfing, Ron	0.333	2	2	6	1	0	1	1	0	0	1
Richert, Bob	0.333	0	1	3	1	0	0	2	0	2	1
Liskey, Bill	0.250	0	1	4	0	0	0	1	0	0	0
Pinion, Carl	0.000	1	0	4	0	0	0	0	0	1	0
Totals	0.310	357	490	1582	93	10	43	324	101	287	190

PITCHERS	IP	H	R	ER	BB	SO	CG	SHO	W	L	ERA
Adamson, Jon	162 2/3	147	45	33	31	109	15	3	17	5	1.83
Dillinger, Dick	152 2/3	157	51	42	35	81	14	6	17	2	2.48
Weinhoff, Don	41 2/3	32	13	9	16	32	3	1	4	1	1.94
Douchant, Mike	36 1/3	40	16	12	17	30	0	1	3	1	2.97
Moehrs, Vern	9	10	2	2	0	4	0	0	1	0	2.00
Totals	402 1/3	386	127	98	99	256	32	11	42	9	2.19

Individual Statistics: 1973

BATTERS	AVG	R	H	AB	2B	3B	HR	RBI	SB	BB	SO
Braun, Carl	0.412	50	75	182	12	1	3	60	8	18	15
Adamson, Jon	0.394	17	28	71	6	2	1	16	2	11	10
Harres, Mike	0.370	38	51	138	9	2	6	31	5	20	21
McEntire, Mike	0.363	22	33	91	11	0	5	37	1	8	15
Frech, Dennis	0.357	49	70	196	23	0	9	50	4	17	11
Mernick, Dennis	0.355	35	33	93	3	1	0	17	21	34	8
Fulte, Lon	0.351	57	59	168	9	5	10	48	6	51	21
Dillinger, Dick	0.348	40	64	184	10	0	1	27	2	36	10
Douchant, Mike	0.296	31	40	135	6	3	3	37	10	19	18
Studt, Alan	0.288	33	40	139	8	1	2	19	3	23	15
Moehrs, Vern	0.353	16	18	51	3	0	0	18	2	16	8
Hirstein, Gary	0.263	8	10	38	2	0	2	5	4	5	5
Thomas, Barry	0.234	6	11	47	1	1	0	6	6	4	2
Thomas, Tommy	0.263	5	5	19	1	0	0	3	0	3	6
Moore, Larry	0.182	7	8	44	1	0	0	1	0	6	27
Gill, Rich	0.265	7	9	34	1	0	1	10	2	4	5
Ludwig, Mark	0.238	4	5	21	0	0	0	2	0	6	5
Keefe, Rick	0.444	6	4	9	0	0	0	2	5	6	3
Doerr, Mark	0.250	2	2	8	1	0	0	0	0	4	5
Phillips, Tim	0.636	2	7	11	2	0	0	6	0	2	1
Beck, J.	0.000	0	0	4	0	0	0	0	0	0	2
Totals	0.340	435	572	1683	109	16	52	395	81	293	213

PITCHERS	IP	H	R	ER	BB	SO	CG	W	L	ERA
Adamson, Jon	119 1/3	115	39	27	24	65	13	14	2	2.04
Moore, Larry	97	82	36	27	39	81	7	9	2	2.51
McEntire, Mike	59 2/3	39	31	11	26	45	4	7	2	1.66
Dillinger, Dick	46	56	27	23	10	25	3	5	2	4.50
Ludwig, Mark	36 1/3	30	15	11	6	20	2	4	1	2.73
Douchant, Mike	14 2/3	15	9	8	11	18	0	1	0	4.91
Doerr, Mark	3 1/3	0	0	0	1	1	0	0	0	0.00
Beck, J.	6	6	3	2	5	4	0	0	1	3.00
Moehrs, Vern	1	5	3	3	0	0	0	0	0	27.00
Totals	383 1/3	348	163	112	122	259	29	40	10	2.63

Individual Statistics: 1974

BATTERS	AVG	R	H	AB	2B	3B	HR	RBI	SB	BB	SO
Hirstein, Gary	0.358	24	24	67	6	1	6	27	2	7	10
Frech, Dennis	0.346	43	65	188	6	2	7	60	5	15	14
Fulte, Lon	0.398	64	64	161	22	3	14	62	5	54	17
Keefe, Rick	0.380	56	65	171	16	3	5	45	20	36	34
Braun, Carl	0.492	60	95	193	24	5	4	69	11	30	12
Mernick, Dennis	0.305	20	25	82	1	4	0	6	14	15	7
Dillinger, Dick	0.266	38	49	184	7	0	1	23	2	33	9
McEntire, Mike	0.330	23	33	100	10	0	6	37	3	9	15
Adamson, Jon	0.330	20	30	91	4	1	3	17	3	7	15
Hasenstab, Chuck	0.254	6	16	63	2	0	0	7	0	8	7
Moehrs, Vern	0.278	7	10	36	1	0	0	4	1	6	6
Ludwig, Mark	0.289	6	11	38	0	1	1	5	2	4	3
Schlemmer, D.	0.440	14	11	25	0	0	0	2	6	9	2
Studt, Alan	0.333	1	1	3	1	0	0	1	0	2	0
Doerr, Mark	0.167	1	1	6	0	0	0	1	0	0	2
Matzenbacher, Bob	0.444	5	4	9	1	0	2	4	0	4	3
Phillips, Tim	0.500	2	7	14	0	0	1	4	0	0	0
Hines, Darrell	0.000	0	0	3	0	0	0	0	0	0	0
Nobbe, Mike	0.278	2	5	18	1	0	0	4	0	4	9
Hacker, Rich	0.000	0	0	4	0	0	0	0	0	2	2
Sanderson, Scott	0.276	9	8	29	1	0	0	5	3	6	2
Doerr, Matt	0.200	6	3	15	0	0	0	2	1	8	4
Deml, Jerry	0.304	11	14	46	3	0	1	13	0	7	9
Totals	0.350	418	541	1546	106	20	52	398	78	266	182

PITCHERS	IP	H	R	ER	BB	SO	CG	W	L	ERA
Adamson, Jon	153	127	41	34	37	100	16	19	1	2.00
Deml, Jerry	66 2/3	61	26	19	27	80	6	8	1	2.57
Moore, Larry	82 2/3	70	31	25	47	72	6	8	2	2.72
McEntire, Mike	58 2/3	43	14	8	25	56	5	9	0	1.23
Dillenger, Dick	13	16	14	8	6	12	0	0	0	5.54
Keefe, Rick	1	1	1	1	0	0	0	0	0	9.00
Lynn, J.	4	8	5	4	3	4	0	1	0	9.00
Moehrs, Vern	0	0	0	0	0	0	0	0	0	0.00
Ludwig, Mark	53 1/3	56	24	18	16	36	3	6	1	3.04
Totals	432 1/3	382	156	117	161	360	36	51	5	2.44

Individual Statistics: 1975

BATTERS	AVG	R	H	AB	2B	3B	HR	RBI	SB	BB	SO
Braun, Carl	0.417	51	83	199	18	2	12	78	2	20	24
Fulte, Lon	0.406	52	69	170	15	2	9	44	7	32	11
Hirstein, Gary	0.391	23	50	128	10	1	10	39	2	7	24
Phillips, Tim	0.391	29	50	128	8	1	5	39	0	16	20
Keefe, Rick	0.347	46	59	170	11	3	2	27	16	19	19
Adamson, Jon	0.378	17	28	74	8	2	3	25	1	4	8
Ludwig, Mark	0.345	18	20	58	3	2	0	11	2	13	12
Mernick, Dennis	0.337	29	35	104	1	1	0	15	14	31	5
Wheat, Kevin	0.327	14	16	49	2	2	2	7	3	4	5
Dillinger, Dick	0.301	37	49	163	2	1	0	17	2	34	4
Hughes, Bob	0.263	27	44	167	9	0	1	17	2	15	22
Frech, Dennis	0.228	28	34	149	4	1	5	24	0	22	19
Deml, Jerry	0.171	1	6	35	1	0	0	1	0	1	14
Moore, Larry	0.364	4	4	11	0	0	1	2	0	5	2
Novack, Mark	0.154	2	2	13	0	0	0	2	0	5	2
McEntire, Mike	0.600	2	6	10	1	0	0	1	0	3	1
Beekwith, Joe	0.375	12	15	40	3	0	2	8	0	3	8
Moehrs, Vern	0.300	3	3	10	0	0	0	3	0	1	2
Nobbe, Mike	0.091	1	1	11	0	0	0	1	0	1	4
Cosman, Jim	0.000	0	0	2	0	0	0	0	0	0	1
Pugh, Darren	0.250	1	2	8	0	0	0	1	0	0	2
Prescher, Roger	0.000	0	0	1	0	0	0	0	0	3	1
Studt, Alan	0.500	0	1	2	0	0	0	0	0	0	1
Totals	0.339	397	577	1702	96	18	52	362	51	239	211

PITCHERS	IP	H	R	ER	BB	SO	CG	SHO	W	L	ERA
Deml, Jerry	119	80	33	23	30	120	9	4	14	1	1.74
Adamson, Jon	96	115	57	37	19	72	11	1	12	2	3.47
Moore, Larry	59	74	33	28	26	57	4	1	5	1	4.27
Phillips, Tim	28 2/3	38	21	10	6	23	2	0	2	1	3.14
Dillinger, Dick	42 1/3	43	21	9	5	8	2	0	4	1	1.91
McEntire, Mike	17 2/3	21	10	8	11	15	0	0	2	0	4.08
Nobbe, Mike	5	2	0	0	3	2	0	0	1	0	0.00
Pugh, Darren	4	6	4	3	4	0	0	0	0	0	6.75
Cosman, Jim	15	11	5	1	7	7	1	0	1	0	0.60
Ludwig, Mark	15 1/3	19	11	10	10	7	0	0	2	1	5.87
Restoff, Joe	8	17	13	9	3	3	0	0	1	0	10.13
Forfeit	0	0	0	0	0	0	0	0	2	0	0.00
Totals	410	426	208	138	124	314	29	6	46	7	3.03

Individual Statistics: 1976

BATTERS	AVG	R	H	AB	2B	3B	HR	RBI	SB	BB	SO
Braun, Carl	0.361	38	61	169	13	6	6	56	8	18	13
Mernick, Dennis	0.369	34	41	111	6	2	0	20	28	35	7
Adamson, Jon	0.322	18	29	90	6	1	8	31	3	10	13
Fulte, Lon	0.320	29	47	147	9	1	1	27	1	40	23
Keefe, Rick	0.361	40	39	108	7	0	0	15	20	34	8
Phillips, Tim	0.347	28	41	118	10	1	1	22	2	26	15
Hirstein, Gary	0.318	19	34	107	7	1	2	26	1	5	18
Frech, Dennis	0.296	30	42	142	5	2	6	37	3	21	11
Ludwig, Mark	0.277	19	28	101	6	1	1	19	2	22	11
Wheat, Kevin	0.244	13	19	78	2	0	0	8	6	20	18
Dillinger, Dick	0.178	25	24	135	2	0	0	13	3	24	5
Junge, Rich	0.348	6	8	23	1	1	2	4	0	3	4
Mauser, Gary	0.273	1	3	11	0	0	0	1	0	2	0
Moehrs, Vern	0.278	4	5	18	1	0	0	5	0	5	2
Hughes, Bob	0.235	11	4	17	1	0	0	3	1	5	1
Nobbe, Mike	0.333	0	1	3	0	0	0	0	0	1	0
Yeager, Mark	0.200	2	2	10	0	0	0	1	0	5	3
Rolfing, Ron	0.400	0	2	5	1	1	0	2	0	0	0
Greenwald, Jim	0.389	6	7	18	1	1	1	9	0	4	3
Borger, Mike	0.231	2	3	13	0	1	0	0	0	1	5
Hesterberg, Brett	0.167	1	1	6	0	0	0	6	0	0	0
Novack, Mark	0.208	10	5	24	3	0	0	0	4	15	6
Restoff, Joe	0.500	11	2	4	0	0	0	0	0	0	1
Goldschmidt, A.	0.250	0	1	4	0	0	0	0	0	0	2
Goldschmidt, T.	0.250	0	1	4	0	0	0	0	0	0	2
Totals	0.307	347	450	1466	81	19	28	305	82	296	171

PITCHERS	IP	H	R	ER	BB	SO	CG	SHO	W	L	ERA
Adamson, Jon	131	126	41	31	35	86	16	5	15	4	2.13
Moore, Larry	62 1/3	64	36	21	36	33	6	0	5	2	3.03
Hesterberg, Brett	9	9	2	2	1	7	1	0	1	0	2.00
Moehrs, Vern	1	3	2	2	0	1	0	0	0	0	18.00
Nobbe, Mike	20 1/3	22	17	14	11	16	2	0	1	2	4.82
Dillinger, Dick	15 2/3	23	15	15	5	9	0	0	2	0	8.62
Keefe, Rick	1 2/3	2	0	0	0	0	0	0	0	0	0.00
Ludwig, Mark	28 1/3	24	19	6	12	10	3	0	2	2	1.91
Phillips, Tim	12 2/3	14	7	7	5	9	1	0	1	1	4.97
Huston,	21 2/3	21	14	11	10	5	2	0	3	0	4.57
Restoff, Joe	50 2/3	53	37	19	31	31	3	0	4	3	3.38
Borger, Mike	5	11	12	8	4	4	0	0	0	2	14.40
Totals	359.3	372	202	136	150	211	34	5	34	16	3.41

Individual Statistics: 1977

BATTERS	AVG	R	H	AB	2B	3B	HR	RBI	SB	BB	SO
Mernick, Dennis	0.357	49	51	143	8	0	1	25	31	24	3
Keefe, Rick	0.333	43	48	144	9	0	4	26	27	33	17
Ludwig, Mark	0.305	27	43	141	17	0	1	30	4	27	18
Braun, Carl	0.429	56	67	156	11	1	10	59	7	34	17
Matzenbacher, Bob	0.372	58	64	172	11	3	16	63	21	29	38
Fulte, Lon	0.335	64	57	170	12	1	9	51	8	39	16
Frech, Dennis	0.362	31	46	127	5	0	8	37	2	22	14
Wheat, Kevin	0.336	27	47	140	8	4	2	22	16	19	23
Adamson, Jon	0.367	11	29	79	3	0	1	20	6	4	7
Novack, Mark	0.304	6	7	23	0	0	0	1	1	8	10
Wahlig, Jim	0.303	22	27	89	9	1	2	18	3	4	10
Dillinger, Dick	0.000	0	0	7	0	0	0	0	0	0	3
Moehrs, Vern	0.000	0	0	1	0	0	0	0	0	0	0
Modglin, Don	0.000	2	0	5	0	0	0	0	0	2	4
Baxmeyer, Dave	0.200	6	4	20	1	0	0	1	0	9	4
Hesterberg, Brett	0.250	4	7	28	2	0	0	6	1	2	8
Doerr, M.	0.600	3	3	5	1	1	0	2	0	0	1
Greenwald, Jim	0.429	3	3	7	1	0	1	3	1	2	0
Pullium, Larry	0.214	4	3	14	0	0	0	2	2	4	2
Range, Dale	0.200	3	3	15	1	1	0	4	1	4	3
Totals	0.343	419	509	1486	99	12	55	370	131	266	198

PITCHERS	IP	H	R	ER	BB	SO	W	L	ERA
Adamson, Jon	126	145	63	51	27	61	13	6	3.64
McFarland, J.	90	84	43	29	27	79	11	0	2.90
Doerr, M.	95	82	35	31	28	50	10	2	2.94
Hesterberg, Brett	53	48	15	10	11	38	6	2	1.70
Moehrs, Vern	3	1	0	0	0	0	0	0	0.00
Totals	367	360	156	121	93	228	40	10	2.97

Individual Statistics: 1978

BATTERS	AVG	R	H	AB	2B	3B	HR	RBI	SB	BB	SO
Keefe, Rick	0.327	46	50	153	9	1	4	26	16	37	21
Mernick, Dennis	0.274	40	37	135	5	0	2	18	21	25	8
Fulte, Lon	0.353	39	53	150	10	1	9	38	3	33	16
Braun, Carl	0.379	44	64	169	9	3	10	64	6	24	14
Matzenbacher, Bob	0.309	37	46	149	7	1	14	39	5	28	34
Frech, Dennis	0.267	25	36	135	7	0	5	25	2	22	11
Wheat, Kevin	0.325	24	41	126	7	1	4	19	5	11	16
Wahlig, Jim	0.462	49	66	143	15	4	5	41	14	21	10
Ludwig, Mark	0.336	30	43	128	11	4	3	31	4	25	12
Toal, John	0.167	8	7	42	2	1	0	2	7	11	14
Neeman, Cal	0.351	9	13	37	2	1	4	12	0	1	2
Pitchford, Jerry	0.222	7	6	27	0	0	1	2	3	4	10
Doerr, M.	0.207	3	6	29	2	1	0	5	0	5	11
Adamson, Jon	0.333	4	6	18	2	0	1	4	0	5	1
Hesterberg, Brett	0.000	0	0	6	0	0	0	0	0	0	3
Hirth, Steve	0.333	1	1	3	0	0	1	3	0	0	0
McFarland, J.	0.111	0	1	9	0	0	0	0	0	0	3
Range, Dale	0.000	1	0	2	0	0	0	0	0	2	1
Moehrs, Vern	0.000	3	0	3	0	0	0	0	0	2	0
Baxmeyer, Dave	0.250	2	1	4	1	0	0	0	0	2	0
Totals	0.325	372	477	1468	89	18	63	329	86	258	187

PITCHERS	IP	H	R	ER	BB	SO	CG	GS	W	L	ERA
Doerr, M.	100 2/3	95	37	34	48	59	10	15	12	0	3.04
McFarland, J.	102	91	36	28	22	58	10	14	12	0	2.47
Keefe, Rick	44 2/3	26	9	6	14	30	1	1	6	3	1.21
Hirth, Steve	28	35	15	15	13	19	1	6	4	1	4.82
Hesterberg, Brett	66 2/3	60	27	24	18	36	3	9	7	0	3.24
Voelker, Don	42 1/3	40	22	18	10	29	1	5	3	1	3.83
Totals	384 1/3	347	146	125	125	231	26	50	44	5	2.93

Individual Statistics: 1979

BATTERS	AVG	R	H	AB	2B	3B	HR	RBI	SB	BB	SO
Keefe, Rick	0.268	42	42	157	6	1	4	23	14	27	12
Mernick, Dennis	0.265	23	26	98	3	1	0	13	17	32	2
Wahlig, Jim	0.419	35	49	117	13	0	3	26	15	25	10
Braun, Carl	0.347	40	50	144	13	2	7	42	10	27	13
Fulte, Lon	0.338	39	50	148	14	0	6	42	6	36	11
Matzenbacher, Bob	0.333	33	44	132	8	2	11	41	6	20	30
Munden, Jim	0.313	33	42	134	9	0	4	24	8	38	11
Ludwig, Mark	0.315	27	41	130	4	0	5	37	6	36	13
Frech, Dennis	0.297	22	30	101	7	0	2	21	0	33	6
Wheat, Kevin	0.231	7	12	52	1	0	0	9	1	3	10
Baxmeyer, Dave	0.222	1	4	18	0	0	0	4	0	3	4
Doerr, M.	0.143	3	3	21	2	0	0	1	0	3	6
Adamson, Jon	0.214	2	3	14	0	0	0	0	1	6	5
Shadowens, Chris	0.125	3	1	8	0	0	0	2	0	1	2
Kreher, Dennis	0.000	0	0	3	0	0	0	0	0	0	3
McFarland, J.	0.100	3	1	10	0	0	0	1	1	2	9
Moehrs, Vern	0.250	1	1	4	0	0	0	1	1	0	1
Hesterberg, Brett	0.083	1	1	12	0	0	0	0	0	0	6
Totals	0.307	315	400	1303	80	6	42	287	86	292	154

PITCHERS	IP	H	R	ER	BB	SO	CG	GS	W	L	ERA
McFarland, J.	49 1/3	61	34	32	18	36	3	8	5	2	5.84
Doerr, M.	74	80	40	36	24	55	4	11	8	4	4.38
Kreher, Dennis	80	66	35	22	28	49	9	14	9	2	2.48
Hesterberg, Brett	75	74	32	31	18	48	7	9	9	1	3.72
Keefe, Rick	35	32	12	8	11	26	1	1	3	1	2.06
Adamson, Jon	21	26	9	9	10	9	2	2	2	0	3.86
Ehlers, Ryan	11	17	16	12	10	5	0	3	1	0	9.82
Totals	345 1/3	356	178	150	119	228	26	48	37	10	3.91

Individual Statistics: 1980

BATTERS	AVG	R	H	AB	2B	3B	HR	RBI	SB	BB	SO
Matzenbacher, Bob	0.374	67	70	187	14	4	12	54	14	32	26
Wahlig, Jim	0.492	75	89	181	13	1	10	56	23	33	11
Wirth, Mike	0.424	40	56	132	12	1	6	35	5	24	9
Braun, Carl	0.403	52	79	196	15	0	7	55	5	29	12
Fulte, Lon	0.349	58	65	186	17	1	11	57	4	48	10
Ludwig, Mark	0.335	36	59	176	6	2	3	52	10	44	18
Frech, Dennis	0.255	20	38	149	8	2	6	36	3	25	16
Mernick, Dennis	0.239	26	28	117	6	1	0	13	10	26	6
Kilman, Eric	0.280	21	26	93	2	2	0	5	9	8	8
Keefe, Rick	0.288	18	23	80	2	0	3	17	4	18	11
Niswonger	0.276	20	21	76	4	2	1	14	5	16	11
Roy, Mike	0.295	9	13	44	1	0	0	8	0	2	4
Baxmeyer, Dave	0.095	2	2	21	0	0	0	4	0	3	5
Adamson, Jon	0.400	5	8	20	3	1	0	7	0	3	2
Roy, Jeff	0.167	0	1	6	0	0	0	1	0	1	1
Moehrs, Vern	0.667	2	2	3	0	0	0	2	0	2	0
Doerr, Ma.	0.333	4	4	12	0	0	0	3	1	3	3
Doerr, M.	0.000	3	0	6	0	0	0	0	0	1	1
Hesterberg, Brett	0.333	1	4	12	1	0	0	2	0	0	4
Zalasky, R.	1.000	2	4	4	1	1	1	2	0	0	0
Thies, Scott	0.000	1	0	3	0	0	0	1	1	1	1
Latimore, Bryan	0.000	2	0	6	0	0	0	1	0	2	2
Shadowens, Chris	0.333	0	3	9	0	0	0	1	2	2	2
Totals	0.346	464	595	1719	105	18	60	426	96	323	163

PITCHERS	IP	H	R	ER	BB	SO	CG	GS	W	L	ERA
Kreher, Dennis	117	125	50	40	43	92	11	17	15	2	3.08
Keefe, Rick	96	78	47	27	39	54	9	14	10	5	2.53
Doerr, M.	73 1/3	82	48	34	26	37	4	9	8	1	4.17
Hesterberg, Brett	63	11	39	32	25	39	5	8	8	3	4.57
Tiernan, J.	16 1/3	21	10	9	13	7	0	3	2	0	4.96
Adamson, Jon	19 1/3	22	14	10	7	11	0	2	1	0	4.66
Dillenberger, Dave	18	21	12	10	9	11	0	2	1	0	5.00
Meyer, Mike	16	20	8	7	2	11	0	2	3	0	3.94
Wahlig, Jim	2 2/3	6	4	4	3	1	0	0	0	0	13.50
Ludwig, Mark	3 1/3	3	2	2	1	1	0	0	0	0	5.40
Moehrs, Vern	3 1/3	5	2	2	0	2	0	0	0	0	5.40
Baxmeyer, Dave	1 2/3	0	0	0	2	2	0	0	0	0	0.00
Totals	430	394	236	177	170	268	29	57	48	11	3.70

Individual Statistics: 1981

BATTERS	AVG	R	H	AB	2B	3B	HR	RBI	SB	BB	SO
Wahlig, Jim	0.722	9	13	18	2	0	3	11	3	2	0
Frech, Dennis	0.250	22	36	144	8	0	5	28	1	18	8
Keefe, Rick	0.243	35	37	152	6	3	4	22	8	25	24
Mernick, Dennis	0.262	22	39	149	6	2	0	15	20	27	10
Braun, Carl	0.333	19	43	129	5	0	5	25	0	19	9
Roy, Mike	0.398	26	41	103	5	0	8	22	0	6	10
Ludwig, Mark	0.309	23	43	139	11	1	3	35	3	27	11
Fulte, Lon	0.338	37	48	142	8	1	7	40	2	38	17
Matzenbacher, Bob	0.435	32	57	131	6	0	11	57	4	29	20
Kilman, Eric	0.303	13	23	76	1	0	0	11	7	9	6
Adamson, Jon	0.250	7	7	28	0	1	1	3	1	7	4
Range, Dale	0.309	18	29	94	6	0	1	19	0	10	7
Shadowens, Chris	0.310	5	13	42	3	0	0	4	0	6	5
Schulte, Mark	0.385	7	15	39	6	0	2	18	0	6	1
Vandiver, Kevin	0.160	4	4	25	0	0	0	4	0	5	3
Dillenberger, Dave	0.100	0	1	10	0	0	0	1	0	4	3
Doerr, M.	0.000	1	0	5	0	0	0	0	0	0	2
Malone, Chris	0.000	0	0	5	0	0	0	0	0	0	1
Hosick, Steve	0.250	0	1	4	0	0	0	2	0	1	2
Meyer, Mike	0.143	0	1	7	0	0	0	1	0	3	2
Wuelling, John	0.250	1	1	4	0	0	0	0	0	0	0
Hesterberg, Brett	0.167	1	1	6	0	0	0	2	0	0	0
Totals	0.312	282	453	1452	73	8	50	320	49	242	145

PITCHERS	IP	H	R	ER	BB	SO	W	L	ERA
Keefe, Rick	24	16	1	0	9	14	3	1	0.00
Hesterberg, Brett	25 1/3	31	16	6	4	12	3	1	2.13
Adamson, Jon	24	23	6	6	9	12	2	0	2.25
Kreher, Dennis	89	84	42	31	27	48	10	4	3.13
Hirth, Steve	56	71	19	24	17	26	7	2	3.86
Dillenberger, Dave	40	53	28	23	17	16	4	3	5.18
Meyer, Mike	36	45	23	19	18	16	1	4	4.75
Malone, Chris	44	27	23	17	19	15	3	1	3.48
Wuelling, John	7	14	7	5	2	2	0	0	6.43
Doerr, M.	13	15	9	5	4	7	2	0	3.46
Klindworth, Mike	2	5	7	2	3	0	0	0	9.00
Totals	360.3	384	181	138	129	168	35	16	3.45

Individual Statistics: 1982

BATTERS	AVG	R	H	AB	2B	3B	HR	RBI	SB	BB	SO	HP
Roy, Mike	0.473	59	88	186	15	2	22	72	3	28	12	4
Mernick, Dennis	0.407	35	44	108	4	1	0	23	23	21	2	2
Ludwig, Mark	0.379	37	61	161	18	0	2	33	9	30	14	0
Votrain, Craig	0.374	54	58	155	15	2	4	37	8	32	13	1
Haberl, Scott	0.364	41	55	151	12	2	6	37	8	34	20	1
Fulte, Lon	0.360	45	62	172	13	1	11	53	6	46	17	3
Matzenbacher, Bob	0.331	40	53	160	10	4	8	31	3	30	27	3
Frech, Dennis	0.321	26	44	137	9	2	5	30	1	17	9	0
Hines, Ken	0.317	6	13	41	3	0	1	8	4	7	5	0
Ries, Bret	0.276	20	27	98	6	0	1	13	9	28	12	3
Shadowens, Chris	0.265	25	35	132	7	1	2	23	5	19	11	2
Roy, Jeff	0.238	11	15	63	2	0	3	12	0	13	15	0
Dillenberger, Dave	0.125	3	1	8	0	0	0	1	0	5	3	0
Doerr, M.	0.000	0	0	9	0	0	0	1	0	3	1	0
Braun, Carl	0.400	2	2	5	0	0	0	0	0	0	0	0
Stanberry, Tim	1.000	0	1	1	0	0	0	0	0	0	0	0
Keefe, Rick	0.300	2	3	10	1	0	1	6	0	3	1	0
Moehrs, Vern	1.000	0	1	1	0	0	0	1	0	0	0	0
Fehrenz, Warren	0.000	0	0	1	0	0	0	0	0	0	1	0
Totals	0.352	406	563	1599	115	15	66	381	79	316	163	19

Team Record: 42 wins - 14 losses
No Pitching Records Recorded

Individual Statistics: 1983

BATTERS	AVG	R	H	AB	2B	3B	HR	RBI	SB	BB	SO	HP
Wahlig, Jim	0.486	54	67	138	13	0	16	51	4	14	13	0
Wirth, Mike	0.374	49	52	139	14	4	11	56	0	12	11	0
Matzenbacher, Bob	0.368	67	63	171	16	1	10	38	12	25	22	2
Fulte, Lon	0.394	66	56	142	10	1	14	60	4	49	11	1
Roy, Mike	0.395	56	60	152	10	2	15	55	8	21	16	4
Haberl, Scott	0.391	52	61	156	12	0	20	69	7	31	31	1
Ludwig, Mark	0.369	33	59	160	11	1	3	37	1	15	13	1
Roy, Jeff	0.309	24	25	81	5	1	2	19	0	14	12	1
Mernick, Dennis	0.299	22	26	87	2	0	0	12	5	15	2	0
Votrain, Craig	0.317	38	40	126	7	2	2	26	4	26	11	0
Ries, Bret	0.186	15	11	59	1	1	0	11	1	11	11	0
Dillenberger, Dave	0.373	20	19	51	3	2	6	22	0	12	7	0
Doerr, M.	0.359	13	14	39	4	0	2	10	1	5	6	0
Wahlig, John	0.500	7	15	30	4	0	1	8	3	3	3	0
Hines, Ken	0.316	4	6	19	0	0	0	4	1	6	1	0
Shadowens, Chris	0.182	6	4	22	0	0	0	3	1	4	3	0
Adamson, Jon	1.000	1	3	3	0	0	0	0	0	0	0	0
Moehrs, Vern	0.200	0	1	5	0	0	0	0	0	0	1	0
Fehrenz, Warren	0.333	0	1	3	0	0	0	0	0	0	2	1
Keefe, Rick	0.857	2	6	7	3	0	0	1	0	1	0	0
Lucht, Kevin	0.250	1	1	4	0	0	0	0	0	0	1	1
Totals	0.370	530	590	1594	115	15	101	482	52	264	177	12

PITCHERS	IP	H	R	ER	BB	SO	W	L	S	ERA
Kreher, Dennis	94 2/3	80	34	27	24	62	12	1	1	2.57
Fehrenz, Warren	83	79	38	30	27	40	10	1	0	3.25
Dillenberger, Dave	71 2/3	55	37	24	38	52	11	2	0	3.01
Adamson, Jon	63 1/3	66	31	25	7	28	10	0	1	3.55
Meyer, Gene	27	33	23	18	17	17	3	0	1	6.00
Lucht, Kevin	14	16	24	18	17	17	1	2	0	11.57
Keefe, Rick	11	10	5	4	5	9	1	0	0	3.27
Moehrs, Vern	1	3	1	1	0	0	0	0	0	9.00
Haberl, Scott	1	0	1	0	0	0	0	0	0	0.00
Totals	366.7	342	194	147	135	225	48	6	3	3.61

"The stats our guys put up in the early days are unbelievable. Jimmy's twenty-four-year .442 average and 278 home runs, Lon's 800 walks. Think of all the games we had to play to get those kinds of stats. The divorce rate was 80%!"
—Vern Moehrs

Individual Statistics: 1984

BATTERS	AVG	R	H	AB	2B	3B	HR	RBI	SB	BB	SO	HP
Wahlig, John	0.342	59	64	187	11	4	5	28	13	25	19	1
Wahlig, Jim	0.506	67	85	168	22	3	20	73	3	31	13	3
Wirth, Mike	0.397	50	60	151	12	2	14	60	2	24	10	0
Ludwig, Mark	0.437	56	73	167	21	1	7	47	6	31	12	0
Fulte, Lon	0.337	58	58	172	7	0	12	50	7	44	13	1
Matzenbacher, Bob	0.422	44	49	116	11	1	10	34	4	17	13	0
Haberl, Scott	0.380	45	57	150	9	2	10	33	9	17	12	2
Mernick, Dennis	0.382	38	50	131	6	2	1	32	8	24	2	1
Doerr, M.	0.270	29	27	100	6	0	3	15	2	16	16	2
Snodgrass, Brian	0.379	23	33	87	5	0	1	17	2	15	11	1
Keefe, Rick	0.313	19	21	67	2	0	1	12	3	10	11	0
Adamson, Jon	0.409	5	9	22	1	0	1	5	1	4	3	0
Roy, Mike	0.273	2	6	22	1	1	0	7	3	0	3	0
Dillenberger, Dave	0.343	10	12	35	3	0	3	10	2	8	6	0
Wheat, Kevin	0.167	3	5	30	1	0	0	4	1	5	9	0
Fehrenz, Warren	0.143	5	2	14	0	0	1	3	0	3	7	0
Kreher, Dennis	0.000	1	0	0	0	0	0	0	0	2	0	0
Moehrs, Vern	1.000	1	1	1	1	0	0	1	1	1	0	0
Moehrs, Clay	0.222	2	2	9	0	0	0	1	0	1	7	0
Baxmeyer, Dave	0.000	1	0	3	0	0	0	0	0	0	2	0
Lucht, Kevin	0.200	1	1	5	1	0	0	0	0	0	2	0
Kaiser, Jeff	0.143	1	1	7	1	0	0	0	0	0	0	0
Harres, Jeff	0.125	1	1	8	0	0	0	0	0	2	1	0
Tedder, Ron	0.000	0	0	3	0	0	0	0	0	1	1	0
Totals	0.373	521	617	1655	121	16	89	432	67	281	173	11

PITCHERS	IP	H	R	ER	BB	SO	W	L	ERA
Dillenberger, Dave	31 1/3	24	12	10	10	18	6	0	2.23
Fehrenz, Warren	91 2/3	96	52	45	24	59	13	1	3.44
Kreher, Dennis	101	102	43	37	22	71	13	1	2.56
Keefe, Rick	47 1/3	53	34	26	11	46	5	1	3.85
Lucht, Kevin	51 1/3	48	38	28	12	30	5	1	3.82
Ludwig, Mark	14	13	8	6	5	9	2	0	3.00
Adamson, Jon	27	29	15	12	4	6	2	1	3.11
Roy, Mike	4	4	3	2	4	2	0	0	3.50
Wheat, Kevin	8	10	9	7	5	7	0	0	7.88
Wahlig, Jim	1 1/3	1	0	0	2	0	0	0	0.00
Totals	377	380	214	173	99	248	46	5	4.13

Individual Statistics: 1985

BATTERS	AVG	R	H	AB	2B	3B	HR	RBI	SB	BB	SO	HP	SAC
Wahlig, Jim	0.485	58	64	132	7	3	13	52	5	28	6	1	1
Ludwig, Mark	0.387	47	60	155	11	0	11	50	0	20	12	0	3
Wirth, Mike	0.363	37	58	160	9	1	5	39	3	17	11	1	4
Haberl, Scott	0.404	55	69	171	3	0	26	75	5	24	23	0	2
Fulte, Lon	0.340	53	49	144	7	1	10	37	6	47	19	2	4
Wahlig, John	0.357	50	61	171	10	1	10	42	6	23	14	1	3
Purshke, Ray	0.348	39	56	161	6	0	11	49	2	17	19	1	4
Doerr, M.	0.223	20	23	103	2	2	0	15	0	22	13	0	3
Mernick, Dennis	0.405	13	17	42	3	0	1	11	4	7	2	1	0
Snodgrass, B.	0.229	16	16	70	1	0	0	10	0	7	18	0	1
Keefe, Rick	0.371	18	23	62	5	2	1	12	7	12	6	0	1
Jones, David	0.429	11	15	35	0	1	0	4	1	7	2	0	0
Ferguson, Roger	0.200	3	4	20	0	1	1	4	0	5	5	0	0
Moehrs, Clay	0.231	4	3	13	0	0	0	1	1	1	6	0	0
Fehrenz, Warren	0.250	0	1	4	0	0	0	0	0	3	0	0	1
Moehrs, Vern	1.000	0	1	1	0	0	0	0	0	1	0	0	0
Goudey, Rob	0.000	0	0	1	0	0	0	0	0	0	1	0	0
Totals	0.360	424	520	1445	64	12	52	401	40	241	157	7	27

PITCHERS	IP	H	R	ER	BB	SO	W	L	S	ERA
Keefe, Rick	74 2/3	44	37	29	14	47	10	0	4	3.50
Fehrenze, Warren	60	54	34	29	23	32	7	1	0	4.35
Ferguson, Roger	67 1/3	57	53	37	49	60	7	3	0	4.95
Jones, David	42	39	34	27	19	36	7	3	1	5.79
Gray, David	62	54	43	32	15	46	8	0	0	4.65
Kreher, Dennis	13 2/3	20	8	7	5	12	2	0	0	4.61
Lucht, Kevin	19	25	20	15	18	15	0	1	0	7.11
Tedder, Ron	9 2/3	6	5	5	6	6	0	0	0	4.66
Ludwig, Mark	4 1/3	2	2	2	0	3	0	0	0	4.15
Roy, Mike	2/3	0	0	0	0	1	1	0	0	0.00
Rabberman, Doug	1	2	0	0	1	2	0	0	0	0.00
Adamson, Jon	3	6	2	2	1	1	0	0	1	6.00
Totals	357 1/3	309	238	185	151	261	42	8	6	4.66

Individual Statistics: 1986

BATTERS	AVG	R	H	AB	2B	3B	HR	RBI	SB	BB	SO	HP
Wahlig, John	0.392	50	58	148	11	3	13	38	16	12	12	2
Wahlig, Jim	0.464	51	78	168	10	1	23	61	3	11	14	1
Roy, Mike	0.444	60	71	160	14	2	22	72	8	28	6	0
Haberl, Scott	0.344	45	56	163	7	1	14	39	9	30	12	1
Dillenberger, Dave	0.335	36	54	161	7	0	12	53	1	14	20	0
Fulte, Lon	0.393	44	55	140	5	0	15	35	3	34	18	0
Thies, Scott	0.340	42	51	150	4	2	14	43	26	12	23	1
Kaiser, Jeff	0.353	33	42	119	5	0	3	30	1	12	14	3
Doerr, M.	0.306	17	22	72	2	1	0	14	2	13	13	0
Kilman, Eric	0.222	5	6	27	0	0	0	1	2	3	2	0
Snodgrass, Brian	0.313	21	21	67	3	0	0	15	0	4	13	0
Prewitt, Marty	0.000	2	0	3	0	0	0	0	0	1	0	0
Keefe, Rick	0.615	7	8	13	2	0	2	8	0	2	1	1
Ferguson, Roger	0.294	5	5	17	2	1	1	1	0	3	2	0
Moehrs, Clay	0.000	3	0	15	0	0	0	0	0	1	5	0
Pitchford, Gerry	0.125	3	2	16	0	0	1	2	0	3	1	0
Basse, Greg	0.538	5	7	13	0	0	0	1	1	2	0	0
Jones, D.J.	0.000	0	0	2	0	0	0	0	0	0	0	0
Roy, Jeff	0.333	1	1	3	0	0	0	1	0	0	0	0
Moehrs, Vern	1.000	1	1	1	0	0	0	0	0	1	0	0
Price, Chris	0.500	1	2	4	0	0	0	2	0	1	2	0
Totals	0.369	432	540	1462	72	11	120	416	72	187	158	9

PITCHERS	IP	H	R	ER	BB	SO	G	W	L	ERA
Keefe, Rick	96	78	35	32	18	51	21	14	2	3.00
Ferguson, Roger	84	64	29	23	24	54	16	11	0	2.46
Fehrenz, Warren	81 1/3	82	48	44	18	46	14	8	3	4.87
Dillenberger, Dave	43	52	32	31	22	33	11	6	0	6.49
Gray, David	27	21	15	10	6	8	7	3	0	3.33
Jones, David	7	6	2	0	0	5	2	1	0	0.00
Thies, Scott	8	13	5	3	1	3	2	1	0	3.38
Moehrs, Vern	0	2	0	1	0	0	1	0	0	0.00
Roy, Mike	2/3	2	3	3	0	0	1	0	0	40.50
Lueht, Kevin	9	9	8	3	2	9	3	0	0	3.00
Totals	356	329	177	150	91	209	78	44	5	3.79

Individual Statistics: 1987

BATTERS	AVG	R	H	AB	2B	3B	HR	RBI	SB	BB	SO	HP	SAC
Matzenbacher, Bob	0.326	45	45	138	9	0	11	37	1	16	18	0	0
Keefe, Rick	0.406	10	13	32	0	0	3	9	0	1	0	0	0
Roy, Mike	0.507	73	77	152	14	1	25	64	5	22	3	2	0
Wahlig, Jim	0.482	63	68	141	10	2	20	56	0	21	12	1	0
Haberl, Steve	0.412	42	56	136	5	2	17	39	7	15	12	0	0
Dillenberger, Dave	0.399	42	59	148	9	1	15	51	0	13	21	0	1
Thies, Scott	0.314	35	48	153	8	0	17	44	12	14	12	1	0
Fulte, Lon	0.261	32	36	138	4	0	5	21	3	39	14	0	0
Vogel, Mark	0.234	26	26	111	3	0	0	9	2	20	23	0	1
Doerr, M.	0.267	15	20	75	3	0	1	9	0	8	4	1	4
Price, Chris	0.217	13	13	60	4	0	1	6	3	6	6	0	0
Moehrs, Clay	0.308	10	16	52	2	0	1	10	2	5	13	0	0
Basse, Greg	0.600	3	6	10	0	0	0	1	0	2	2	0	0
Rippelmeyer, Ray	0.000	2	0	3	0	0	0	0	0	0	2	0	0
Ferguson, Roger	0.667	1	2	3	1	0	0	0	0	0	0	0	0
Biekert, M.	0.750	0	3	4	0	0	0	1	1	1	0	0	0
Fehrenz, Warren	0.000	0	0	1	0	0	0	0	0	0	0	0	0
Fulte, Tim	0.333	0	1	3	0	0	0	1	0	0	1	0	0
Wahlig, John	0.600	2	3	5	1	0	1	3	0	0	0	0	0
Totals	0.360	414	492	1365	73	6	117	361	36	183	143	5	6

PITCHERS	IP	H	R	ER	BB	SO	W	L	ERA
Keefe, Rick	78	90	55	46	21	55	9	2	5.31
Ferguson, Roger	55	76	56	48	27	54	8	2	7.85
Fehrens, Warren	51	56	38	29	9	20	3	2	5.12
Gray, David	9	10	7	8	3	5	2	0	8.00
Moehrs, Vern	1	2	1	1	0	0	0	0	9.00
Dillenberger, Dave	22	20	15	12	13	21	2	0	4.91
Collson, Ron	39	42	38	28	25	36	4	1	6.46
Roy, Mike	2	0	0	0	0	0	0	0	0.00
Kreher, Dennis	2	2	2	1	0	0	0	0	4.50
Jones, David	7 1/3	15	7	7	3	5	0	1	8.59
Wahlig, Jim	2/3	2	0	0	0	1	0	0	0.00
Thies, Scott	9 2/3	12	13	12	5	5	1	1	9.32
Pierson, Larry	14	13	10	10	1	8	2	0	6.43
Kossina, Tony	6	4	9	6	2	0	1	0	9.00
Totals	298	344	251	208	109	210	35	9	6.28

Individual Statistics: 1988

BATTERS	AVG	R	H	AB	2B	3B	HR	RBI	SB	BB	SO	HP	SAC
Matzenbacher, Bob	0.333	25	35	105	9	1	6	17	4	6	28	2	0
Wahlig, John	0.510	45	50	98	9	2	12	34	5	4	8	0	0
Roy, Mike	0.553	58	73	132	12	1	18	58	4	17	6	0	0
Wahlig, Jim	0.443	53	54	122	7	0	24	60	1	23	10	1	4
Haberl, Scott	0.462	51	61	132	8	3	2	67	7	18	27	1	1
Moehrs, Clay	0.333	32	45	135	5	2	3	26	5	14	26	0	0
Keefe, Rick	0.295	15	18	61	6	1	2	14	5	14	9	0	0
Price, Chris	0.388	23	33	85	2	1	10	29	4	5	10	1	1
Thies, Scott	0.400	52	56	140	11	2	2	51	21	18	18	1	0
Doerr, M.	0.253	20	19	75	1	0	4	21	2	18	17	1	0
Purschke, Ray	0.280	27	28	100	4	0	1	14	3	16	15	0	2
Ferguson, Roger	0.304	5	14	46	2	0	5	8	1	3	2	0	3
Dillenberger, Dave	0.468	20	22	47	30	0	0	19	0	5	11	0	1
Vogel, Mark	0.250	2	5	20	1	0	0	3	0	0	1	1	0
Fulte, Tim	0.300	3	3	10	0	0	0	2	0	0	1	0	0
Fehrenz, Warren	0.500	1	2	4	0	0	0	2	0	0	2	0	0
Howell, J.	0.500	0	1	2	0	0	0	0	0	0	0	0	0
Frech, Dennis	0.167	6	2	12	0	0	0	3	0	6	1	0	0
Werth, Donnie	0.467	11	7	15	2	1	0	3	0	0	1	0	0
Rippelmeyer, Ray	0.125	1	1	8	0	0	0	1	0	1	1	0	0
Schulte, Mark	0.364	27	32	88	7	1	6	21	7	8	1	0	7
Totals	0.390	477	561	1437	116	15	95	453	69	176	195	8	19

PITCHERS	IP	H	R	ER	BB	SO	W	L	SV	ERA
Fehrens, Warren	70	69	54	49	28	45	6	0	2	6.30
Ferguson, Roger	80	89	64	56	26	73	13	2	0	6.30
Keefe, Rick	73	89	48	42	29	40	8	2	5	5.18
Dieckman, J.	52	69	59	47	19	32	4	4	1	8.13
Parker, J.	23	22	12	13	12	14	3	0	0	5.09
Dillenberger, Dave	7	7	7	5	7	4	1	0	0	6.43
Schulte, Mark	4	8	12	8	3	4	0	0	0	18.00
Thies, Scott	4	3	5	5	1	2	0	0	0	11.25
Hempen, Hal	4	3	1	1	6	4	0	0	0	2.25
Roy, Mike	3	1	0	0	0	4	0	0	0	0.00
Totals	320	360	261	226	131	222	35	8	8	6.36

Individual Statistics: 1989

BATTERS	AVG	R	H	AB	2B	3B	HR	RBI	SB	BB	SO	HP	SAC
Wahlig,John	0.409	46	65	159	10	2	12	40	5	12	6	2	1
Wahlig, Jim	0.460	54	69	150	11	1	14	36	6	12	6	3	0
Wirth, Mike	0.383	28	36	94	6	0	8	36	1	15	7	0	1
Roy, Mike	0.424	39	59	139	8	0	12	47	2	6	4	1	0
Thies, Scott	0.336	43	50	149	8	0	9	37	13	16	7	2	0
Moehrs, Clay	0.301	24	41	136	2	0	3	24	4	11	22	1	0
Baxmeyer, John	0.347	12	25	72	5	0	6	23	1	4	7	1	0
Price, Chris	0.321	24	34	106	8	0	0	14	7	10	12	0	0
Werth, Donnie	0.232	5	16	69	3	0	0	6	8	7	7	0	1
Fulte, Tim	0.174	3	4	23	0	0	0	4	0	2	2	0	0
Biekert, Dan	0.240	8	12	50	0	0	2	6	2	2	8	1	3
Steinbach, Tyler	0.500	2	6	12	0	0	1	6	0	0	2	0	0
Fehrenz, Warren	0.286	8	8	28	1	0	2	4	1	1	2	1	0
Finochio, Tim	0.333	1	3	9	0	0	0	2	0	1	1	0	0
Doerr, Merle	0.000	0	0	1	0	0	0	0	0	2	0	0	0
Keefe, Rick	0.333	0	1	3	0	0	0	0	0	0	1	0	0
Schulte, Mark	0.385	10	15	39	2	0	3	12	1	3	2	0	0
Mullens, Ed	0.000	2	0	12	0	0	0	0	0	1	6	0	0
Haberl, Scott	0.355	29	38	107	7	1	8	29	2	14	13	0	0
Totals	0.355	338	482	1358	71	4	80	326	53	119	115	12	6

PITCHERS	IP	H	R	ER	BB	SO	W	L	SV	ERA
Steinbach, Tyler	76	72	50	37	14	46	9	3	0	4.38
Beattie, Larry	39	32	20	13	8	33	4	1	0	3.00
Hempen, Hal	80 1/3	63	42	31	38	44	9	1	0	3.47
Fehrenz, Warren	47	37	25	16	21	31	5	1	0	3.06
Keefe, Rick	40	41	24	19	11	22	4	2	0	4.28
Schulte, Mark	2 1/3	1	3	3	4	1	1	1	0	11.57
Finochio, Tim	15	21	15	12	10	6	2	1	1	7.20
Roy, Mike	4	3	4	2	3	2	0	0	1	4.50
Biekert, Dan	8	9	12	8	10	3	0	0	0	9.00
Haberl, Scott	2/3	0	0	0	1	0	0	0	0	0.00
Stellhorn, J.	1	1	1	1	1	0	0	0	0	9.00
Mullens, Ed	12	10	11	10	11	15	1	1	0	7.50
Wahlig, Jim	1	2	5	2	2	0	0	0	0	18.00
Totals	326 1/3	292	212	154	134	203	35	11	2	4.25

Individual Statistics: 1990

BATTERS	AVG	R	H	AB	2B	3B	HR	RBI	SB	BB	SO	HP	SAC
Baxmeyer, John	0.353	31	54	153	8	0	16	55	6	16	23	2	5
Fulte, Tim	0.161	7	5	31	0	0	0	0	0	6	10	0	0
Haberl, Scott	0.423	27	33	78	7	0	8	19	3	11	13	0	1
Kaiser, Jeff	0.430	29	40	93	7	2	2	11	5	8	4	1	5
Moehrs, Clay	0.292	29	45	154	15	0	3	27	10	8	32	2	1
Moerhs, Vern	0.000	0	0	1	0	0	0	0	0	0	0	0	0
Price, Chris	0.241	19	19	79	3	0	1	15	4	16	13	1	3
Roy, Mike	0.351	46	61	174	12	1	13	42	2	22	20	1	1
Schulte, Mark	0.426	60	83	195	13	3	26	82	1	12	11	2	2
Thies, Scott	0.341	37	42	123	12	0	6	32	22	27	18	1	3
Wahlig, Jim	0.451	54	64	142	15	2	18	56	2	26	7	3	3
Wahlig, John	0.484	57	89	184	17	2	20	62	4	18	11	3	3
Werth, Donnie	0.206	19	13	63	4	0	1	7	5	10	10	2	0
Wirth, Mike	0.394	53	65	165	16	0	8	31	3	20	18	0	4
Totals	0.375	468	613	1635	129	10	122	439	67	200	190	18	31

PITCHERS	IP	H	R	ER	BB	SO	HP	CG	SHO	W	L	SV	ERA
Brewer, J.	37	65	43	42	26	24	4	5	1	7	2	0	10.22
Champagne, Bo	29	31	16	14	8	21	1	2	0	3	0	1	4.34
Donius, Bob	60 1/3	87	56	50	27	16	1	1	0	7	3	0	7.46
Fehrenz, Warren	88 1/3	83	65	59	27	43	5	7	2	9	3	0	6.01
Hefner, Brett	7	5	5	5	4	4	0	0	0	0	0	0	6.43
McQuary, J.	20 1/3	22	13	9	14	5	0	1	0	1	1	0	3.98
Montgomery, Jim	5 1/3	5	4	3	5	2	0	0	0	1	0	0	5.06
Mosbacher, Don	29 2/3	51	26	25	6	3	1	1	0	2	1	0	7.58
Roy, Mike	37 2/3	28	16	16	27	34	2	0	0	4	1	2	3.82
Scheller, Larry	38	51	35	34	25	19	2	0	0	2	3	0	8.05
Schulte, Mark	2	7	6	5	1	4	0	0	0	0	0	0	22.50
Stellhorn, J.	2	2	0	0	2	2	0	0	0	0	0	1	0.00
Totals	356 2/3	437	285	262	172	177	16	17	3	36	14	4	6.61

Individual Statistics: 1991

BATTERS	AVG	R	H	AB	2B	3B	HR	RBI	SB	BB	SO	HP	SAC
Baxmeyer, John	0.310	34	48	155	9	0	6	28	5	17	26	6	4
Bovinette, J.	0.316	14	25	79	4	0	0	12	3	8	6	4	2
Fulte, Lon	0.147	5	5	34	2	0	0	8	0	4	11	1	2
Huber, Ryan	0.000	0	0	1	0	0	0	0	0	0	0	0	0
Judge, Fred	0.317	20	26	82	5	0	4	19	1	20	6	2	4
Kaiser, Jeff	0.372	39	61	164	15	1	5	21	8	28	14	3	2
Lance, Sam	0.222	5	4	18	0	0	1	3	0	2	5	0	0
Moehrs, Clay	0.351	31	52	148	8	0	7	31	5	8	23	0	1
Price, Chris	0.087	4	2	23	0	0	0	0	2	6	6	0	0
Roy, Mike	0.435	50	67	154	10	1	18	62	2	18	13	2	0
Schulte, Mark	0.387	47	65	168	12	1	22	63	1	12	14	4	2
Vogel, Mark	0.185	2	5	27	1	0	0	8	0	4	4	0	1
Wahlig. Jim	0.476	70	80	168	17	0	15	47	7	32	3	2	1
Wahlig. John	0.364	50	56	154	11	2	12	43	4	25	8	0	0
Werth, Donnie	0.264	12	14	53	5	0	0	4	1	7	9	4	2
Wirth, Mike	0.454	59	83	183	16	2	10	67	0	32	11	0	2
Totals	0.368	442	593	1611	115	7	100	416	39	223	159	28	23

PITCHERS	IP	H	R	ER	BB	SO	HP	CG	SHO	W	L	SV	ERA
Beattie, Larry	6 1/3	7	1	1	0	8	0	0	0	2	0	0	1.42
Donius, Bob	35	43	24	20	13	10	2	0	0	5	1	0	5.14
Fehrenz, Warren	68	79	44	40	11	12	1	1	0	6	2	2	5.29
Hefner, Brett	16 1/3	21	17	13	13	15	1	1	0	2	1	0	7.16
Hollander, J.	18	32	21	15	15	11	1	1	0	2	2	0	7.50
Huber, Ryan	67	80	46	33	21	25	3	3	0	6	2	0	4.43
Jarvis, Jim	2	3	2	2	3	1	0	0	0	0	0	0	9.00
Lance, Sam	34 2/3	34	40	34	36	34	4	4	0	2	3	0	8.83
McClure, Todd	5	2	0	0	2	10	0	0	0	0	0	0	0.00
Roy, Mike	9	5	3	3	1	4	0	0	0	0	0	4	3.00
Scheller, Larry	19	25	19	17	13	6	0	0	0	0	0	0	8.05
Schlecht, Jim	103 2/3	83	37	30	34	35	6	8	2	13	1	1	2.60
Totals	384	414	254	208	162	171	18	18	2	38	12	7	4.88

Individual Statistics: 1992

BATTERS	AVG	R	H	AB	2B	3B	HR	RBI	SB	BB	SO	HP	SAC
Baxmeyer, John	0.310	26	45	145	4	2	8	30	3	10	13	2	2
Degener, J.	0.667	1	2	3	0	1	0	1	0	1	0	1	0
Fehrenz, Warren	0.357	2	5	14	2	0	0	4	0	0	1	1	1
Fulte, Tim	0.125	0	1	8	0	0	0	1	0	0	5	0	0
Judge, Fred	0.275	30	33	120	5	0	4	11	1	21	20	4	2
Kaiser, Jeff	0.380	45	62	163	7	3	8	57	6	31	15	1	2
Markert, Josh	0.250	1	3	12	1	0	0	2	0	2	1	0	0
Moehrs, Clay	0.376	70	73	194	8	0	13	45	13	31	31	1	1
Roy, Mike	0.387	64	72	186	9	1	17	65	3	28	14	1	4
Schulte, Mark	0.273	13	15	55	3	0	2	16	0	8	7	1	3
Thies, Scott	0.261	4	6	23	2	0	0	3	2	5	7	0	0
Vogel, Jason	0.182	3	2	11	0	0	1	2	1	2	5	0	0
Vogel, Mark	0.326	26	28	86	4	0	0	19	2	9	15	0	0
Wahlig, Jim	0.440	73	80	182	10	0	24	69	6	22	9	6	4
Wahlig, John	0.404	68	67	166	10	2	21	84	5	28	15	2	4
Werth, Donnie	0.381	21	32	84	4	1	0	25	8	15	11	4	6
Wirth, Mike	0.441	74	79	179	17	1	14	49	7	36	22	2	3
Totals	0.371	521	605	1631	86	11	112	483	57	249	191	26	32

PITCHERS	IP	H	R	ER	BB	SO	HP	CG	SHO	W	L	SV	ERA
Burris, Duane	34 1/3	22	10	10	15	29	0	2	0	4	0	3	2.62
Daniel, Dale	73	75	33	32	20	42	4	6	2	9	0	0	3.95
Donius, Bob	30 1/3	35	14	14	12	8	2	1	0	4	0	0	4.15
Farrell, Torrey	11 1/3	19	19	17	8	5	0	0	0	1	0	0	13.50
Fehrenz, Warren	43	57	41	31	24	29	4	0	0	6	1	4	6.49
Hefner, Brett	58	76	36	20	17	27	4	2	1	7	2	0	3.10
Huber, Ried	42	53	32	25	25	11	2	0	0	4	1	0	5.36
Keen, J.	5 2/3	5	6	6	4	5	0	0	0	0	0	0	9.53
McClure, Todd	2 1/3	1	0	0	1	2	0	0	0	0	0	0	0.00
Roy, Mike	7	6	4	4	8	3	0	0	0	1	0	0	5.14
Schlecht, Jim	67 2/3	75	45	35	29	41	3	7	2	5	4	0	4.66
Vogel, Jason	2 1/3	2	0	0	0	0	0	0	0	0	0	0	0.00
Forfeit	0	0	0	0	0	0	0	0	0	2	0	0	0.00
Totals	377	426	240	194	163	202	19	18	5	43	8	7	4.63

Individual Statistics: 1993

BATTERS	AVG	R	H	AB	2B	3B	HR	RBI	SB	BB	SO	HP	SAC
Baxmeyer, John	0.426	40	66	155	14	1	16	54	8	13	16	1	1
Chetwood, Chris	0.118	6	2	17	2	0	0	4	0	1	1	1	1
Daniel, Dale	0.000	0	0	1	0	0	0	0	0	0	1	0	0
Davis, J.	0.000	0	0	3	0	3	0	0	0	1	0	0	0
Fiala, Neil	0.419	48	57	136	8	0	12	41	5	23	3	3	1
Gardner, Matt	0.200	3	4	20	1	0	1	5	0	0	6	0	1
Kaiser, Jeff	0.374	46	61	163	15	0	5	25	6	19	20	0	1
Kempfer, Jason	0.182	2	2	11	0	3	1	1	0	0	2	0	0
Moehrs, Clay	0.285	28	41	144	7	0	5	24	2	14	30	0	0
Neff, Ben	0.250	4	2	8	1	0	0	1	0	0	3	0	0
Roy, Mike	0.111	2	1	9	0	0	0	0	0	4	3	0	0
Shields, Jim	0.333	11	10	30	2	0	1	5	4	4	3	1	0
Smith, Brian	0.375	2	9	24	1	0	1	6	0	2	2	1	0
Thies, Scott	0.179	4	7	39	3	0	1	4	0	1	4	0	0
Vogel, Jason	0.367	5	18	49	2	0	1	13	0	7	12	0	1
Vogel, Mark	0.331	41	52	157	8	0	9	20	4	15	11	0	0
Wahlig, Jim	0.426	36	43	101	8	0	9	34	4	23	6	4	4
Wahlig, John	0.299	32	52	174	8	0	0	35	2	16	13	1	2
Werth, Donnie	0.360	21	32	89	5	1	0	16	6	16	9	4	2
Wetzler, J.	0.000	0	0	3	0	0	0	0	1	1	1	0	0
Wirth, Mike	0.398	42	68	171	13	0	11	45	1	25	16	4	1
Totals	0.350	373	527	1504	98	8	73	333	43	185	162	20	15

PITCHERS	IP	H	R	ER	BB	SO	HP	CG	SHO	W	L	SV	ERA
Daniel, Dale	70 2/3	84	55	46	28	39	5	2	0	4	3	0	5.86
Donius, Bob	8 1/3	14	8	7	6	2	0	0	0	1	0	0	7.56
Fehrens, Warren	2 1/3	3	3	3	4	1	0	0	0	0	0	1	11.57
Fortner, Greg	42 1/3	35	29	19	29	19	2	2	0	5	2	1	4.04
Hefner, Brett	5 1/3	7	6	4	5	5	0	0	0	0	0	0	6.75
Kempfer, Jason	46 1/3	36	17	14	32	59	3	5	0	6	2	0	2.72
Proffer, Cole	59	65	38	26	21	34	2	1	0	6	1	0	3.97
Schlecht, Jim	92 2/3	43	34	28	8	47	5	7	3	11	3	0	2.72
Smith, Brian	1	5	6	6	2	0	0	0	0	0	0	0	54.00
Vogel, Jason	48 1/3	43	23	23	20	20	1	1	0	3	1	1	4.28
Forfeit	0	0	0	0	0	0	0	0	0	2	0	0	0.00
Totals	376 1/3	335	219	176	155	226	18	18	3	38	12	3	4.21

Individual Statistics: 1994

BATTERS	AVG	R	H	AB	2B	3B	HR	RBI	SB	BB	SO	HP	SAC
Baxmeyer, John	0.366	42	60	164	10	2	18	48	3	32	16	2	3
Brueggeman, J.	0.400	3	4	10	2	0	0	1	0	1	1	0	0
Burris, Duane	1.000	0	1	1	0	0	0	0	0	0	0	0	0
Donius, Bob	1.000	0	1	1	1	0	0	3	0	0	0	0	0
Fiala, Neil	0.530	72	88	166	18	1	16	61	6	27	2	2	4
Frierdich, Grant	0.419	20	31	74	5	1	1	16	4	4	6	4	3
Hewitt, Ben	0.375	7	9	24	1	0	0	4	1	4	4	1	1
Kaiser, Jeff	0.335	55	62	185	13	3	10	46	7	21	15	1	0
Markert, John	0.391	18	27	69	3	0	6	21	5	9	2	3	0
Martin, J.	0.615	10	16	26	0	0	0	4	4	2	0	2	0
McClure, Todd	1.000	1	1	1	0	0	0	3	0	1	0	0	1
Moehrs, Clay	0.379	51	72	190	11	3	7	55	9	13	26	2	4
Neff, Ben	0.500	3	6	12	0	0	0	1	0	0	2	3	4
Shields, Jim	0.167	6	4	24	1	1	0	3	0	5	5	0	0
Shikles, Larry	0.333	3	2	6	0	0	1	2	0	2	0	0	0
Smith, Brian	0.000	1	0	2	0	0	0	0	0	0	1	0	0
Vogel, Jason	0.333	4	7	21	0	0	0	1	1	3	4	2	0
Vogel, Mark	0.296	35	45	152	5	2	0	12	6	16	21	2	7
Wahlig, Jim	0.425	56	74	174	9	2	14	65	8	33	5	4	2
Wahlig, John	0.408	67	78	191	19	0	27	108	4	31	12	0	6
Werth, Donnie	0.369	26	24	65	4	1	0	13	8	18	6	2	2
Wirth, Mike	0.471	75	98	208	19	3	14	70	4	27	14	2	1
Totals	0.402	555	710	1766	121	19	114	537	70	249	142	32	38

PITCHERS	IP	H	R	ER	BB	SO	HP	CG	SHO	W	L	SV	ERA
Brueggeman,	3	4	2	1	1	5	0	0	0	0	0	0	3.00
Burris, Duane	43 1/3	42	28	28	12	17	0	0	0	3	1	1	5.82
Donius, Bob	8	6	6	6	4	4	0	0	0	2	1	0	6.75
Gummesheimer,	1	0	0	0	2	1	0	0	0	0	0	0	0.00
McClure, Todd	51	38	14	13	17	74	3	0	0	4	0	3	2.29
Mosbacher, J.	38	44	26	20	11	33	2	0	0	4	1	0	4.74
Proffer, Cole	40 2/3	44	31	21	21	19	1	0	0	4	0	0	4.65
Schlecht, Jim	36	45	26	23	8	20	4	0	0	4	2	0	5.75
Shikles, Larry	111 1/3	87	39	28	17	72	3	12	4	15	1	0	2.26
Smith, Brian	60 2/3	56	25	21	23	64	1	2	1	9	1	2	3.12
Vogel, Jason	8 2/3	14	12	6	6	1	0	0	0	0	0	0	6.23
Totals	401 2/3	380	209	167	122	310	14	14	5	45	7	6	3.74

Individual Statistics: 1995
Records lost but memories not forgotten

Individual Statistics: 1996

BATTERS	AVG	R	H	AB	2B	3B	HR	RBI	SB	BB	SO	HP	SAC
Wahlig, John	0.445	56	69	155	7	0	19	66	1	14	13	0	3
Wahlig, Jim	0.419	49	62	148	12	0	7	36	1	23	11	1	0
Fiala, Neil	0.453	59	73	161	14	3	17	49	12	22	6	0	0
Moehrs, Clay	0.348	45	56	161	14	2	5	33	12	17	24	0	3
Anderson, Jim	0.333	36	41	123	6	1	10	39	1	10	8	1	6
Kaiser, Jeff	0.340	32	48	141	10	0	10	33	1	15	18	4	2
Baxmeyer, John	0.388	32	47	121	8	1	9	45	2	12	21	1	0
Vogel, Mark	0.319	21	22	69	3	0	0	10	3	13	13	0	4
Cepicky, Scott	0.385	24	20	52	4	0	11	30	0	12	6	1	2
Wirth, Mike	0.442	59	68	154	8	0	7	37	0	19	12	6	2
Work, Rich	0.267	8	12	45	2	0	0	7	0	4	5	0	0
Werth, Donnie	0.200	10	5	25	1	0	0	3	2	5	10	1	0
Hewitt, Ben	1.000	0	1	1	0	0	0	0	0	0	0	0	0
Smith, Brian	0.250	0	1	4	0	0	0	1	0	0	0	0	0
Henneberry, J.	0.250	2	2	8	0	0	0	3	0	2	1	0	0
Matzenbacher, Brian	0.333	0	1	3	0	0	0	0	0	0	0	0	0
Frierdich, Grant	0.000	0	0	8	0	0	0	1	0	0	1	0	0
Totals	0.383	433	528	1379	89	7	95	393	35	168	149	15	22

PITCHERS	IP	H	R	ER	BB	SO	W	L	SV	ERA
Braun, Chris	2	0	0	0	0	2	1	0	0	0.00
Blackwell, Corey	13	9	4	3	2	7	3	0	0	2.08
Hargan, Chris	92	75	55	43	47	66	9	2	1	4.21
Matzenbacher, Brian	65	65	52	40	36	61	7	0	0	5.54
Lattimore, Matt	33	54	22	19	19	23	3	0	0	5.18
Proffer, Cole	82	85	56	49	32	64	11	2	0	5.38
Schlect, Jim	5	7	7	5	2	4	1	1	0	9.00
Smith, Brian	63	76	44	30	21	54	5	1	1	4.29
Totals	355	371	240	189	159	281	40	6	2	4.79

Individual Statistics: 1997

BATTERS	AVG	R	H	AB	2B	3B	HR	RBI	SB	BB	SO	HP	SAC
Anderson, Jim	0.467	52	70	150	18	0	12	60	3	24	6	0	3
Baxmeyer, John	0.376	29	50	133	8	0	10	41	2	16	12	0	2
Breidigam, J.	0.125	0	1	8	1	0	0	1	0	0	2	0	0
Cepicky, Scott	0.414	12	12	29	1	0	3	10	1	6	0	1	1
Fiala, Neil	0.474	71	73	154	13	1	22	77	12	31	3	1	2
Frierdich, Grant	0.000	0	0	4	0	0	0	1	0	0	2	0	0
Grant, Barry	0.358	18	38	106	9	1	1	21	4	12	10	3	3
Johnson, Steve	0.347	26	26	75	4	2	2	13	6	18	11	1	0
Kaiser, Jeff	0.417	43	63	151	8	1	8	34	4	18	24	5	0
Miller, Matt	0.250	1	1	4	0	0	0	0	0	1	0	0	0
Moehrs, Clay	0.318	49	54	170	13	0	1	27	11	19	34	1	0
Proffer, Cole	0.455	3	5	11	1	0	0	1	0	0	1	0	0
Schlecht, Jim	0.000	0	0	1	0	0	0	0	0	0	0	0	0
Smith, Brian	0.000	0	0	0	0	0	0	1	0	1	0	0	0
Vogel, Mark	0.269	12	18	67	1	0	0	5	4	9	8	1	3
Wahlig, Jim	0.489	48	67	137	8	0	10	51	3	30	10	4	6
Wahlig, John	0.439	65	72	164	11	0	23	60	0	25	13	0	1
Werth, Donnie	0.404	15	19	47	3	0	0	13	4	13	7	5	1
Totals	0.403	444	569	1411	99	5	92	416	54	223	143	22	22

PITCHERS	IP	H	R	ER	BB	SO	HP	CG	SHO	W	L	SV	ERA
George, Chris	58	37	16	13	27	55	2	4	2	8	0	0	2.02
Johnson, Steve	1	2	1	1	0	2	1	0	0	0	0	0	9.00
Lattimore, Matt	1 2/3	4	1	1	0	0	0	0	0	0	0	0	5.40
Mowry, J.	3 1/3	4	5	4	3	6	0	0	0	1	0	0	10.80
O'Keefe, Don	20 1/3	30	23	19	8	22	0	1	1	1	2	0	8.41
Proffer, Cole	30 2/3	49	32	27	10	18	3	1	0	3	1	0	7.92
Paul, Ryan	82	96	67	63	36	54	5	4	2	8	4	1	6.91
Schlecht, Jim	56 2/3	60	30	26	16	40	3	2	0	7	0	6	4.13
Sherman, Lance	2	6	4	3	0	0	0	0	0	0	1	0	13.50
Smith, Brian	50 1/3	61	25	23	10	47	0	3	1	7	1	0	4.11
Wiggins, Chris	23 2/3	31	40	18	13	10	1	1	1	3	0	0	6.85
Totals	329 2/3	380	244	198	123	254	15	16	7	38	9	7	5.41

Individual Statistics: 1998

BATTERS	AVG	R	H	AB	2B	3B	HR	RBI	SB	BB	SO	HP	SAC
Fiala, Neil	0.512	82	86	168	14	2	19	57	27	29	3	1	1
Margalski, Ben	0.480	8	12	25	3	1	1	9	0	2	5	0	0
Wirth, Mike	0.436	52	71	163	19	0	3	51	4	24	12	1	4
Moehrs, Clay	0.435	62	70	161	10	2	2	35	25	16	27	0	4
Wahlig, John	0.431	56	69	160	15	0	16	72	3	24	8	0	4
Anderson, Jim	0.410	41	57	139	9	0	12	52	3	19	7	3	6
Wahlig, Jim	0.401	57	65	162	7	0	11	42	0	13	9	1	3
Baxmeyer, John	0.377	37	52	138	10	0	10	50	1	25	15	2	2
Musso, Brandon	0.364	2	4	11	0	0	1	2	0	3	3	0	1
Johnson, Steve	0.352	22	19	54	6	0	4	10	2	14	6	1	1
Kaiser, Jeff	0.346	33	36	104	4	0	8	33	0	9	6	5	3
Haake, Steve	0.316	18	24	76	4	0	1	12	4	8	11	2	0
Smith, Brian	0.300	5	3	10	0	0	0	1	0	5	1	2	0
Pickett, Adam	0.267	4	4	15	1	0	0	2	1	0	5	1	0
Hendrickson, Darin	0.227	2	5	22	4	0	0	0	1	1	1	0	0
Unger, Brian	0.179	5	5	28	1	0	0	0	2	0	4	0	1
Miller, Matt	0.167	2	2	12	0	0	0	2	0	0	3	0	1
Werth, Donnie	0.000	1	0	11	0	0	0	0	0	2	1	0	0
Almond, Kevin	0.000	0	0	2	0	0	0	0	0	0	2	0	0
Totals	0.400	489	584	1461	107	5	88	430	73	194	129	19	31

PITCHERS	IP	H	R	ER	BB	SO	HP	CG	W	L	SV	ERA
Musso, Brandon	29	22	13	6	13	30	1	1	6	1	0	1.86
Hendrickson, Darin	71	53	24	17	11	49	6	9	10	0	0	2.15
Unger, Brian	12 1/3	13	3	3	1	6	0	1	2	0	1	2.19
Almond, Kevin	35 1/3	32	15	12	22	31	2	1	5	0	3	3.06
Braun, Chris	32 2/3	36	15	15	7	25	1	1	5	0	0	4.13
Hargan, Chris	56	67	37	27	18	51	2	6	9	0	0	4.34
Phillips, Bill	31 1/3	38	23	17	16	17	0	0	3	0	2	4.88
Schlecht, Jim	33	36	22	21	6	24	2	1	2	0	10	5.73
George, Chris	5	6	4	4	1	8	0	0	1	0	1	7.20
Smith, Brian	11	17	12	11	3	13	1	0	2	0	0	9.00
Blackwell, Corey	4	6	5	5	0	2	0	0	0	0	1	11.25
Margalski, Ben	2 1/3	0	0	0	2	0	0	0	0	0	1	0.00
Forfeit	0	0	0	0	0	0	0	0	2	0	0	0.00
Totals	323	326	173	138	100	256	15	20	47	1	19	3.85

Individual Statistics: 1999

BATTERS	AVG	R	H	AB	2B	3B	HR	RBI	SB	BB	SO	HP	SAC
Fiala, Neil	0.435	40	57	131	10	2	9	49	23	23	2	1	7
Kaiser, Jeff	0.431	32	56	130	7	1	8	34	2	7	11	3	5
Wirth, Mike	0.421	35	53	126	15	2	3	27	2	18	11	5	1
Haake, Steve	0.407	29	46	113	7	0	4	30	7	14	12	1	4
Wahlig, Jim	0.380	14	19	50	1	0	4	15	2	7	6	1	0
Baxmeyer, John	0.364	38	40	110	10	1	8	28	1	23	15	3	0
Moehrs, Clay	0.356	46	57	160	7	2	6	36	17	10	23	0	2
Anderson, Jim	0.345	29	40	116	8	2	4	23	2	20	6	1	1
Anderson, Jon	0.333	0	1	3	0	0	0	0	0	1	0	0	0
Grant, Barry	0.324	33	35	108	9	3	2	25	9	14	24	6	4
Wahlig, John	0.288	28	34	118	8	0	6	29	2	21	10	1	2
Blackwell, Corey	0.273	3	3	11	1	0	0	5	0	0	6	0	1
Vogel, Mark	0.185	6	5	27	1	0	1	2	1	6	6	0	1
Unger, Brian	0.143	6	1	7	0	0	0	3	0	0	1	2	0
Hendrickson, Darin	0.091	1	1	11	1	0	0	0	0	0	0	0	0
Musso, Brandon	0.000	0	0	2	0	0	0	0	0	1	2	0	0
Braun, Chris	0.000	0	0	1	0	0	0	0	0	0	1	0	0
Torisky, John	0.000	0	0	1	0	0	0	0	0	0	0	0	0
Totals	0.366	340	448	1225	85	13	55	306	68	165	136	24	28

PITCHERS	IP	H	R	ER	BB	SO	HP	CG	W	L	SV	ERA
Schlecht, Jim	24 2/3	17	9	4	4	19	0	2	4	0	3	1.46
Musso, Brandon	62 2/3	51	22	18	20	72	2	5	7	1	0	2.59
Unger, Brian	26 2/3	25	14	11	8	21	0	1	5	1	1	3.71
Blackwell, Corey	74 2/3	100	46	38	16	47	1	7	8	0	2	4.58
Hendrickson, Darin	83 2/3	93	53	43	19	77	5	8	8	4	0	4.63
Braun, Chris	11	16	9	6	3	9	1	0	2	0	0	4.91
George, Chris	1	1	0	0	0	2	1	0	0	0	0	0.00
Forfeit	0	0	0	0	0	0	0	0	2	0	0	0.00
Totals	284 1/3	303	153	120	70	247	10	23	36	6	6	3.80

Individual Statistics: 2000

BATTERS	AVG	R	H	AB	2B	3B	HR	RBI	SB	BB	SO	HP	SAC
Moehrs, Clay	0.399	38	55	138	7	1	5	29	23	13	15	0	1
Wahlig, Jim	0.351	16	27	77	6	1	1	13	1	11	7	1	0
Haake, Steve	0.344	36	42	122	6	0	2	19	15	25	20	2	0
Wahlig, John	0.315	23	28	89	3	1	6	35	0	18	12	0	6
Frederich, Jake	0.347	25	35	101	5	2	5	22	1	3	12	7	1
Williams, J.	0.286	0	2	7	0	0	0	0	0	0	3	0	0
Hurst, Jake	0.318	19	27	85	5	0	2	12	1	13	10	1	2
Dill, Mark	0.167	1	3	18	0	0	0	4	2	2	1	0	3
Vogel, Mark	0.267	17	24	90	1	0	0	10	1	12	11	1	8
Jennings, J.	0.301	13	22	73	4	0	2	13	1	16	16	0	2
Neff, Ben	0.301	18	22	73	3	1	1	16	2	14	14	0	1
Gansmann, Jeff	0.255	13	12	47	0	0	0	5	4	8	10	0	2
Unger, Brian	1.000	0	2	2	0	0	0	2	0	0	0	0	0
Baxmeyer, Jon	0.433	7	13	30	2	0	3	11	0	5	1	0	0
Blackwell, Corey	0.088	2	3	34	0	0	0	1	0	2	1	1	0
Anderson, Jim	0.162	9	11	68	0	0	2	4	1	1	1	1	0
Piatt, Ben	0.397	13	27	68	7	0	1	12	1	2	6	2	1
Totals	0.316	250	355	1122	49	6	30	208	53	145	140	16	27

PITCHERS	IP	H	R	ER	BB	SO	HP	W	L	SV	ERA
Blackwell, Corey	75 2/3	73	30	22	21	54	1	9	3	2	2.62
Frech, John	65	86	49	39	17	44	5	7	2	1	5.40
Unger, Brian	53	50	25	22	12	61	1	8	0	0	3.74
Musso, Brandon	53	52	30	21	20	67	3	4	2	0	3.56
Schlecht, Jim	17	9	5	5	7	10	0	2	1	2	2.65
Hendrickson, Darin	7	4	2	2	0	7	0	1	0	0	2.57
Forfeit	0	0	0	0	0	0	0	2	0	0	0.00
Totals	270 2/3	274	141	111	77	243	10	33	8	5	3.69

Individual Statistics: 2001

BATTERS	AVG	R	H	AB	2B	3B	HR	RBI	SB	BB	SO	HP	SAC
Moehrs, Clay	0.367	45	51	139	8	0	4	23	29	14	21	3	1
Wahlig, Jim	0.421	9	16	38	2	0	0	9	1	8	1	1	1
Ohlau, Craig	0.361	23	35	97	5	1	0	18	9	19	9	8	2
Wahlig, John	0.329	24	25	76	4	1	5	21	5	21	1	1	3
Riva, Buck	0.385	25	45	117	13	0	4	29	5	11	17	2	3
Hurst, Jake	0.294	16	25	85	5	1	0	16	6	7	14	1	1
LaPlantz, J.	0.286	3	2	7	0	0	0	0	1	3	1	1	0
Vogel, Mark	0.319	21	29	91	6	0	0	17	1	11	14	1	7
Blackwell, Corey	0.111	3	2	18	0	0	0	1	2	3	4	0	0
Neff, Ben	0.218	9	12	55	3	0	2	15	2	5	13	2	1
Wells, Fory	0.500	8	8	16	1	0	4	14	0	8	3	1	0
Wheatley	0.250	1	2	8	1	0	0	1	0	0	0	0	0
Beatty, Brad	0.253	11	20	79	5	0	2	19	0	11	16	3	1
Wells, Randy	0.303	14	20	66	2	0	1	11	1	4	10	2	1
Piatt, Ben	0.371	20	26	70	5	0	6	24	4	9	7	1	1
Friedrich, Jake	0.356	19	26	73	3	0	0	9	5	10	12	6	3
Unger, Brian	1.000	0	1	1	0	0	0	0	0	0	0	0	0
Totals	0.333	251	345	1036	63	3	28	227	71	144	143	33	25

PITCHERS	IP	H	R	ER	BB	SO	HP	W	L	SV	ERA
Blackwell, Corey	78 2/3	85	49	43	20	55	7	10	1	1	3.83
Dugan, Bob	34	31	17	16	4	23	6	5	0	1	3.29
Unger, Brian	60 1/3	65	34	27	18	43	2	7	1	0	3.13
Musso, Brandon	18	21	11	9	9	21	2	1	0	0	3.50
Schlecht, Jim	49 2/3	51	28	26	20	35	5	7	1	2	3.66
Waeltz, Brandon	15	20	19	17	6	16	6	0	2	0	7.93
Hendrickson, Darin	2 1/3	4	2	2	1	1	0	0	0	0	6.00
Beatty, Brad	5	7	2	2	2	7	1	0	0	0	2.80
Totals	263	284	162	142	80	201	29	30	5	4	3.78

Individual Statistics: 2002

BATTERS	AVG	R	H	AB	2B	3B	HR	RBI	SB	BB	SO	HP	SAC
Moehrs, Clay	0.388	52	59	152	9	0	6	32	35	17	18	0	1
Wahlig, Jim	0.442	16	19	43	4	0	6	19	0	8	7	1	0
Ohlau, Craig	0.453	28	34	75	9	1	3	34	1	21	8	0	1
Wright, C.J.	0.407	52	44	108	10	2	8	39	13	14	18	4	1
Riva, Buck	0.481	54	64	133	16	0	13	70	10	20	16	5	4
Hurst, Jake	0.397	38	54	136	10	1	6	50	5	20	12	0	3
Grau, Phil	0.220	13	9	41	1	0	1	9	3	13	5	1	0
Vogel, Mark	0.372	42	42	113	8	0	1	24	12	33	13	2	2
Blackwell, Corey	0.250	5	6	24	2	0	0	4	0	11	7	0	0
Gansmann, Jeff	0.200	5	5	25	1	0	0	5	0	3	10	5	2
Link, Derek	0.400	1	4	10	1	0	0	4	1	0	4	0	0
Wheatley, M	0.310	6	9	29	0	0	0	4	0	3	4	2	0
Caby, Eric	0.378	41	45	119	6	1	9	46	2	22	27	9	0
Marruth, Glenn	0.313	5	5	16	1	0	2	11	0	2	2	0	1
Hepp, Clay	0.259	31	30	116	7	0	1	19	4	15	17	2	4
Wealtz, Brandon	0.000	0	0	1	0	0	1	0	0	0	0	0	0
Unger, Brian	0.000	1	0	2	0	0	0	0	0	2	0	0	1
Musso, Brandon	0.083	0	1	12	0	0	0	2	0	2	6	0	0
Haake, Steve	0.214	4	6	28	0	0	1	3	1	1	4	1	0
Thompson, Aaron	0.321	22	18	56	3	2	2	14	9	11	4	1	0
Totals	0.366	416	454	1239	88	7	60	389	96	218	182	33	20

PITCHERS	IP	H	R	ER	BB	SO	HP	W	L	SV	ERA
Blackwell, Corey	76	65	29	21	13	65	4	14	0	0	2.49
Dugan , Bob	36 1/3	45	28	23	13	32	3	1	0	4	5.70
Unger, Brian	63	85	49	39	13	37	0	6	3	1	5.57
Musso, Brandon	4	4	1	0	1	6	0	0	0	0	0.00
Schlecht, Jim	19 2/3	32	24	22	6	14	1	1	2	1	10.07
Waeltz, Brandon	64 1/3	71	34	31	13	58	5	7	1	0	4.34
Backs, Ron	4	6	6	6	1	2	0	0	1	0	13.50
Link, Derek	29	32	17	17	20	21	1	4	1	0	5.28
Klahs, Dave	2 1/3	1	0	0	0	4	0	1	0	0	0.00
Totals	298 2/3	341	188	159	80	239	14	34	8	6	4.79

Individual Statistics: 2003

BATTERS	AVG	R	H	AB	2B	3B	HR	RBI	SB	BB	SO	HP	SAC
Moehrs, Clay	0.372	23	32	86	4	0	3	14	8	4	11	0	0
Schulte, Mark	0.414	29	29	70	7	1	4	15	2	18	11	2	0
Wright, C.J.	0.389	38	42	108	8	1	7	35	13	12	15	2	1
Riva, Buck	0.402	32	33	82	8	0	10	33	4	8	14	6	3
Ohlau, Craig	0.430	45	55	128	11	1	12	46	3	18	14	3	5
Hurst, Jake	0.380	37	46	121	9	0	10	44	4	22	19	1	2
Mckee, John	0.500	2	6	12	0	1	1	4	0	0	1	1	1
Thompson, Aaron	0.330	26	32	97	4	1	5	27	8	12	22	2	2
Smith, Brian	0.250	1	1	4	1	0	0	4	0	4	1	0	1
Hepp, Clay	0.156	23	10	64	1	0	0	5	6	13	15	5	3
Blackwell, Corey	0.273	5	6	22	1	0	0	7	0	5	10	0	1
Wahlig, Jim	0.375	3	3	8	0	0	0	2	0	0	1	0	0
Grant, Barry	0.508	25	32	63	8	1	4	22	2	0	10	11	3
Poling, Erik	0.381	41	43	113	5	1	7	35	3	11	16	3	4
Friedrich, Jake	0.369	40	41	111	6	3	3	28	15	3	17	11	0
Unger, Brian	0.556	8	5	9	0	0	0	3	0	11	0	1	0
Link, Derek	0.538	5	7	13	2	0	0	5	0	1	2	1	0
Vogel, Mark	0.667	1	2	3	0	0	0	0	0	1	0	0	0
Thompson, Jordan	0.000	1	0	3	0	0	0	2	0	0	0	0	0
Caby, Eric	0.273	3	3	11	1	0	1	3	0	0	0	0	0
Totals	0.379	388	428	1128	76	10	67	334	68	143	179	49	26

PITCHERS	IP	H	R	ER	BB	SO	HP	W	L	SV	ERA
Blackwell, Corey	64 1/3	74	39	32	14	42	6	7	2	0	4.48
Caron, Jeff	6 1/3	11	6	7	3	9	0	1	0	0	9.95
Unger, Brian	12 1/3	20	8	8	2	11	0	1	0	0	5.84
Musso, Brandon	67	50	31	22	14	88	5	11	0	0	2.96
Waeltz, Brandon	30	29	15	12	12	27	0	4	0	0	3.60
Bahr, Jessie	22 1/3	18	13	10	9	37	1	3	2	0	4.03
Warnecke, Ryan	18 1/3	22	12	12	2	20	0	0	0	1	5.89
Dugan, Bob	6 2/3	8	9	8	2	2	1	0	0	0	10.80
Smith, Brian	12 2/3	3	2	2	3	18	0	1	1	0	1.42
Meyer, Blake	15	19	10	8	8	15	0	2	1	0	4.80
Link, Derek	6	11	11	10	3	3	2	1	2	0	15.00
Totals	261	265	156	131	72	272	15	31	8	1	4.52

Individual Statistics: 2004

BATTERS	AVG	R	H	AB	2B	3B	HR	RBI	SB	BB	SO	HP	SAC
Friedrich, Jake	0.381	43	48	126	5	0	1	20	22	19	8	9	4
Moehrs, Clay	0.324	26	34	105	5	2	0	20	9	14	20	1	2
Piatt, Ben	0.395	32	47	119	11	0	4	34	4	7	10	2	5
Bolstad, Joe	0.405	25	32	79	6	2	5	30	0	13	14	2	1
Ohlau, Craig	0.389	42	49	126	8	0	4	37	5	25	8	2	5
Grau, Phil	0.413	42	43	104	7	1	9	37	16	24	9	1	0
Kaiser, Jeff	0.380	15	30	79	5	0	2	17	1	5	7	2	0
Caby, Eric	0.291	30	34	117	6	0	8	35	13	17	21	9	3
Grant, Barry	0.270	6	10	37	1	0	0	6	3	2	7	2	0
Hurst, Jake	0.296	22	32	108	6	2	2	25	5	15	16	2	6
Smith, Brian	0.000	0	0	1	0	0	0	0	0	0	0	0	0
Blackwell, Corey	0.400	4	4	10	0	0	1	2	7	3	4	0	1
Arzola, J.	0.600	5	3	5	0	0	0	0	4	2	0	2	0
Rayfield, John	0.250	3	4	16	2	0	0	3	0	2	1	0	3
McBride, M	0.000	0	0	2	0	0	0	0	0	0	1	1	1
Thompson, Aaron	0.354	28	34	96	7	0	0	11	16	22	12	1	0
Riva, Buck	0.405	17	15	37	2	0	4	12	5	4	4	3	0
Powell, James	0.000	1	0	0	0	0	0	0	0	0	0	0	0
Anderson, Jim	0.250	6	6	24	1	1	0	8	0	3	1	1	2
Totals	0.357	347	425	1191	72	8	40	297	110	177	143	40	33

PITCHERS	IP	H	R	ER	BB	SO	HP	W	L	SV	ERA
Musso, Brandon	61 1/3	46	21	18	17	67	1	10	0	0	2.64
Waeltz, Brandon	74 1/3	76	35	30	21	81	9	9	0	0	3.63
Blackwell, Corey	87 1/3	70	34	24	12	53	6	8	2	2	2.47
Unger, Brian	12 1/3	12	5	4	3	9	2	2	0	2	2.92
Mueller, Mark	23 1/3	25	14	14	7	19	1	2	1	1	5.40
Smith, Brian	12 2/3	19	14	11	5	15	0	1	2	0	7.82
Briette,	11 1/3	9	12	12	10	16	2	0	1	0	9.53
Braun, Chris	1	2	3	3	1	1	0	0	0	0	27.00
Buck, Peter	32	22	8	5	4	32	1	3	0	2	1.41
Powell, James	1	1	0	0	0	0	0	0	0	0	0.00
Totals	316 2/3	282	146	121	80	293	22	35	6	7	3.44

Individual Statistics: 2005

BATTERS	AVG	R	H	AB	2B	3B	HR	RBI	SB	BB	SO	HP	SAC
Friedrich, Jake	0.444	51	60	135	11	0	1	22	28	16	5	10	5
Hardin, Pat	0.398	24	35	88	8	0	2	21	3	9	11	3	2
Thompson, Aaron	0.375	44	45	120	10	2	4	26	26	24	19	2	2
Ohlau, Craig	0.395	47	49	124	10	1	7	47	14	19	9	8	3
Wigger, Chas	0.388	24	38	98	12	1	5	34	12	14	15	14	4
Kaiser, Jeff	0.368	20	35	95	8	0	2	20	3	5	7	3	2
Caby, Eric	0.297	30	35	118	10	0	1	30	12	12	17	4	0
Bergheger, Jeremiah	0.257	8	9	35	1	0	0	9	1	6	3	1	0
Hurst, Jake	0.342	22	39	114	8	0	4	26	3	10	13	1	8
Smith, Brian	0.091	5	1	11	0	0	1	3	0	2	6	1	0
Blackwell, Corey	0.538	4	7	13	3	0	0	5	0	1	4	0	1
Baxmeyer, John	0.389	7	7	18	4	0	0	5	1	3	1	2	0
Bradfield, J.	0.182	5	4	22	1	0	0	4	0	4	11	1	0
Thompson, Jordan	0.304	6	7	23	2	0	0	2	5	1	3	1	2
Queern, Jim	0.316	26	36	114	12	2	4	35	11	7	15	2	3
Waeltz, Brandon	1.000	3	3	3	1	0	0	1	0	3	3	0	1
Totals	0.363	326	410	1131	101	6	31	290	119	136	142	53	33

PITCHERS	IP	H	R	ER	BB	SO	HP	W	L	SV	ERA
Musso, Brandon	61	48	18	14	4	60	3	8	0	0	2.07
Waeltz, Brandon	52	40	21	17	12	40	2	7	1	3	2.94
Blackwell, Corey	73 1/3	61	22	16	11	59	5	10	1	2	1.96
Unger, Brian	3	0	0	0	0	0	0	0	0	0	0.00
Mueller, Mark	44 1/3	34	24	19	11	39	4	5	2	0	3.86
Smith, Brian	11 2/3	9	3	2	0	8	0	2	0	0	1.54
Buck, Peter	34	27	9	7	6	31	2	4	0	2	1.85
Powell, James	7 1/3	12	10	8	3	5	1	0	0	0	9.82
Totals	286 2/3	231	107	83	47	242	17	36	4	7	2.61

Individual Statistics: 2006

BATTERS	AVG	R	H	AB	2B	3B	HR	RBI	SB	BB	SO	HP	SAC
Friederich, Jake	0.424	52	59	139	13	1	1	38	18	13	15	5	5
Fuess, Brian	0.424	34	61	144	13	1	7	59	2	7	5	4	8
Hardin, Pat	0.315	25	34	108	7	1	1	19	2	18	16	1	2
Thompson, Aaron	0.329	20	27	82	7	0	1	20	6	28	14	1	5
Ohlau, Craig	0.472	46	58	123	19	2	6	53	1	28	10	2	2
Wigger, Chas	0.392	41	38	97	8	2	1	20	10	5	17	12	9
Kaiser, Jeff	0.429	11	9	21	1	0	1	9	0	12	1	2	1
Caby, Eric	0.366	39	45	123	8	0	14	55	7	32	22	5	4
Dawson, Travis	0.347	48	41	118	10	1	2	21	13	24	14	0	0
Hurst, Jake	0.321	43	36	112	9	0	2	30	4	14	14	1	5
Thompson, Jordan	0.338	23	25	74	5	0	2	18	13	0	12	3	2
Thompson, Harry	0.000	0	0	1	0	0	0	0	0	0	0	0	0
Blackwell, Corey	0.500	3	2	4	0	0	0	3	0	5	1	0	0
Powell, James	1.000	0	1	1	0	0	0	1	0	0	0	0	0
Totals	0.380	385	436	1147	100	8	38	346	76	186	141	36	43

PITCHERS	IP	H	R	ER	BB	SO	HP	W	L	SV	ERA
Musso, Brandon	72	51	13	10	15	65	4	10	0	1	1.25
Waeltz, Brandon	58	39	28	18	14	49	10	7	0	0	2.79
Blackwell, Corey	61 1/3	50	19	13	13	55	5	10	1	0	1.91
Fitch, M.	11 1/3	6	3	3	7	21	2	0	0	1	2.38
Mueller, Mark	10	12	11	11	5	6	3	2	0	0	9.90
Powell, James	10	8	5	5	8	6	1	1	0	0	4.50
Schlecht, Jim	1	0	0	0	0	1	0	0	0	1	0.00
Unger, Brian	2 1/3	3	1	1	0	2	0	0	0	1	0.20
Otten, Chris	45 2/3	36	17	14	13	41	5	6	0	1	2.76
Fuess, Brian	3 2/3	6	5	4	0	3	0	1	1	0	9.82
Totals	275 1/3	211	102	79	75	249	30	37	2	5	2.58

Individual Statistics: 2007

BATTERS	AVG	R	H	AB	2B	3B	HR	RBI	SB	BB	SO	HP	SAC
Friederich, Jake	0.385	63	57	148	7	2	5	14	21	17	16	11	4
Fuess, Brian	0.393	27	59	150	13	2	7	64	0	16	5	2	3
Amann, Scott	0.352	31	50	142	7	3	2	27	9	11	11	3	1
Thompson, Jordan	0.280	29	37	132	6	1	4	37	11	17	28	4	2
Ohlau, Craig	0.403	40	48	119	17	0	4	50	1	29	13	5	4
Wigger, Chas	0.254	31	29	114	2	2	6	24	14	3	29	11	2
Blackwell, Corey	0.267	5	4	15	0	0	0	1	0	12	6	0	0
Caby, Eric	0.290	30	40	138	11	0	11	37	3	37	20	1	5
Dawson, Travis	0.439	62	58	132	12	3	5	36	13	18	7	1	2
Hurst, Jake	0.275	32	36	131	5	0	5	29	4	12	19	1	2
Thompson, Aaron	0.306	6	11	36	0	0	1	5	2	4	7	0	1
Toenjes, Shane	0.361	6	13	36	5	0	0	4	0	0	10	2	1
Moehrs, Clay	0.250	0	1	4	0	0	0	0	0	0	2	0	0
Waeltz, Brandon	0.250	1	1	4	0	0	0	2	0	0	2	0	0
Galle, Andy	0.500	1	1	2	0	0	1	3	0	0	1	0	0
Totals	0.342	364	445	1303	85	13	51	333	78	176	176	41	27

PITCHERS	IP	H	R	ER	BB	SO	HP	W	L	SV	ERA
Musso, Brandon	66 1/3	64	36	30	19	87	5	7	1	0	4.07
Waeltz, Brandon	15 1/3	11	7	5	9	19	1	1	0	2	2.93
Blackwell, Corey	73	58	19	17	11	62	3	11	1	0	2.10
Parke, Rusty	6 1/3	6	2	2	2	0	0	1	0	0	2.84
Mueller, Mark	52	31	22	19	22	58	6	7	1	0	3.29
Galle, Andy	64 2/3	62	27	14	20	56	1	9	1	2	1.95
Otten, Chris	48 2/3	42	24	17	15	38	4	5	2	0	3.14
Unger, Brian	0	0	0	0	0	0	0	0	0	0	0.00
Fuess, Brian	2	2	0	0	0	2	0	0	0	0	0.00
Totals	271 2/3	276	137	104	98	322	20	41	6	4	3.45

Individual Statistics: 2008

BATTERS	AVG	R	H	AB	2B	3B	HR	RBI	SB	BB	SO	HP	SAC
Friederich, Jake	0.475	47	47	99	15	1	9	34	11	16	13	4	3
Dawson, Travis	0.490	51	51	104	16	1	3	33	15	25	4	5	4
Fuess, Brian	0.433	22	45	104	11	0	2	38	1	9	6	0	3
Harrison, Jason	0.350	24	35	100	5	1	4	35	2	12	14	3	5
Amann, Scott	0.310	31	36	116	3	1	1	25	13	17	16	3	1
Thompson, Jordan	0.341	27	31	91	6	1	6	23	15	7	22	5	5
Ohlau, Craig	0.413	28	43	104	9	0	2	33	2	16	10	3	1
Wigger, Chas	0.317	33	32	101	8	1	4	32	13	12	18	16	4
Lepere, Dusty	0.167	0	1	6	0	0	0	0	0	0	1	0	0
Hurst, Jake	0.363	27	33	91	6	0	6	31	2	26	17	0	0
Thompson, Aaron	0.324	30	24	74	5	0	4	18	12	19	17	0	1
Toenjes, Shane	0.303	11	10	33	5	0	0	8	0	8	11	2	2
Blackwell, Corey	0.500	3	3	6	0	0	0	2	0	4	3	0	1
Galle, Andy	0.000	0	0	2	0	0	0	0	0	0	2	0	0
Grau, Phil	0.357	5	10	28	2	0	0	4	2	2	1	0	0
Totals	0.379	339	401	1059	91	6	41	316	88	173	155	41	30

PITCHERS	IP	H	R	ER	BB	SO	HP	W	L	SV	ERA
Musso, Brandon	45 1/3	44	20	17	19	64	0	6	1	1	3.38
Waeltz, Brandon	14	15	4	4	4	12	1	1	0	1	2.57
Blackwell, Corey	65 1/3	54	24	17	16	60	4	9	2	0	2.34
Mueller, Mark	44	40	22	15	9	49	5	5	1	0	3.07
Galle, Andy	36	28	16	11	11	36	0	5	0	0	2.75
Otten, Chris	32 2/3	37	24	19	14	35	1	4	0	2	5.23
Schlecht, Jim	2	2	0	0	1	2	0	0	0	0	0.00
Fuess, Brian	2	3	3	3	2	0	0	1	0	0	13.50
Koeningstein, Brandon	3	3	2	2	1	2	0	0	0	0	6.00
Forfeit	0	0	0	0	0	0	0	2	0	0	0.00
Totals	271 2/3	226	115	88	77	260	11	33	4	4	2.92

Individual Statistics: 2009

BATTERS	AVG	R	H	AB	2B	3B	HR	RBI	SB	BB	SO	HP	SAC
Amann, Scott	0.260	12	13	50	1	0	0	5	11	15	18	1	3
Blackwell, Corey	0.125	3	2	16	0	0	0	0	2	5	8	0	1
Dawson, Travis	0.329	27	27	82	6	2	1	15	11	17	1	3	0
Degener, Mark	0.387	8	12	31	2	0	1	5	4	4	5	3	1
Elliot, Zack	0.324	17	33	102	6	1	4	29	4	8	21	8	2
Friederich, Jake	0.336	28	36	107	9	0	1	11	12	17	21	5	2
Hurst, Jake	0.284	17	21	74	1	0	2	21	3	14	10	0	1
LePere, Dusty	0.370	19	30	81	7	2	2	25	16	8	11	3	3
Miesner, Patrick	0.343	15	24	70	6	0	2	14	10	12	11	0	0
Ohlau, Craig	0.471	28	40	85	6	0	7	37	6	18	4	2	1
Thompson, Jordan	0.280	7	7	25	2	0	1	7	4	4	9	0	2
Thompson, Aaron	0.000	0	0	6	0	0	0	0	0	0	1	0	0
Thigpen, Andrew	0.339	21	19	56	5	1	5	14	4	5	13	7	0
Waeltz, Brandon	0.000	1	0	1	0	0	0	0	0	1	1	0	0
Wahlig, Sam	1.222	9	11	9	5	0	1	9	1	2	4	1	5
Wigger, Chas	1.600	15	24	15	6	0	2	11	8	7	18	6	0
Totals	0.369	227	299	810	62	6	29	203	96	137	156	39	21

PITCHERS	IP	H	R	ER	BB	SO	HP	W	L	SV	ERA
Amann, Scott	5	5	0	3	1	3	0	0	0	0	5.40
Blackwell, Corey	41 2/3	56	0	28	9	41	1	4	3	0	6.05
Jones, Ron	14	11	0	7	5	15	2	2	0	1	4.50
LePere, Dusty	2	0	0	0	1	5	0	1	0	0	0.00
Mueller, Mark	64 2/3	60	0	28	29	67	7	5	4	1	3.90
Musso, Brandon	67 1/3	59	0	19	16	71	6	6	4	1	2.54
Otten, Chris	29 1/3	41	0	20	11	25	2	3	0	1	6.14
Waeltz, Brandon	13	13	0	11	2	6	2	1	1	0	7.62
Totals	237	245	0	116	74	233	20	22	12	4	4.41

Individual Statistics: 2010

BATTERS	AVG	R	H	AB	2B	3B	HR	RBI	SB	BB	SO	HP	SAC
Miesner, Patrick	0.287	34	35	122	4	0	7	22	6	29	25	1	1
Hurst, Jake	0.313	31	42	134	11	1	4	35	1	20	22	3	4
Ohlau, Craig	0.293	26	34	116	7	0	6	35	4	24	9	5	2
Wigger, Chas	0.318	45	41	129	11	0	4	28	15	22	17	14	3
Schweirjohn, Jeff	0.391	35	50	128	13	0	5	48	6	31	13	2	2
Degener, Mark	0.380	31	46	121	10	0	4	30	3	8	17	5	4
Wahlig, Sam	0.365	31	50	137	8	1	3	33	8	7	16	3	2
LePere, Dusty	0.327	15	18	55	4	0	0	10	7	7	9	0	0
Hopkins, Gabe	0.281	11	18	64	3	0	0	4	3	9	15	0	1
Schmidt, Jonah	0.527	20	29	55	4	1	4	18	2	2	3	3	0
Blackwell, Corey	0.333	4	5	15	0	0	0	3	0	3	3	0	0
Schaake, Jake	0.357	7	5	14	0	0	1	1	2	2	0	1	0
Dunning, Nick	0.333	0	3	9	0	0	0	5	0	0	3	0	0
Otten, Chris	0.000	0	0	1	0	0	0	0	0	0	0	0	0
Wetzler, Lucas	0.000	0	0	0	0	0	0	0	0	1	1	0	0
Mueller, Mark	1.000	0	1	1	0	0	0	0	0	0	0	0	0
Weidmann, Zack	0.313	5	5	16	0	0	0	0	0	1	0	2	2
Dunningan, Brad	0.500	0	2	4	0	0	0	0	0	0	0	0	0
Day, Lucas	0.143	3	1	7	0	0	0	0	3	1	0	0	0
Galle, Clinton	0.217	2	5	23	0	0	0	2	1	3	10	0	0
Unger, Brian	0.500	1	1	2	0	0	0	0	0	0	0	0	0
Miller, Ian	0.625	3	5	8	1	0	1	3	1	0	0	0	0
Totals	0.341	304	396	1161	76	3	39	277	62	170	163	39	21

PITCHERS	IP	H	R	ER	BB	SO	HP	W	L	SV	ERA
Otten, Chris	29	41	31	14	12	8	1	3	1	0	4.34
Unger, Brian	11 1/3	14	9	6	2	8	2	1	0	2	4.76
Musso, Brandon	59 2/3	72	35	30	18	56	5	6	3	1	4.53
Mueller, Mark	63 2/3	57	28	17	29	62	9	8	0	0	2.40
Blackwell, Corey	62	87	47	34	17	48	4	7	3	1	4.94
Waeltz, Brandon	17 2/3	30	18	15	4	12	3	1	0	0	7.64
Phelps, Joe	6	8	2	0	5	3	1	1	0	0	0.00
Galle, Andy	49 2/3	61	37	27	17	45	2	3	3	0	4.89
Gradel, Jeff	3 2/3	8	5	5	2	3	0	1	0	0	12.27
Forfiet	0	0	0	0	0	0	0	1	0	0	0.00
Totals	302 2/3	378	212	148	106	245	27	32	10	4	4.40

Individual Statistics: 2011

BATTERS	AVG	R	H	AB	2B	3B	HR	RBI	SB	BB	SO	HP	SAC
Aycock, Aaron	0.364	11	16	44	2	0	0	7	10	5	5	1	0
Nowak, Brady	0.211	1	4	19	1	0	0	0	1	4	6	1	0
Wigger, Chas	0.245	8	12	49	3	0	1	7	4	5	11	6	3
Otten, Chris	0.000	0	0	0	0	0	0	0	0	0	0	0	0
Blackwell, Corey	0.500	1	2	4	0	0	0	2	1	3	2	0	3
Myers, Devon	0.361	13	26	72	6	1	0	9	8	11	12	4	1
Parkinson, David	0.217	4	5	23	0	0	0	1	2	1	12	1	1
Hopkins, Gabe	0.250	6	11	44	1	0	0	5	6	2	15	1	2
Hurst, Jake	0.211	17	19	90	3	0	1	14	6	23	7	1	2
Wetzler, Lucas	0.262	4	17	65	4	0	1	16	1	3	13	1	1
Degener, Mark	0.337	16	30	89	6	0	1	14	8	7	12	4	0
Vallandngham, Marshall	0.363	27	45	124	14	0	3	23	11	5	14	7	1
Dunning, Nick	0.338	18	27	80	6	0	1	15	3	17	15	0	5
Wahlig, Sam	0.372	21	32	86	8	0	1	12	8	5	12	4	4
Skaer, A.J.	0.167	2	1	6	0	0	0	0	0	0	4	0	0
Kunkel, Adam	0.268	17	22	82	3	0	0	10	10	13	12	4	4
Miesner, Patrick	0.290	6	9	31	1	1	1	6	2	11	5	3	3
Crutchfield, A.J.	0.333	1	2	6	0	0	0	0	2	0	1	0	0
Ohlau, Craig	0.250	3	5	20	2	0	0	3	1	7	1	1	0
Stepping, Nick	0.250	0	1	4	0	0	0	1	0	0	2	0	0
McGlynn, Pat	0.143	3	3	21	0	0	0	0	1	3	6	2	1
Degener, Jake	0.000	0	0	4	0	0	0	0	0	0	0	1	0
Bergheger, Jeremiah	1.000	3	3	3	1	0	0	0	1	2	0	0	0
Totals	0.302	182	292	966	61	2	10	145	86	127	167	42	31

PITCHERS	IP	H	R	ER	BB	SO	HP	W	L	SV	ERA
Galle, Andy	53 1/3	54	0	15	11	35	3	6	3	0	2.53
Nowak, Brady	13 2/3	14	0	5	7	12	4	1	0	0	3.29
Musso, Brandon	36 1/3	38	0	9	16	34	5	4	3	0	2.23
Waeltz, Brandon	18 2/3	17	0	8	8	22	2	0	1	0	3.86
Wine, Cale	13	9	0	3	6	13	2	0	1	1	2.08
Otten, Chris	10 1/3	12	0	4	2	6	0	0	0	0	3.48
Blackwell, Corey	47	49	0	10	12	41	2	4	3	1	1.91
Parkinson, David	8 1/3	12	0	5	7	8	5	1	1	0	5.40
Phelps, Joe	15 1/3	14	0	5	4	8	1	0	2	0	2.94
Mueller, Mark	2 1/3	7	0	2	2	3	0	0	1	0	7.73
Roberts, Otto	26 2/3	12	0	3	12	26	1	3	0	1	1.01
Cructhfield, A.J.	8	12	0	2	1	12	1	1	0	0	2.25
Totals	253	250	0	71	88	220	26	20	15	3	2.53

Individual Statistics: 2012

BATTERS	AVG	R	H	AB	2B	3B	HR	RBI	SB	BB	SO	HP	SAC
Ballard, Matt	0.250	16	14	56	1	0	0	3	14	11	7	3	2
Rheinicker, John	0.289	13	22	76	2	0	1	19	2	10	19	4	2
Kunkel , Adam	0.178	11	13	73	4	0	1	12	4	12	13	3	5
Blackwell, Corey	0.000	3	0	5	0	0	0	2	0	3	1	1	1
Aycock, Aaron	0.268	17	22	82	1	2	0	11	10	10	20	1	3
Campbell,	0.067	5	1	15	0	0	0	0	1	3	5	2	1
Dillenberger, Brad	0.284	41	38	134	6	0	1	16	13	13	12	2	3
Dunning , Nick	0.340	21	36	106	11	0	3	26	8	8	14	3	3
Winkel, Joe	0.298	4	14	47	5	2	0	16	3	6	5	1	3
Hamilton, Alex	0.333	4	6	18	0	0	0	2	0	3	3	1	0
Reinholz, John	0.281	15	18	64	5	1	0	11	0	4	14	0	0
Bergheger, Jeremiah	0.189	30	20	106	7	3	1	16	5	22	6	3	7
Wetzler, Lucas	0.219	8	16	73	2	0	0	10	3	11	11	3	2
Hopkins, Gabe	0.129	17	12	93	7	0	2	18	7	11	26	1	3
Haake, Steve	0.000	1	0	5	0	0	0	0	0	0	4	0	0
Crutchfield, A.J.	0.000	1	0	0	0	0	0	0	0	0	0	0	0
Musso, Brandon	0.000	7	0	7	0	0	0	1	0	2	3	1	1
Galle, Andy	0.000	0	0	6	1	0	0	1	0	1	2	0	0
Dunning, Justin	0.292	4	7	24	2	0	0	7	0	3	3	2	1
Klein, Jason	0.000	0	0	3	0	0	0	0	0	0	0	0	0
Totals	0.241	218	239	993	54	8	9	171	70	133	168	31	37

PITCHERS	IP	H	R	ER	BB	SO	HP	W	L	SV	ERA
Blackwell, Corey	45	46	0	5	12	47	4	6	1	0	1.00
Galle, Andy	30 1/3	35	0	9	4	22	2	2	3	0	2.67
Dunning, Nick	1	0	0	0	1	2	0	0	0	0	0.00
Dillenberger, D.J.	2 2/3	1	0	0	4	1	0	0	0	0	0.00
Mueller, Mike	59 2/3	60	0	16	13	54	8	4	2	0	2.41
Crutchfield, A.J.	34 1/3	36	0	14	8	21	3	4	1	2	3.67
Mueller, Mark	51 2/3	37	0	8	25	46	6	4	2	0	1.39
Musso, Brandon	43	39	0	7	9	51	6	5	1	0	1.47
Totals	267 2/3	254	0	59	76	244	29	25	10	2	1.98

Individual Statistics: 2013

BATTERS	AVG	R	H	AB	2B	3B	HR	RBI	SB	BB	SO	HP	SAC
Dunning, Nick	0.345	18	39	113	9	0	4	28	1	5	14	0	1
Dunning, Justin	0.402	22	43	107	10	1	6	38	3	8	17	5	1
Watson, L.J.	0.455	24	40	88	8	1	4	21	11	4	13	2	2
Bastein, Bryce	0.388	34	47	121	8	8	2	26	16	9	22	4	1
Dillenberger, Brad	0.273	30	36	132	10	1	1	12	10	10	11	2	1
Bergheger, Jeremiah	0.393	25	33	84	9	0	3	15	7	16	15	2	4
Hall, Ryan	0.355	23	33	93	4	1	1	10	10	7	9	1	2
Wetzler, Lucas	0.250	9	18	72	1	0	0	7	0	4	16	3	3
Friedrich, Jake	0.268	20	30	112	6	0	0	20	6	8	15	1	4
Winckel, Joe	0.366	4	15	41	3	1	1	9	3	3	5	2	0
Stoulph, Jordan	0.458	4	11	24	1	0	0	6	1	1	3	0	0
Hopkins, Gabe	0.129	4	4	31	0	0	0	2	3	10	11	0	3
Reinholz, John	0.200	3	6	30	0	0	0	2	1	1	6	0	0
Ruff, Ethan	0.412	7	7	17	2	0	0	6	4	0	3	0	0
Wittenaur, Alex	0.118	4	2	17	0	0	0	1	2	0	5	1	0
Ohlau, Craig	0.400	3	4	10	1	0	2	2	0	0	0	1	0
Connor, Chris	0.250	3	1	4	0	0	0	0	0	1	0	0	0
Totals	0.337	237	369	1096	72	13	24	205	78	87	165	24	22

PITCHERS	IP	H	R	ER	BB	SO	HP	W	L	SV	ERA
Blackwell, Corey	55	59	14	14	15	41	4	6	2	0	2.29
Musso, Brandon	61	39	15	5	19	58	1	7	2	2	0.74
Galle, Andy	44	42	12	10	10	30	3	7	1	2	2.05
Vanover, Brett	32	34	9	7	3	24	3	4	1	0	1.97
Mueller, Mark	31	23	13	10	8	29	3	2	3	0	2.90
Osborne, John	13	10	9	5	10	6	0	2	0	0	3.46
Wittenaur, Alex	5 1/3	7	3	3	1	4	0	1	0	0	5.07
Connor, Chris	3	1	4	2	5	3	1	0	1	0	6.00
Leible, Dan	2	1	0	0	2	2	0	0	0	0	0.00
Phelps, Joe	10	11	7	5	1	8	0	1	0	0	4.50
Anthony, J.	6	3	1	0	1	4	0	0	0	0	0.00
Totals	262 1/3	230	87	61	75	209	15	30	10	4	2.09

Individual Statistics: 2014

BATTERS	AVG	R	H	AB	2B	3B	HR	RBI	SB	BB	SO	HP	SAC
Dunning, Justin	0.321	16	34	106	8	0	7	30	6	7	21	8	3
Dunning, Nick	0.400	25	40	100	7	0	6	31	2	19	14	1	4
Friedrich, Jake	0.400	35	52	130	5	0	3	25	16	18	9	4	3
Ohlau, Craig	0.293	16	29	99	7	0	1	21	2	21	4	3	3
Dillenberger, Brad	0.271	22	29	107	4	0	0	11	9	15	13	6	2
Ruff, Ethan	0.430	35	58	135	1	0	0	17	35	9	5	0	0
Watson, L.J.	0.321	24	36	112	8	4	3	32	7	8	14	2	4
Bergheger, Jeremiah	0.289	21	26	90	7	1	1	11	6	21	5	1	1
Oquendo, Eduardo	0.378	19	28	74	2	0	0	12	5	7	12	2	3
Wittenaur, Alex	0.214	14	6	28	1	0	0	3	7	6	2	1	0
Wetzler, Lucas	0.237	1	18	76	2	0	0	10	0	5	6	2	4
Curtis, Drew	0.444	8	12	27	7	0	1	7	0	3	5	2	0
Hopkins, Gabe	0.222	6	2	9	0	0	0	3	5	2	6	0	0
Galle, Andy	0.000	0	0	3	0	0	0	0	0	0	0	0	0
Hall, Ryan	0.304	4	7	23	0	0	0	5	0	2	1	0	1
Miller, Ian	0.286	2	2	7	1	0	0	0	0	1	2	0	0
Totals	0.337	248	379	1126	60	5	22	218	100	144	119	32	28

PITCHERS	IP	H	R	ER	BB	SO	HP	W	L	SV	ERA
Crutchfield, A.J.	15 1/3	21	18	4	5	4	0	1	1	0	2.35
Auble, John	50	29	15	14	14	29	0	7	1	0	2.52
Musso, Brandon	71 1/3	49	20	11	18	53	0	8	0	2	1.39
Galle, Andy	52	58	13	5	15	29	1	5	2	0	0.87
Miller, Ian	31	22	28	6	15	26	2	4	0	0	1.74
Wittenaur, Alex	25	23	14	6	8	9	1	3	0	0	2.16
Rettig, Jeremy	12 2/3	21	15	9	5	13	2	4	0	0	6.39
Meyer, Blake	12 2/3	14	11	10	5	11	0	1	2	0	7.11
Dunning, Nick	8 2/3	1	0	0	3	6	0	0	0	2	0.00
Nunnery, Austin	3	3	0	0	0	4	0	0	0	0	0.00
Feldmann, Brendan	2	0	0	0	0	0	0	0	0	0	0.00
Totals	283 2/3	241	134	65	88	184	6	33	6	4	2.06

Individual Statistics: 2015

BATTERS	AVG	R	H	AB	2B	3B	HR	RBI	SB	BB	SO	HP	SAC
Albers, Johnny	0.100	4	2	20	0	0	0	3	0	1	6	1	2
Harrison, Jason	0.311	8	14	45	3	0	1	12	1	8	12	1	2
Ohlau, Craig	0.476	23	39	82	9	0	3	28	1	17	8	3	1
Wittenauer, Alex	0.192	12	5	26	1	0	0	4	6	0	7	1	0
Koester, Wade	0.321	20	25	78	6	0	1	12	1	10	8	1	1
Ruff, Ethan	0.429	29	42	98	3	0	0	16	21	10	5	0	4
Wilson, Ken	0.360	16	18	50	2	0	0	11	1	9	4	3	2
Miller, Jacob	0.500	1	1	2	0	0	0	0	0	0	1	0	1
Schimsa, Larry	0.450	28	45	100	13	0	7	42	0	11	13	1	3
Dillenberger, Brad	0.370	20	27	73	5	1	0	12	6	7	10	6	2
Schlecht, Garrett	0.447	15	34	76	7	0	3	29	2	10	8	2	2
Klaustermeier, Ben	0.000	1	0	2	0	0	0	0	0	0	1	0	1
Friedrich, Jake	0.356	31	31	87	5	2	3	16	3	8	6	2	4
Nunnery, Austin	0.000	0	0	3	0	0	0	0	0	0	0	0	0
McDaniel, Parker	0.091	2	1	11	1	0	0	1	0	2	6	0	0
Dunning, Nick	0.353	2	24	68	6	0	3	22	0	8	7	0	1
Dunning, Justin	0.300	10	24	80	5	0	2	20	2	12	12	5	3
Miller, Ian	0.000	0	0	3	0	0	0	0	0	0	2	0	0
Totals	0.367	222	332	904	66	3	23	228	44	113	116	26	29

PITCHERS	IP	H	ER	BB	SO	HP	W	L	SV	ERA
Auble, John	16 1/3	22	13	7	8	0	2	1	0	7.16
Wittenauer, Alex	11	17	11	4	5	1	1	0	0	9.00
Bearden, Ryan	6	4	3	3	5	0	1	0	0	4.50
Miller, Jacob	7	14	5	4	6	1	0	1	0	6.43
Tiefenthaler, Eric	27 2/3	24	6	11	15	1	3	0	0	1.95
Schlecht, Garrett	1/3	2	1	3	1	0	0	1	0	27.00
Klaustermeier, Ben	23 1/3	28	11	7	10	2	3	1	0	4.24
Nunnery, Austin	25 1/3	21	8	10	21	0	3	1	0	2.84
McDaniel, Parker	16 2/3	11	4	12	21	2	1	1	2	2.16
Dunning, Nick	12 2/3	19	4	5	9	0	1	0	3	2.84
Vogel, Corey	1 2/3	10	5	1	0	0	0	1	0	27.00
Rettig, Jeremy	43	36	9	16	24	3	5	0	0	1.88
Saeckels, Mark	13	7	1	14	8	2	1	1	0	0.69
Miller, Ian	7 1/3	11	4	9	6	1	1	1	0	4.91
Burris, Joey	5	3	0	2	0	2	1	0	0	0.00
Galle, Andy	7	7	0	2	4	0	1	0	0	0.00
Totals	223 1/3	236	85	110	143	15	24	9	5	3.43

Individual Statistics: 2016

BATTERS	AVG	R	H	AB	2B	3B	HR	RBI	SB	BB	SO	HP	SAC
Rettig, Jeremy	0.000	0	0	1	0	0	0	0	0	0	1	0	0
Vogel, Corey	0.000	0	0	2	0	0	0	0	0	0	1	0	0
Albers, Johnny	0.000	9	9	29	0	0	0	3	0	5	4	3	1
Perry, James	0.342	8	13	38	4	0	0	9	1	3	5	2	2
Kaiping, Cole	0.333	3	3	9	0	0	0	0	0	0	2	0	0
Ohlau, Craig	0.307	18	27	88	5	0	2	20	2	14	5	4	1
Wittenauer, Alex	0.353	20	30	85	4	1	0	3	5	7	13	3	0
Ruff, Ethan	0.377	33	43	114	4	2	0	8	25	12	11	0	2
Wilson, Ken	0.358	21	29	81	3	1	0	13	8	15	9	3	2
Wetzler, Lucas	0.411	20	37	90	8	1	1	20	3	5	10	1	1
Schimsa, Larry	0.400	2	2	5	0	0	1	2	0	1	0	6	0
Dillenberger, Brad	0.307	16	23	75	3	0	0	12	2	12	10	3	1
Schlecht, Garrett	0.266	17	29	109	5	2	2	23	4	9	18	0	3
Klaustermeier, Ben	0.250	1	2	8	1	0	0	7	0	0	3	0	2
King, Mason	0.214	3	3	14	1	0	0	4	3	4	1	0	0
Nunnery, Austin	0.000	0	0	2	0	0	0	0	0	0	2	2	0
Schambliss, Corey	0.214	6	6	28	1	1	0	1	0	3	9	0	1
Galle, Andy	0.000	0	0	2	0	0	0	0	0	0	1	0	0
Gleason, Dre	0.357	2	5	14	0	0	0	2	0	1	3	0	0
Baxmeyer, Keegan	0.263	4	10	38	2	1	0	5	0	3	8	0	0
Harrison, Jason	0.222	3	4	18	1	0	0	0	0	0	2	0	0
Totals	0.324	186	275	850	42	9	6	132	53	94	118	27	16

PITCHERS	IP	H	ER	BB	SO	HP	CG	W	L	SV	ERA
Rettig, Jeremy	44 2/3	61	25	7	8	1	1	4	3	0	5.04
Vogel, Corey	20	17	7	4	5	0	0	3	2	4	3.15
Hummel, Nick	46 2/3	54	27	4	6	2	3	5	2	0	5.21
Wittenauer, Alex	2 2/3	4	2	11	15	0	0	0	0	0	6.75
Thaggard, Noah	10	3	2	3	1	3	0	0	0	0	1.80
Klaustermeier, Ben	11 2/3	13	4	7	10	1	0	1	0	0	3.09
Nunnery, Austin	50 1/3	43	19	10	21	0	3	6	1	1	3.40
Galle, Andy	33 1/3	35	16	12	21	1	1	4	1	0	4.32
Totals	219 1/3	230	102	58	87	8	8	23	9	5	4.19

Individual Statistics: 2017

BATTERS	AVG	R	H	AB	2B	3B	HR	RBI	SB	BB	SO	HP	SAC
Shakeel, Fahd	0.667	4	2	3	1	0	0	0	1	1	0	1	0
Lubinski, Cory	0.520	21	26	50	9	2	6	28	2	6	5	0	1
Purcell, Chandler	0.443	31	39	88	8	1	6	37	2	16	3	2	3
Bender, Hayden	0.429	4	3	7	2	0	0	0	0	1	2	0	0
Krebs, Mitchell	0.421	31	45	107	7	5	1	21	4	5	4	3	1
Davis, Trevor	0.400	8	14	35	1	0	0	7	5	3	2	0	0
Ruff, Ethan	0.385	16	15	39	2	2	0	7	2	2	3	0	1
Ohlau, Craig	0.354	16	28	79	11	0	0	12	4	17	1	3	2
Wetzler, Lucas	0.348	19	40	115	6	1	1	27	4	12	13	0	2
Vogel, Corey	0.333	0	1	3	0	0	0	0	0	1	0	1	1
Henry, Tyler	0.333	1	1	3	0	0	0	0	0	1	0	0	0
Dillenberger, Brad	0.316	24	25	79	4	1	0	18	1	13	7	8	7
Wittenauer, Alex	0.315	21	23	73	3	1	0	8	3	8	8	4	3
Baxmeyer, Keegan	0.314	18	33	105	5	1	2	15	4	5	23	2	1
Hovey, Jordan	0.300	4	3	10	1	0	0	2	1	3	3	0	1
Jackson, Aaron	0.294	14	25	85	8	0	0	13	2	9	16	0	0
Hardin, Mike	0.279	11	12	43	2	0	1	6	2	7	8	0	1
Gaul, Pat	0.148	3	4	27	1	0	0	1	2	1	3	0	0
Albers, Johnny	0.000	19	22	72	3	0	0	8	1	10	11	6	3
Klaustermeier, Ben	0.000	0	0	2	0	0	0	1	0	1	2	0	0
Zielonko, Matt	0.000	0	0	8	0	0	0	0	0	0	8	0	0
Totals	0.422	131	172	408	41	10	13	112	20	51	20	9	8

PITCHERS	IP	H	ER	BB	SO	HP	CG	W	L	SV	ERA
Nunnery, Austin	4 1/3	1	0	3	4	1	0	0	0	1	0.00
Hummel, Nick	14	15	4	2	11	0	2	2	0	0	2.57
Jackson, Aaron	3 1/3	2	0	2	1	0	0	0	0	2	0.00
Davis, Trevor	2/3	1	0	0	2	0	0	0	0	0	0.00
Galle, Andy	63 2/3	56	19	10	45	2	6	8	2	0	2.69
Unger, Brian	3 1/3	5	1	0	3	0	0	1	0	0	2.70
Lubinski, Cory	6	2	2	3	1	0	0	0	0	0	3.00
Mauer, Ben	24	21	8	8	12	0	0	3	1	0	3.00
Thaggard, Noah	40	42	15	16	23	7	0	4	1	0	3.38
Klaustermeier, Ben	31 2/3	40	16	9	18	1	2	3	2	0	4.55
Dillenberger, D.J.	6 2/3	6	4	7	6	2	0	1	0	0	5.40
Rettig, Jeremy	38 2/3	40	25	13	26	2	2	6	1	0	5.82
Vogel, Corey	14 2/3	13	11	5	11	1	0	1	0	1	6.75
Totals	251	244	105	78	163	16	12	29	7	4	3.76

Individual Statistics: 2018

BATTERS	AVG	R	H	AB	2B	3B	HR	RBI	SB	BB	SO	HP	SAC
Rettig, Jeremy	0.000	2	0	1	0	0	0	0	0	0	1	0	0
Lubinski, Cory	0.349	16	29	83	3	3	3	21	1	4	8	0	1
Albrecht, Quinn	0.348	13	24	69	2	0	1	11	2	14	15	5	0
Ohlau, Craig	0.350	5	7	20	4	0	0	5	1	3	3	1	0
Mueth, Logan	0.341	19	31	91	4	0	0	12	10	13	18	1	2
Hardin, Mike	0.230	9	14	61	0	0	2	15	5	9	8	5	1
Ruff, Ethan	0.412	34	49	119	6	2	0	16	30	7	6	6	2
Wetzler, Lucas	0.364	15	28	77	6	1	0	12	3	5	8	2	2
Thaggard, Noah	0.000	0	0	2	0	0	0	0	0	0	1	2	0
Dillenberger, Brad	0.246	11	15	61	0	0	0	4	1	21	6	8	0
Purcell, Chandler	0.298	10	28	94	5	0	0	15	4	6	5	0	3
Klaustermeir, Ben	0.000	1	0	3	0	0	0	0	0	1	0	0	0
Yancik, Andrew	0.239	10	11	46	1	0	2	7	1	10	17	0	1
Davis, Trevor	0.214	7	12	56	1	1	0	10	2	4	14	1	1
Bender, Hayden	0.000	1	0	3	0	0	0	0	0	1	1	2	0
Galle, Andy	0.308	1	4	13	1	0	1	5	0	1	3	0	0
Baxmeyer, Keegan	0.376	14	32	85	2	0	1	10	4	4	16	1	0
Krebs, Mitchell	0.200	20	3	15	0	1	0	2	1	1	0	1	0
Rushing, Lee	0.000	0	0	2	0	0	0	0	0	0	0	0	0
Totals	0.317	113	182	901	25	6	6	92	52	55	67	20	8

PITCHERS	IP	H	ER	BB	SO	HP	CG	W	L	SV	ERA
Rettig, Jeremy	60	64	32	33	59	5	2	6	4	0	3.73
Vogel, Cory	11	14	9	4	9	0	0	1	2	0	5.73
Lubinski, Cory	2	1	0	0	0	0	0	0	0	0	0.00
Shill, Marshall	27	16	6	8	26	1	0	4	1	0	1.56
Killian, Brenden	15	21	11	2	14	3	0	1	1	0	5.13
Thaggard, Noah	30	39	25	14	14	2	0	0	3	0	5.83
Klaustermeir, Ben	18	19	12	9	11	1	0	0	1	0	4.67
Yancik, Andrew	38	32	7	10	38	3	1	3	1	1	1.29
Davis, Trevor	1	1	0	0	0	0	0	0	0	0	0.00
Wolf, Joe	8	14	9	4	6	0	0	1	0	0	7.87
Galle, Andy	5	2	0	1	1	0	0	0	0	0	0.00
Hebel, Tyler	6	13	11	9	4	0	0	0	0	0	12.83
Jackson, Aaron	5	6	4	3	3	0	0	0	1	0	5.60
Kohrman, Trevor	6	3	2	4	1	2	0	0	1	0	2.33
Totals	232	245	128	101	186	17	3	16	15	1	4.00

Individual Statistics: 2019

BATTERS	AVG	R	H	AB	2B	3B	HR	RBI	SB	BB	SO	HP	SAC
Sutton, Dusty	0.167	1	1	6	0	0	0	0	0	1	2	0	0
Mayberry, Holden	0.000	0	0	1	0	0	0	0	0	0	0	0	0
Goss, Adam	0.500	4	4	8	1	0	0	3	1	2	1	0	0
Krebs, Mitchell	0.333	19	33	99	4	0	0	14	2	7	2	1	1
Burns, Kade	0.250	9	16	64	1	0	0	5	2	16	13	1	2
Wade, Alex	0.200	6	7	35	2	0	0	5	0	5	14	1	0
Zimmer, Bailey	0.321	12	17	53	5	0	0	13	0	6	15	2	0
Mueth, Logan	0.292	12	19	65	3	1	0	15	1	5	9	2	1
Kueper, Tyler	0.250	0	1	4	0	0	0	0	0	2	1	1	1
Ruff, Ethan	0.342	25	40	117	7	0	0	15	23	10	11	0	3
Ward, Mike	0.237	17	18	76	1	0	2	9	3	22	20	8	2
Jones, Jared	0.377	13	23	61	2	0	2	15	0	5	12	5	2
Davis, Trevor	0.188	11	9	48	2	0	0	6	1	6	8	0	1
Dillenberger, Brad	0.328	9	21	64	2	0	0	9	0	13	8	1	3
Hendrickson, Reid	0.200	0	1	5	0	0	0	15	0	1	2	0	0
Seiler, Zack	0.203	10	15	74	2	0	0	15	1	2	7	5	1
Jausel, Grant	0.000	0	0	0	0	0	0	0	1	0	0	0	1
Kueper, Tyler	0.125	1	1	8	0	0	0	0	0	2	5	0	0
Miller, D.J.	0.471	7	16	34	2	0	0	4	1	0	4	2	0
Baxmeyer, Keegan	0.367	16	29	79	5	0	2	13	5	10	12	0	0
Totals	0.301	172	271	901	39	1	6	141	41	115	146	29	18

PITCHERS	IP	H	ER	BB	SO	W	L	SV	ERA
Thaggard, Noah	2.00	0	0	0	3	0	0	0	0.00
Mayberry, Holden	0.00	0	0	0	0	0	0	0	0.00
Parkinson, Nathan	2.33	2	1	0	2	0	0	0	3.00
Rettig, Jeremy	10.34	15	7	8	9	1	0	0	4.74
Burns, Kade	1.00	1	0	0	1	0	0	0	0.00
Zimmer, Bailey	3.33	11	11	3	5	0	0	0	23.12
Stidham, Parker	44.66	45	22	6	42	4	4	0	3.45
Davis, Trevor	25.33	31	10	6	18	3	0	0	2.76
Erger, Dalton	8.00	8	4	5	6	1	0	0	3.50
Dillenberger, Brad	0.67	0	0	0	0	0	0	0	0.00
Hendrickson, Reid	61.00	45	13	27	62	6	1	1	1.49
Klaustermeir, Ben	9.00	18	7	1	3	0	1	0	5.44
Jausel, Grant	26.00	29	16	11	24	2	2	0	4.31
Garza, Brandon	41.33	46	27	22	34	5	3	0	4.57
Totals	235.00	251	118	89	209	22	11	1	3.52

Waterloo Buds

Waterloo Baseball Club, Inc. (APPLICATION)

1. Name _____
   (Last)   (Middle)   (First)

2. Address _____
   (Street)   (State)   (Zip)

3. Age _____ Phone (___) (___) (___)

4. Number of years a member of the Buds _____.

5. Were did you play College or Professional Baseball.
   _____

6. Below is a copy of contract with the Waterloo Baseball Club, Inc. while playing in the Mon-Clair League

7. The Waterloo Baseball Club, Inc. does not have any medical or accident Insurance. Please note with your signature.
   X (Sign) _____.

8. Attached is a copy of release requested by Koerber Dist. Co. Please sign, and return. _____

9. You assigned uniform number _____.

PLAYER CONTRACT
MON-CLAIR BASEBALL LEAGUE, Inc.

The undersigned player agrees to play with the ....WATERLOO Baseball Club and will not hold that Club, its sponsor, the owner of property on which games are played, or the Mon-Clair Baseball League, Inc. responsible for any injuries incurred by him. It is further recognized that the undersigned player shall not sign a player contract with any other Club in the Mon-Clair Baseball League, Inc., until he has obtained his release from the undersigned manager, notice of such release to be received by League headquarters prior to signing of new contract.

NOTE — Signing of contract by person other than designated player shall void contract and make designated player ineligible for participation with team, and shall subject team to forfeiture of any games in which said player participates.

_____
(Player's Signature)

_____
(If player is of minor age, parent or guardian shall also sign)

_____
(Manager's Signature)

Please PRINT Player's Name on Reverse Side

Waterloo Buds original contract and application

BASEBALL
THORBURG ACRES
SUNDAY, JUNE 17, 2:30 p.m.
WATERLOO BUDS
vs.
MAEYSTOWN STAGS
Refreshments Available

Everyone Welcome

No Admission Charge

Columbia Monroe County Clarion, May 27, 1964

WATERLOO BUDS

BASEBALLL QUEEN DANCE
SATURDAY. JUNE 6
8:00 to 12:00
V. F. W. Hall
WATERLOO

CORONATION 9:30 P. M.

Music by Stan Nelson Orchestra

BUY YOUR TICKETS FROM ONE OF THESE CANDIDATES:

CONNIE CORTNER	ELLEN NOBBE
SHERYL LUHR	JUDY SIEGFRIED
SUSAN METZGER	PAT TOAL

Columbia Monroe County Clarion, May 27, 1964

Columbia Drops Season Opener To Waterloo

The Columbia Legionnaires dropped the opening game of the Mon-Clair League season to the Waterloo Bubs, 9-4, here Sunday afternoon.

Waterloo opened the scoring with two runs in the third but Columbia came back with one in the fourth. Waterloo added two more in the sixth, before Columbia came up with three runs in the eighth. In the ninth Waterloo runners crossed the plate four times to ice up the game.

The game was rather close throughout the contest until the ninth when Hoffmann opened the inning for Waterloo by getting on base as the result of an error. Dillinger then was hit by a pitch. Madd advanced the runners with a sacrifice bunt and Rahn walked to fill the bases. A double by Fults scored two runs and a single by Braun produced two more.

Columbia scored one in the fourth and three in the eighth in which they had only one hit but were helped by three walks, an error and a passed ball.

Columbia committed three errors in the game against two for Waterloo.

Ralph Mathews led Columbia's attack with a triple and a single. Rehg, Roessler, Barker and Holden rounded out the hitting with a single each.

Dick Dillinger was the winning pitcher although he got help from Fr. Ed Hustedde in the eighth while Bob Roessler took the loss.

In other games:

Valmeyer over Dupo, 5-1, East St. Louis beat Fults, 11-1, O'Fallon topped Lebanon, 9-2, St. Libory beat Tilden 4-0 and Millstadt took a 4-3 decision from Belleville.

MON-CLAIR BASEBALL LEAGUE STANDINGS
Mon-Clair Division

Team	Won	Lost
Waterloo	1	0
E. St. Louis	1	0
Valmeyer	1	0
Fults	0	1
Dupo	0	1
Columbia	0	1

Greater County Division

Team	Won	Lost
Millstadt	1	0
O'Fallon	1	0
St. Libory	1	0
Belleville	0	1
Lebanon	0	1
Tilden	0	1

Next Sunday's Schedule

Fults at Waterloo, Valmeyer at E. St. Louis, Columbia at Dupo, St. Libory at Millstadt, Belleville at Lebanon, O'Fallon at Tilden (Sparta).

Columbia Monroe County Clarion, May 12, 1966

1966

WILLIAM H. MOHR, President
331 S. Missouri Ave.
Belleville, Illinois
Phone: AD. 3-1005

WILLIS T. KOENIGSMARK, Vice-Pres.
403 Hanover Ave.
Waterloo, Illinois
Phone: 939-6511

NORMAN RUTTER, Sec.-Treas.
St. Libory, Illinois
Phone: 768-6160

MON-CLAIR BASEBALL LEAGUE

Serving the
Southwestern Illinois Independent Baseball Area

COMBINED MON-CLAIR, GREATER COUNTY
BASEBALL LEAGUES OPEN PLAY MAY 8

The Mon-Clair Baseball League, consisting of the newly-merged
Mon-Clair and Greater County Baseball Leagues, will open its 1966
season Sunday, May 8, when all 12 of the participating teams will
be in action.

The league will be divided into two divisions. Competing as
Mon-Clair Division teams are Columbia, Dupo, East St. Louis, Fults,
Valmeyer and Waterloo. The Greater County Division will consist of
Belleville, Lebanon, Millstadt, O'Fallon, St. Libory and Tilden.
Each team will play clubs in its own division twice and oppose
teams of the other division once, for a total of 16 games. Division
champions will be recognized and, at the conclusion of the regular
schedule, the top three teams in final standings of each division
will participate in playoffs for the league championship.

Four of the clubs will have new managers this year. The fledgling
pilots are Arnold Stechmesser at Columbia; Robert Mason, Dupo; Ray
Brooks, Lebanon, and Earl Roy of Valmeyer. Returning for another
year at the helm of their respective teams are Ferd Beiler, Belleville; Joe Cook, East St. Louis; Gerald Fausz, Fults; Wpl Smoth,
Millstadt; Jack Waltman, O'Fallon; Elmer Lange, St. Libory; Tom
Kirkman, Tilden, and Vern Moehrs, Waterloo.

Columbia, Dupo, East St. Louis, Fults, Millstadt, Valmeyer and
Waterloo were Mon-Clair League participants in 1965, while Belleville,
O'Fallon, Tilden and St. Libory were listed as Greater County League
members. Millstadt captured both the season and playoff championships in the Mon-Clair last year, and O'Fallon duplicated that feat
in the Greater County circuit. Lebanon was in the St. Louis Tandy
League in 1965.

An all-star game, pitting division against division, will be
played at Columbia Sunday, July 3. The season, prior to playoffs,
is scheduled to end August 28.

Bill Mohr of Belleville, who formerly headed both the Mon-Clair
and Greater County circuits, is president of the merged league.
Willis Koenigsmark of Waterloo is vice-president, and Norm Rutter
of St. Libory is secretary-treasurer. The league statistician is
John Goodman of O'Fallon.

The complete schedule is as follows:

(See enclosed schedule.)

OFFICERS

PRESIDENT—William H. Mehr, 321 S. Missouri Ave., Belleville, Ill.; phone Belleville ADams 3-1055.

VICE-PRESIDENT—Willis T. Koenigsmark, 405 Morrison Ave., Waterloo, Ill.; phone Waterloo 939-6311.

SECRETARY-TREASURER—Norman Rutter, St. Libory, Ill.; phone St. Libory 768-2160.

STATISTICIAN—John Goodman, 306 S. Smiley, O'Fallon, Ill.; phone O'Fallon East Office, ME. 2-4691.

1966 MEMBERS

BELLEVILLE—Manager, Ford Sailor, 12 N. 39th St., Belleville, Ill.; phone Belleville AD. 3-8834.

COLUMBIA—Manager, Arnold Stechmesser, R. R. 2, Columbia, Ill.; phone Columbia BU. 1-0351.

DUPO—Manager, Robert Mason, Sr., 512 S. Main St., Dupo, Ill.; phone Dupo 286-3298.

EAST ST. LOUIS—Manager, Joseph Cook, 828 N. 71st St., East St. Louis, Ill.; phone East St. Louis EX. 7-7771.

FULTS—Manager, Gerald Feuss, Fults, Ill.; phone Fults 458-6587.

LEBANON—Manager, Ray Brooks (contact Louis Edison, 316 North St., Lebanon, Ill.; phone Lebanon KE. 7-2485).

MILLSTADT—Manager, Syl Muwih, 512 W. Mill St., Millstadt, Ill.; phone Millstadt OR. 6-5771.

O'FALLON—Manager, John Feltman, R. R. 1, O'Fallon, Ill.; phone O'Fallon ME. 2-3516.

ST. LIBORY—Manager, Elmer Lange, St. Libory, Ill.; phone St. Libory 768-2802.

TILDEN—Manager, Tom Kirkman, Tilden, Ill.; phone Tilden 587-3532.

VALMEYER—Manager, Earl Roy, P. O. Box 199, Valmeyer, Ill.; phone Valmeyer 935-3279.

WATERLOO—Manager, Verneil Moehrs, 302 Columbia Ave., Waterloo, Ill.; phone Waterloo 939-7779.

REPORTING GAMES

After each game, home team shall call Waterloo 939-7519 no later than 6:00 p. m. day of game, unless game time goes past 6:00 — then call at completion of game. Person calling is to give score by innings, total runs, hits, errors, complete batteries, along with leading hitters and highlights. IN ADDITION, the home team, within 24 hours of completion of game, shall send to the League Statistician a boxscore report of game, listing players (first and last names) for both teams, their times at bat, runs and hits; and,

1966 SCHEDULE

SUNDAY—

May 8—Waterloo at Columbia; Dupo at Valmeyer; East St. Louis at Fults; Millstadt at Belleville; Lebanon at O'Fallon; Tilden at St. Libory.

May 15—Valmeyer at E. St. Louis; Fults at Waterloo; Columbia at Dupo; O'Fallon at Tilden (Sparta); St. Libory at Millstadt; Belleville at Lebanon.

May 22—Waterloo at Millstadt; Columbia at Belleville; Dupo at Lebanon; Valmeyer at O'Fallon; E. St. Louis at Tilden (Sparta); Fults at St. Libory.

May 29—Dupo at Waterloo; E. St. Louis at Columbia; Fults at Valmeyer; Millstadt at Lebanon; Tilden at Belleville; St. Libory at O'Fallon.

June 5—Belleville at Waterloo; Lebanon at Columbia; O'Fallon at Dupo; Tilden at Valmeyer; St. Libory at E. St. Louis; Millstadt at Fults.

June 12—Columbia at Fults; Waterloo at Valmeyer; Dupo at E. St. Louis; Belleville at St. Libory; Millstadt at O'Fallon; Lebanon at Tilden (Sparta).

June 19—Waterloo at Lebanon; Columbia at O'Fallon; E. St. Louis at Millstadt; Dupo at Tilden (Sparta); Valmeyer at St. Libory; Fults at Belleville.

June 26—E. St. Louis at Waterloo; Fults at Dupo; Valmeyer at Columbia; Tilden at Millstadt; St. Libory at Lebanon; O'Fallon at Belleville.

July 3—All-Star Game at Columbia (Mon-Clair Division vs. Greater County Division).

July 10—Columbia at Waterloo; Valmeyer at Dupo; Fults at E. St. Louis; Belleville at Millstadt; O'Fallon at Lebanon; St. Libory at Tilden (Sparta).

July 17—E. St. Louis at Valmeyer; Waterloo at Fults; Dupo at Columbia; Tilden at O'Fallon; Millstadt at St. Libory; Lebanon at Belleville.

July 24—O'Fallon at Waterloo; Tilden at Columbia; St. Libory at Dupo; Millstadt at Valmeyer; Belleville at E. St. Louis; Lebanon at Fults.

July 31—Waterloo at Dupo; Columbia at E. St. Louis; Valmeyer at Fults; Lebanon at Millstadt; Belleville at Tilden (Sparta); O'Fallon at St. Libory.

Aug. 7—St. Libory at Waterloo; Millstadt at Columbia; Belleville at Dupo; Lebanon at Valmeyer; O'Fallon at E. St. Louis; Tilden at Fults.

Aug. 14—Fults at Columbia; Valmeyer at Waterloo; E. St. Louis at Dupo; St. Libory at Belleville; O'Fallon at Millstadt; Tilden at Lebanon.

Aug. 21—Waterloo at Tilden (Sparta); Columbia at St. Libory; Dupo at Millstadt; Valmeyer at Belleville; E. St. Louis at Lebanon; Fults at O'Fallon.

Aug. 28—Waterloo at E. St. Louis; Dupo at Fults; Columbia at Valmeyer; Millstadt at Tilden (Sparta); Lebanon at St. Libory; Belleville at O'Fallon.

In the pitchers' summary, the pitchers used by both teams, innings pitched by each, hits, runs and earned runs given up, strikeouts and bases on balls, also designating the winning and losing pitchers. Non-compliance with either of these provisions shall result, in a fine of FIVE DOLLARS.

Inaugural Mon-Clair League Memo/Schedule 1966

Waterloo Buds 1975

Waterloo Buds 1978

Jimmy Wahlig 1978

"The biggest day of my minor league career was on August 19, 1982. That was the day my daughter was born. I struck out three times and I popped out, but I couldn't have cared less."
—*Jimmy Wahlig*

RICK KEEFE (left) and MIKE ROY
Voted Co-MVP's for 1982 Season

CARL BRAUN receives a watch from
Manager Vernell Moehrs upon retirement after 22 years of service
to the Waterloo Buds Baseball club.

Waterloo Buds program clipping 1983

Waterloo Buds

1983 SEASON

Official Souvenir
SCORE CARD

Mon-Clair League
Gibault Athletic Field
Waterloo, Illinois

KOERBER DISTRIBUTING CO., Waterloo

CLYDESDALE HORSE at Anheuser-Busch Brewery entrance in Busch Gardens, Tampa, Florida.

Waterloo Buds official souvenir scorecard 1983

MIKE WIRTH (left) and DAVE DILLENBERGER (right) led the Buds in hitting and in pitching respectively last season. Wirth was the batting champion and Dillenberger, the E.R.A. leader.

Waterloo Buds program clipping 1984

MON-CLAIR CHAMPS
1983
Left Back K.Lueht,W.Fehrenz,M.Roy,D.Kreher,M.Wirth,S.Haberl,D.Dillenberger,J.Adamson
R.Matzenbacher-Left Front-John Wahlig,M.Ludwig,M.Doerr,JimWahlig,J.Roy,C.Mernich
C.Vetrian,L.Fulte,Vern Moehrs(Mgr.)

Waterloo Buds 1983

Scott Haberl
Buds
MVP 1983

Scott Haberl 1983

January 29, 1984

Dear Bud Supporter:

Now that we are in the middle of the "Hot Stove League", we would like to take this opportunity to again thank you for your continued support, and also to bring you up to date on the past baseball season.

The Buds in 1983 had one of the finest seasons this area has ever seen. Our 49-6 overall record included winning streaks of 13 and 31 games and a 35 and 1 record from July 1st until Labor Day. A team batting average of .370 may have had something to do with that record as did Mike Wirth's win of the Mon-Clair League Batting title, Dave Dillenberger's win of the League E.R.A. title and Scott Haberl's 22 home runs. Scott was voted the team M.V.P.

Highlights of the season, in more or less chronological order, included the Championship of the Cahokia Fountain of Youth Classic, in which Bob Matzenbacher was named M.V.P. and the Championship of the Valmeyer Holiday Tournament, where Jim Wahlig was M.V.P. Observers say the Buds 3-1 victory over Belleville in the final game at Valmeyer was one of the best games seen in the area in years.

Following the Valmeyer tournament, the Buds went on to win the Monroe Division of the league, and then won four straight for the league playoff championship. Along the way, Lon Fulte recorded his 1000'th career hit, a phenomenal achievement; next year, he should become the Buds' all-time career hit leader.

This upcoming season could be even finer as all starters are returning, with the notable exception of Mike Roy, who will be playing in a collegiate league in the East. Hopefully, young John Wahlig, Jim Wahlig's younger brother, can take up some of the slack left by the absence of Mike's big bat.

We are hoping to see you at many of next year's games; we know you won't be disappointed in the quality of play. Thanks again for your continued support.

Sincerely,

Waterloo Buds supporter letter 1984

Sept 3, 1986 - Memo #1

I would like spare a few moments of happiness with the 1986 Bud players. It was a different group than in past years, it was a "gas house gang" to say the least. If you will look at the stats you will also find that we had a dedicated group with the number at bats in a limited group. This tells me that not many players missed ball games. Congraduation on a great reason (Triple Crown) Div champs, Play-off champs and Valmeyer Tourment. I had a long conversation with Lou Fulte the last of the conor stone of the Best Bud teams, and he is going to play again next reason. 1987. Without Lou's help that he has given the team not in so much with his playing ability but the help behind the seam. "Such as, treasurer, helping get the diamond ready to play, picking up equipment at the end of the games, and helping me to remember the thing that I forget. He peabovy knows me better than I know myself. "That being up a point." I am hoping that in 1987 that many of you older players take on some of these responsiblities.

I am aware that people that have to travel a distance could not help get the diamond ready to play on, but the things that I don't understanding, are some of our ears so big that it would be neither us to put away base, rake the mound and help sack the equipment, also, we are in such a big hurry to leave the diamond after the game to get to the parking lot, but we are not in that big a hurry to get to the parking lot before the game. (Just a few things above that I mentioned piss me off, I personally feel that Lonnie and I work very harder to keep a well run winning organization. One other thing that pisses me off is to hear some one talking about that fucking slow-pitch Donkey Ball if your back with the team next year don't even mention the words "Donkey-ball." I feel very strong that some time in an athletic life that a decision has to be made with priority on which game you want to play. I'll personal feel that everybody was great in letting me know when there was a problem and they were going to be late at other commitments.

I guess the the Old Crab ass got lots of things off his chest after the season and why not, don't mess up a good ball club during the season. I am looking forward to 1987 with great enthusiasm to try and bring our 5th straight championship. to Waterloo, the place were real baseball is played. We have a great group of physically talented player, but with the 5st a stake I wonder how much mental talent we have, I would like to think much. It will be fun to see all the great talent play next season under some pressure, from the fresh and other team because they will be after our ass.

As you well know our banquet will be November 1, 1987 starting at 6:30 Millston V.F.W. Please let me know if your are planning to attend. I'll will need to know by October 20, if you are planning to attend if I don't hear from you by then I will assume you will not be in attendance "Bull shit be there". If I don't hear from you by Jan 1, 1987 you will again be a Bud, from now till Jan 1, 1987 you are a free agent.

I have started, already putting the 1987 team together, have had several quality player enquire about playing with the Buds. I spoke to my east coast scout Craig Vattraw, Jon Adamson, Northern scout Duk Dillinger and Southern Scout Dennis Truck, all have given me people to talk to:

Lonnie reported to me that we ended the season after all bill were paid with $45.⁰⁰ in the treasurer, so men we will asking you next year for some help with our program. I personally feel that each player could sell 5 ads. (Early next year we will have an organization meeting at that time Lon and I will have a detail plan of raising funds.

I feel that I have cover most everything from 1986 till Jan 1, 1987. All of you guys enjoy this years championship because next April we will have to do it all ~~all~~ over again. Have a great winter lets stay in touch. Also if there are things that might help our program please feel free to tell me.

Sincerely yours
Old Crab Ass.

Waterloo Buds memo 1986

Valmeyer catcher Wayne Rohlfing looks to first base after tagging out Waterloo's Jeff Kaiser

Belleville News-Democrat, July 7, 1986

ST. LOUIS POST-DISPATCH

Thurs., Sept. 4, 1986

Buds Didn't Meet Their Waterloo

Baseball

By Steve Overbey

Vern Moehrs knew the answer. He just liked asking the question.

The Waterloo Buds manager was going over his team's successes, which include four straight Mon-Clair League championships.

"I guess you could call this a dynasty, couldn't you?"

Yes, yes, yes, and yes.

The Buds proved once again that they were the best amateur baseball team on the East Side by waltzing to their ninth Mon-Clair League title in the last 14 years. Moehrs club easily disposed of East Alton 8-3 and 16-0 in the first two games of the best-of-three championship series Sunday and Monday.

Waterloo finished the season with an eye-popping 44-5 overall record. It won 22 of 26 league games.

"We don't like to brag but we think we've got something special going here," Moehrs said.

The Buds have had something special going for years now. Winning four straight titles isn't new to the Buds; they also pulled the feat from 1973 through 1976. They have won the Monroe Division championship the past five seasons and six times in the last seven years. Only once in this decade has Waterloo failed to reach the championship series.

And it appears the string of success is not going to be broken in the near future.

"We have what I consider a young team," said the 52-year-old Moehrs. "I don't expect us to have any off years soon."

Moehrs says his team's tradition is what keeps it on top. Good players come looking for good losers and no Mon-Clair team has been more successful than the Buds.

"It's easy to get players when you're winning," Moehrs said. "They hear about us and they come to us looking for a place to play."

Actually the Waterloo lineup has remained about the same the past few years. A perfect blend of veterans and college-age talent has kept the Buds on top.

It was that mix that helped Waterloo hold off upset-minded East Alton over the weekend.

East Alton knocked off Millstadt, the St. Clair Division regular-season champ, in the second round of the playoffs. The Stags entered the championship series with thoughts of another upset. Those hopes were quickly dashed when Waterloo beat East Alton ace Joe Silkwood in the series opener at Waterloo.

First baseman Lou Fulte, 39, ripped three hits, including a home run, to pace the winning attack. His fifth-inning single drove in Dave Dillemberger with the go-ahead run.

Pitcher Rick Keefe, 36, picked up the win by tossing 3½ innings of one-run, two-hit relief. He fanned seven.

After beating East Alton's best pitcher Sunday, the Buds had little trouble Monday at East Alton. Waterloo scored six times in the second inning to erase an early 3-2 deficit. Jim Wahlig and Scott Thies pounded four hits each to pace a 19-hit attack. Once again, Keefe picked up the win in relief. He went the final 3½ innings.

"It was really a disaster," Moehrs said. "Even winning a game like that wasn't too much fun."

The Buds dodged a bullet when Sought upset Valmeyer in the first round of the Monroe Division playoffs. Valmeyer was the only team to beat the Buds more than once this year, winning three of four meetings.

Waterloo split a doubleheader with Valmeyer the final weekend of the regular season to clinch first place. But third-place Sought knocked off Valmeyer in the playoffs 3-2. The Buds then blasted Sought 17-6.

"I think Valmeyer was the second-best team in the league," Moehrs said.

Waterloo used a well-balanced attack to hammer its opposition. All nine regulars hit over .300 with third baseman Jim Wahlig (.458) and shortstop Mike Ray (.440) leading the way. Ray is a former Minnesota Twins farmhand. Jim Wahlig was drafted by the Toronto Blue Jays. Second baseman John Wahlig (.387) and outfielders Scott Haberl (.349) and Jeff Kaiser (.349) were not far behind. First sacker Dillemberger (.336), catcher Meri Doerr (.322) and outfielder Thies (.323) round out the hard-hitting lineup.

Pitchers Roger Ferguson (11-0), Keefe (12-3) and Warren Fehrenz (8-3) handled most of the mound chores.

"There wasn't one player that didn't contribute," Moehrs said. "Everybody did something."

(Steve Overbey is a free-lance writer.)

St. Louis Post-Dispatch, September 4, 1986

Top Row: Mgr. V. Moehrs, C. Moehrs, M. Schulte, M. Roy, F. Schelier, M. Wirth, W. Fahrenz, J. Kaiser, Jim Wahlig.

Bottom: J. Baxmeyer, T. Fulte, R. Mosbacher, C. Price, D. Worth, D. McQuary, S. Thies, John Wahlig.

Waterloo Buds 1990

Clay Moehrs 1990

Mon-Clair All-Star Game 1990

Jimmy Wahlig 1992

Lawrence "Buck" Riva 2002

Waterloo Buds 2004

Rev. Edwin Hustedde, 74; former Gibault principal

6/10/04

BY KIMBERLY RATLIFF
Of the Post-Dispatch

The Rev. Edwin H. Hustedde, an ordained priest and former principal of Gibault High School in Waterloo, died Sunday (June 6, 2004) at Barnes-Jewish Hospital in St. Louis. He was 74 and a longtime resident of Valmeyer.

Father Hustedde was born in Breese to Edwin and Cecilia Hustedde. He was called to the priesthood at the age of 15 and graduated from St. Henry's Preparatory Seminary School in Belleville. He was ordained in 1956 at St. Mary of the Lake Seminary in Mundelein, Ill., and began his work at Sts. Peter and Paul Parish in Waterloo.

A few years later, he was named superintendent of Sts. Peter and Paul High School. He joined Gibault High School in Waterloo as principal in 1967. He served at the school for more than 15 years and later was named director of development.

"Edwin had an intense passion for education and dreamt someday of educating young people," said a sister, Margaret Beckmann of Breese. "He was the one who tried the new flexible modular schedule in helping students learn."

For a time, Father Hustedde was the Gibault baseball coach and was credited with helping to keep the school's athletic program afloat despite a shortage of funds.

He was also a fine southpaw pitcher and was known as the "pitching priest" for the Waterloo Buds amateur baseball team. For many years, he was said to have the best curve ball in Monroe County.

In 1993, he began serving

Hustedde
"Pitching priest"

as pastor of both St. Mary's Catholic Church in Valmeyer and Immaculate Conception Catholic Church in Madonnaville. He held both positions until his death.

"Edwin's greatest gift was the gift of knowledge, and he touched a lot of lives with his direction, caring and vision," said Beckmann. "He was a quiet man who always lived the way of the gospel."

Bishop Wilton D. Gregory will preside at the Eucharist of Christian burial at 11 a.m. today at Sts. Peter and Paul Catholic Church in Waterloo. Burial will be in St. Dominic Catholic Cemetery in Breese.

Father Hustedde is survived by another sister, Mary Theresa Molitor of O'Fallon; and a brother, Richard Hustedde of Breese.

Memorial contributions may be made to Lawlor Funeral Home, c/o Edwin H. Hustedde Scholarship Fund, 218 South Metter Avenue, Columbia, Ill., 62236.

St. Louis Post-Dispatch June 10, 2004

John & Vicki- You asked me to send you a projected budget for 2008.

*Mower Rental	$ 175.00
*League Fee	160.00
*League Umpires	1045.00
(This was 2007 fee)	
*Valmeyer Tourney	225.00
*Non-League Umpires	950.00
*Lights	250.00
*6 doz. baseballs	250.00
*Player picnic	150.00
(End of season)	
*Diamond Paint	100.00
(Paint Foul lines)	
*Diamond rent	200.00
*Liability Ins.	140.00
*Ball chasers	75.00
(Kids chase foul balls)	
*New caps	300.00
	———
	$4020.00

*for your info.
Vickie you should have a copy of this letter
John was giving the funds) $3000.00/yr.*

*Player Picnic: Scott and Lonnie Goeddel barbecue for the players at the end of season.

*If we get new uniforms they will cost approx. $1500. We have approx. $1300 that we have from this year that we have saved to purchase the new uniforms. If we would get new uniforms the caps would be included and that $300.00 can be deducted from our yearly budget.

*Our present uniforms are 10 years old. The tops were donated by our catcher Jim Anderson's friend. He worked for Mutual of Omaha Ins. Co. These are the Red tops that we now wear and they look pretty faded out and old. But we will use them if we have to and buy a few new pairs of pants.

*All players furnish their own bats and catcher's equipment. All bats are $150+ each. To outfit one catcher costs $300+. This an expense that we do not have.

If you have any questions please ask.

Thanks Vernie

Projected Budget before the Buds became the Millers in 2008

Valmeyer Mid-Summer Classic 2008
L-R: Jordan, Harry, and Aaron Thompson

Waterloo Millers 2008

Brandon and Aubrey Waeltz, Craig and Madelyn Ohlau
Valmeyer Mid-Summer Classic 2010

Waterloo Millers 2010

2018 Waterloo Homecoming Parade Honoring Past Waterloo Legends
L-R: Lon Fulte, Carl Braun, Jim Wahlig, Bob Matzenbacher, Rich Hacker, Mark Ludwig, John Wahlig, Tony Musso, Dennis Mernick
2nd Row L-R Backs to Camera: Jon Adamson, Corey Blackwell, Brandon Musso

2018 Waterloo Homecoming Parade (Vern and Lucy)

2019 Valmeyer Midsummer Classic
(Vern's 2005th career win at age 84)
Photo courtesy of the St. Louis Post-Dispatch

Vern and Lucy Moehrs

Valmeyer 4th of July Mid-Summer Classic 2017

ABOUT THE AUTHOR

Craig Ohlau dedicated 18 years to the Mon-Clair League between 2001 and 2018. He was inducted into The National Semi-Pro Baseball Hall of Fame in 2019. Today, Craig is a writer, coach, teacher, and, most importantly, husband and father. Craig is the award-winning author of *The Sons of Chester* and *Kings of the County League*.

Note from the Author

Thank You!

If you enjoyed *Kings of the County League* here are a few things you can do now:

■ Tell a friend who you think would enjoy the book.

■ Write a social media post. Facebook, Twitter, and blog posts are awesome ways to let people know you liked the book.

■ Leave a review wherever you bought the book— even if it is only a sentence or two. Reviews help out a ton and are very much appreciated.

-Craig

Thank you so much for reading
one of our **Sports History** novels.
If you enjoyed the experience, please check out our
recommended title for your next great read!

*The Sons of Chester: A Tale of Small-Town Boys, Baseball,
and Very Big Dreams*

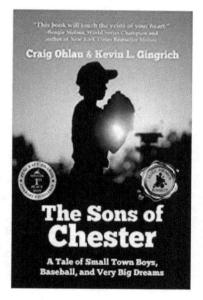

"This book will touch the veins of your heart." –Bengie
Molina, World Series Champion and author of *New York
Times* Bestseller *Molina*

View other Black Rose Writing titles at
www.blackrosewriting.com/books and use promo code
PRINT to receive a **20% discount** when purchasing.

CPSIA information can be obtained
at www.ICGtesting.com
Printed in the USA
BVHW041413111020
590777BV00007B/66

9 781684 335817